The Bulwark of Christendom

The Bulwark of Christendom
The Turkish Sieges of Vienna 1529 & 1683

The Sieges of Vienna by the Turks
Karl August Schimmer

The Great Siege of Vienna, 1683
Henry Elliot Malden

With an Extract from 'The Life of King John Sobieski' by Count John Sobieski

LEONAUR

The Bulwark of Christendom
The Turkish Sieges of Vienna 1529 & 1683
The Sieges of Vienna by the Turks
by Karl August Schimmer
The Great Siege of Vienna, 1683
by Henry Elliot Malden
With an extract from The Life of King John Sobieski
by Count John Sobieski

First published under the titles
The Sieges of Vienna by the Turks
and
Vienna 1683

Leonaur is an imprint of Oakpast Ltd

Copyright in this form © 2016 Oakpast Ltd

ISBN: 978-1-78282-543-2 (hardcover)
ISBN: 978-1-78282-544-9 (softcover)

http://www.leonaur.com

Publisher's Notes

Contents

The Sieges of Vienna by the Turks

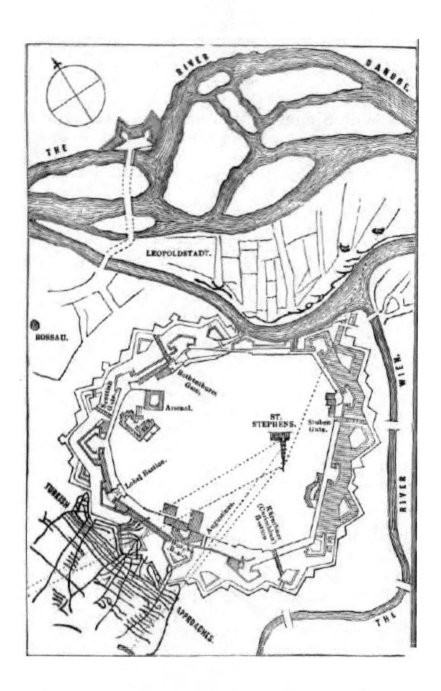

Contents

Think with what passionate delight
The tale was told in Christian halls,
How Sobieski turned to flight
The Muslim from Vienna's walls.
How, when his horse triumphant trod
The Burghers' richest robes upon,
The ancient words rose loud—From God
A man was sent, whose name was John.

Palm Leaves,—Richard Monckton Miles.

Preface

The narrative specified in the Title from which the following pages are in general borrowed, and in great part translated, is the work of a gentleman resident in Vienna, and enjoying as such access to the numerous and valuable sources of information extant in the archives of that city. The other sources to which I have adverted in the title-page, and which I have used for purposes of addition and verification, are principally the well-known Turkish *History of Von Hammer, The Life of Sobieski,* by the French Abbé Coyer; the *History of Poland, by Monsieur de Salvandy*; and the invaluable volume of *John Sobieski's Letters, translated from the Polish by the Count Plater.* I may add that, as many of the rarer printed tracts of the time, cited by Mr. Schimmer, are to be found in the British Museum, I have not failed to avail myself of the assistance of my friend Mr. Panizzi for their examination.

Towards the close of my labour, and in fact through the narrative of the second siege, I have been less faithful as a translator than in the earlier portion. The introduction of such a character as Sobieski on the scene will be my apology to Mr. Schimmer for this divergence, and for the insertion of such matter as I have ventured to embroider on the ground of his narrative. Of the letters of John Sobieski, I have spoken my opinion in the text. The style of the Abbé Coyer seems to me such as might entitle his biography of Sobieski to take rank with Voltaire's Charles XII. and other standard works as a class book for students of the French language. I am indebted to Monsieur de Salvandy for some details of the great battle for the relief of Vienna which have escaped the notice of Ulric and the other German narrators.

Book 1: The First Siege of Vienna

CHAPTER 1

From 1453 to 1526

The fall of Constantinople in 1453 was followed by a rapid extension of the arms and power of the conqueror, Mahomet II. Within a short period, he subjected Persia, the whole of Greece and the Morea, most of the islands of the Archipelago, and Trebisond on the coast of Asia Minor, the seat of the Greek empire of the Comnenes. The last of that dynasty, Daniel Comnenus, he took prisoner, and shortly after caused him with his family to be executed for the alleged offence, probably a mere pretext, of an understanding with the Persians. In 1467 Mahomet took from the Venetians, in addition to several possessions in the Morea, the island of Euboea, and, in 1474, Caffa from the Genoese. The hostilities in which he was soon afterwards involved with Persia hindered him from further pursuing his conquests against the Christian powers, who on their side were prevented by their unhappy dissensions and divisions from attempting to retrieve their losses.

In general, their campaigns against the Turks were confined to purely defensive operations, and it was not till a much later period that common need and danger produced a more general system of aggressive action. In 1480 Mahomet II. attacked the island of Rhodes, the conquest of which he had it much at heart to accomplish; he was, however, repulsed with great loss by its defenders, the Knights of St. John. Upon this repulse he directed his arms against Italy, took Otranto, and would probably have pushed his conquests further in that country, if death had not overtaken him, on an expedition to Persia, in 1481. He had overthrown two empires and ten other sovereignties, and captured more than 200 cities. He directed as an inscription for his tomb the following sentence, simple, but significant to his successors:—

I wished to take Rhodes and subdue Italy.

His two immediate successors, Bajazet II., who reigned from 1481 to 1512, and Selim I. (1512 to 1520), prosecuted schemes of conquest in various directions. The latter was in particular the founder of an extensive naval power, before which those of Venice and Genoa, so considerable at that time, were compelled to quail. He conquered also Mesopotamia, Syria, Palestine, and Egypt, and reduced to subjection the powerful Sheikh of Mecca. In wisdom, however, in power, and in glory, this Soliman was surpassed by his son, the second of that name, the greatest of the Ottoman sovereigns, under whom the Turkish empire attained a pitch of splendour which has not been equalled before or since.

In acquirements he was far beyond his age and country: in addition to the Turkish language, he was master of Persian and Arabic; he also understood Italian; and in that kind of metrical compositions which are called, in Turkish, Misen, the critics of that country pronounced him to exceed all others. In military achievements he was equally distinguished among the sovereigns of his race, and ranks with Mahomet II. as a conqueror. In the first year of his reign, he acquired in Belgrade the key of the Danube, and opened the way for his further advance into Hungary. In the following year, 1522, he carried into execution the unaccomplished wish and dying injunction of Mahomet II. in the subjection of Rhodes, and on Christmas night held his triumphant entry into the conquered city. Soon afterwards he directed his forces again upon Hungary, in which country internal dissensions afforded him a favourable opportunity for the furtherance of his plans of conquest.

King Louis II. of Hungary, the feeble successor of his illustrious father, Ladislaus II., had ascended the throne in 1516, under the guardianship of the Emperor Maximilian I., and of Sigismund, King of Poland, his uncle. At the very commencement of his reign, an insurrection of his nobles threatened to deprive him of the throne. He had, moreover, mortally offended the ambitious John Zapolya, Count of Zips, who held as wayvode the government of Transylvania, and excited him to the most destructive projects by passing him over on the occasion of the election to the office of Palatine. (See note following).

★★★★★★

It is difficult to illustrate the very peculiar institutions of Hungary by reference to those of any other state, as I know of none which presents any near analogy to the office of Palatine. He is chosen by the king out of four magnates presented for election by the states of the kingdom. He represents the king, and is the constitutional mediator between him and his subjects in all matters at issue between them. As President of the highest court of appeal, he resembles our Lord Chancellor, and, like him, takes precedence of all subjects except the primate, the Archbishop of Gran. From 1765 to Joseph II.'s death in 1790 the office remained vacant. It has since been usually filled by an Austrian Archduke.—E.

★★★★★★

This man, whose name, like that of Tekeli, is so intimately connected with the misfortunes of his country, was born in 1487, the son of Stephen Zapolya, one of the best officers of the great king and warrior Mathias Corvinus. Inheriting the rewards of his father's valour in the shape of vast possessions and important governments, he was distinguished through life by restless ambition, great talents for intrigue, and on some occasions by acts of inventive cruelty which exceed in extravagance of horror all that Suetonius has related of the Roman emperors. By a reckless acceptance of Turkish aid, and by treachery as reckless to his engagements with that power, he partially succeeded in the great object of his adventurous life—his establishment on the throne of Hungary. He died a natural death in 1540, leaving an infant son, who succeeded him in the government of Transylvania, but who struggled in vain to establish himself in that of Hungary. With his death in 1570 this race of able and dangerous men fortunately became extinct.

Soliman found little resistance to his invasion of Hungary. Peterwaradin and the Bannat fell quickly into his hands; and on the 20th August, 1526, occurred that disastrous battle which in Hungary still bears the name of the Destruction of Mohacs. Zapolya remained with his forces motionless at Szegedin, careless of the fate of kingdom or king; while the latter, with scarcely 20,000 men and little artillery, stood opposed to a tenfold superior force of the Turks. The wiser heads of the army advised the waiting for reinforcements, but they were overruled by Paul Timoreus, Archbishop of Koloeza, a man who seems to have united every quality which could unfit him for either the sacred functions he had abandoned or those which he had assumed of military command.

The arrival, still hoped for, of Zapolya, with the excellent cavalry of Transylvania, might have saved Hungary, but it would have deprived the prelate of the chief command; and the latter preferred to risk his own life, that of the sovereign, and the fortunes of Hungary, in premature and unequal battle. In less than two hours Soliman had gained a complete victory; the prelate paid the penalty of his presumption with his life, and with him perished the flower of the Hungarian nobility, many of his episcopal brethren, and lastly the unfortunate King Louis himself, suffocated beneath his floundering horse, and borne down by the weight of his armour, in a swamp through which he was urging his flight.

The jewels in which the plume of his helmet was set led ultimately to the discovery and identification of the body. Scarcely 4000 men, led by the Palatine Bathory, escaped under the cover of night from this disastrous battle. Soliman pushed forward his troops, intoxicated with success, as far as the Flatten and Neusiedler lakes, laid waste the country, and burnt Fünfkirchen and Pesth. On the news, however, of disturbances in Asia, he suddenly retired, dragging with him 200,000 persons into captivity, but soon to re-appear in terrible power at the gates of Vienna itself.

The circumstances of the succession to the throne of Hungary were well calculated to invite and facilitate that return. Upon the death of Louis without issue, in virtue of his double connexion by marriage with the Archduke Ferdinand of Austria (afterwards Emperor), and of a treaty concluded between his father Ladislaus and the House of Austria, the right to the throne devolved upon the latter, of which the Archduke was the representative. The royal widow, Mary, sister to Ferdinand, convoked, for the purpose of ratifying this arrangement, a diet at Presburgh, whither she had been compelled to fly when Pesth surrendered.

Her intention, however, was frustrated by the counter measures of John Zapolya, who, after solemnizing the obsequies of Louis at Stuhlweissenburg, had, with the assent of many of the magnates, proclaimed himself king, and had caused himself to be crowned on the 11th November, 1526. He appealed to an ancient law by which no one but a born Hungarian could occupy the throne, although it had never been universally acknowledged, and had been set aside by the recent arrangements. Ferdinand now sent against him an army under the command of a brave man, Nicholas, Count of Salm, who defeated him near Tokay. By the exertions of the faithful Palatine Bathory, a considerable party was created in favour of Ferdinand, and his coronation was celebrated at Pesth on the 21st August, 1527.

After two successive defeats at Erlau and Szinye, Zapolya was compelled to abandon Transylvania and to take refuge in Poland. The magnates of Hungary now came over in great numbers to the party of Ferdinand, and he rejoiced in the prospect of an undisturbed possession of his newly acquired sovereignty. Zapolya, however, though on all sides deserted, and destitute of troops and money, persevered in his designs, and made every exertion to gain over to his cause the nobility of Poland and their king, Sigismund, his brother-in-law by marriage with his sister Barbara.

These attempts were in most instances fruitless; but he succeeded with Jerome Laski, Wayvode of Siradia, a man of resource and enterprise, who showed hospitality to the fugitive, and promised him every possible support. Laski, however, conscious of the inadequacy of his own means to effect his friend's restoration in opposition to the House of Austria, gave him the deplorable advice to betake himself to the *Sultan*.

We are assured by several contemporary writers that Zapolya long hesitated to follow this fatal counsel; and it is not incredible that he felt some compunction in throwing himself into the arms of the arch enemy of Christianity, and in possibly exposing half Europe to Mahometan invasion. The condition, however, of his affairs, and his ambition, urged him to the desperate step, which was somewhat reconciled to his conscience by the knowledge that Ferdinand himself had despatched an embassy to Constantinople to conciliate the good will of the *Sultan*. Zapolya overlooked the distinction that Ferdinand's object was to establish peace, while his own was to kindle a desolating war of race and religion.

So soon as his resolution was adopted, Laski undertook in person a journey to Constantinople, accompanied by a renegade Venetian, Ludovico Gritti, who served him as interpreter. He found ready audience from the *Sultan*, who asked for nothing better than pretext and opportunity to lead his hitherto unconquered forces into the heart of Christendom. The *Sultan* had also been highly irritated by the injudicious behaviour of Ferdinand's envoy, a Hungarian named Hobordansky, who had chosen this unpropitious juncture to demand not merely the unconditional recognition of Ferdinand as king of Hungary, but also to insist with violence on the restoration of Belgrade and Jaicza. Demands such as these, addressed in peremptory language to a sovereign flushed with recent conquest, produced their immediate and natural consequences in facilitating the designs of Zapolya.

A treaty was without delay concluded, by which Soliman undertook to effect his restoration to the throne of Hungary. Zapolya, by secret articles of this compact, engaged in return not merely to pay an annual tribute in money, but to place every ten years at the disposal of the *Sultan* a tenth part of the population of Hungary, of both sexes, and to afford for ever free passage through the kingdom to the Ottoman forces. At the same time Soliman dismissed the envoys of Ferdinand with the menace:

> .... that he would soon come to drive the latter out of a kingdom which he had unjustly acquired; that he would look for him on the field of Mohacs, or even in Pesth; and should Ferdinand shrink from meeting him at either, he would offer him battle under the walls of Vienna itself.

It was thus that through treason in one quarter, ill-timed audacity in another, and the restless spirit of conquest and progression which the Turks derived from their Tartar origin, the crisis arrived so pregnant with evil consequences to an important portion of Christian Europe.

CHAPTER 2

From 1527 to September 11, 1529

The Turkish preparations were pushed forward with great vigour, and in a short time an immense army was assembled in the great plain of Philippopolis. Although the *Sultan* had originally formed the intention of marching with it in person, he nevertheless appointed to its command his famous *Grand Vizier* and favourite Ibrahim. This man was by birth a Greek, of moderate stature, dark complexion, and had been in infancy sold as a slave to Soliman. He soon by his intelligence, his musical talents, his aspiring and enterprising spirit, won the favour of his master, and after Soliman's accession to the throne participated with him in the exercise of the highest powers of the state, in the character of *vizier*, brother-in-law, friend, and favourite, and enjoyed such distinctions as neither Turkish favourite nor minister has ever before or since attained.

He not only often interchanged letters with his master, but frequently his clothes, slept in the same chamber, had his own *seraglio* in the Hippodrome, and his own colour, sky-blue, for the livery of his pages and for his standard. He insisted in his communications with Ferdinand on the title of brother and cousin. In a Latin verse which he addressed to the Venetian ambassador, he signified that while his master had the attributes of Jupiter, he himself was the Caesar of the world. Yet all this exaltation was destined to the usual termination of the career of an Oriental favourite. He was murdered in 1536 by command of Soliman, on suspicion of a design to place himself on the throne.

Soliman had intended to put his army in motion in 1528, but his stores were destroyed, and his arrangements paralysed by rains of such extraordinary violence, that the troops, and even his own person, were endangered. A year's respite was thus afforded to the Austrians, the more valuable to them because, as all accounts concur in stating, they had in the first instance placed little reliance on the accounts of the Turkish preparations for war, and had entertained a very unreasonable disbelief in any serious intention on the part of Soliman to carry his menaces into execution. The threats and vaunting of Oriental despots may generally be received with much allowance for grandiloquence; but in this instance Ferdinand should have remembered that the sovereign who uttered them had already once overrun Hungary to the frontiers of Austria, and had good reason, from past experience, to anticipate success in a renewed invasion.

On the 10th of April, 1529, the *Sultan* left Constantinople at the head of an army of at least 200,000 men. Zapolya, on his part, was not idle. He applied to nearly all the powers of Europe, not excepting even the Pope, Clement VII., whom he knew to be at this period on bad terms with the Emperor, urging them to support what he termed his just cause. These applications were unavailing; the Pope replied by excommunicating him, by exhorting the magnates of Hungary to the support of Ferdinand, and by urging the latter to draw the sword without delay in defence of Christendom.

Zapolya, supported by the money of some Polish nobles, and by some bands of Turkish freebooters, pushed forward early in April into Hungary at the head of about 2000 men, summoning on all sides the inhabitants to his support. Near Kaschan, however, he was attacked and completely routed by the Austrian commander, Da Rewa. Meanwhile the Turkish army advanced without other hindrance than heavy rains and the natural difficulties of the passes of the Balkan, and by the end of June had effected the passage of the rivers of Servia, and had crossed the Hungarian frontier. Before the main body marched a terrible advanced guard of 30,000 men, spreading desolation in every direction. Their leader was a man worthy of such command of blood-thirsty barbarians, the terrible Mihal Oglou, whose ancestor, Kose Mihal, or Michael of the Pointed Beard, derived his origin from the imperial race of the Palaeologi, and on the female side was related to the royal houses of France and Savoy.

His descendants were hereditary leaders of those wild and terrible bands of horsemen called by the Turks *Akindschi*," *i. e.* "hither streaming," or "overflowing;" by the Italians, *Guastadori*, the spoilers; by the French, *Faucheurs* and *Ecorcheurs*, mowers and flayers; but by the Germans universally *Sackman*, possibly because they filled their own sacks with plunder, or emptied those of other people. Whether this explanation be correct or not, it is certain that the name long retained its terrors in Austria, and that down to the beginning of the eighteenth century mothers used it to frighten their unruly children.

Meanwhile Zapolya, encouraged by the progress of the Turk, had ventured his own person in an advance upon Hungary; many of his old adherents joined his standard, and he collected an army of some 6000 men, with which he came on to join the *Sultan*. The meeting took place in the field of Mohacs. Zapolya was received with acclamation by the Turks, and with presents and other marks of honour by the *Sultan*, whose hand he kissed in homage for the sovereignty of Hungary. The *Sultan* assured him of his future protection, and awarded him among other royal honours a body-guard of *Janissaries*. After the army had refreshed itself it proceeded slowly, occupying the fortified places to the right and left; and in thirteen days after its departure from Mohacs the *Sultan's* tents were pitched in the vineyards of Pesth, the inhabitants of which had for the most part fled either to Vienna or Poland.

The garrison consisted of only about a thousand German and Hungarian soldiers, under Thomas Nadasky, who in the first instance showed the best disposition towards a manful defence. The Turks, however, after continuing a well-sustained fire from the neighbouring heights for four days, were proceeding although no breach had been effected to storm the defences, when the courage of the garrison failed them. The latter, with the few remaining inhabitants, retired into the citadel, and the Turks occupied the town. Nadasky was firmly resolved to hold out to the last, with the view of delaying as long as possible the advance of the enemy; but the soldiers had lost all courage, and preferred to obey two of their German officers, who entered into a capitulation with the Turks, and answered Nadasky's remonstrances by putting him into confinement.

The *vizier* rejoiced at the prospect of removing an obstacle which might have materially affected the ulterior plan of his campaign at so advanced a period of the season, and eagerly accepted the conditions, promising them life and liberty; and thus by mutiny and treason was the fortress surrendered on the 7th September. The traitors soon found reason to repent their crime. The event was one which, in justice to the *Sultan*, demands a close investigation, for the naked circumstances were such as to fix a stigma of bad faith on that sovereign, who, however open to the charge of cruelty, was usually distinguished by a rigid and even magnanimous adherence to his word. In many accounts, contemporary and later, he is accused in this instance of a reckless violation of his promises.

It is certain that the garrison was massacred, but there is reason to believe that this occurred neither with the sanction of the Sultan nor without provocation on the part of the victims. The *Janissaries* were in a temper bordering on mutiny on being disappointed of a general plunder of the fortress. Stones were flying at their officers, and the second in their command had been wounded. Through the ranks of these men the garrison had to defile amid expressions of contempt for their cowardice. A German soldier, irritated at this treatment, exclaimed that if he had been in command no surrender would have exposed them to it. This information being received, as might be expected, with redoubled insult, the stout German lost patience, and with his sword he struck a *Janissary* to the ground.

The general massacre which naturally ensued was certainly not by the order, and probably against the will, of the *Sultan*, as indeed the writer, Cantemir, a bitter enemy of the Turk, acknowledges. Not more than sixty men escaped this sweeping execution, part of whom escaped by flight and part were made prisoners. A proof, however, of Soliman's appreciation of honour and courage is to be found in the fact that he not only eulogized the fidelity and firmness of Nadasky, but dismissed him on his parole not to serve against the Turks during the war. This generosity is the more to be praised as it was exercised in the teeth of the resistance not only of the embittered *Janissaries*, but of the Hungarian traitors in the suite of Zapolya. The fortress was placed in the hands of that leader, who remained behind with a sufficient garrison in charge of it, while the Turkish Army pursued its triumphant progress over the Austrian frontier.

On the 14th September Zapolya was solemnly installed on the Hungarian throne, the ceremony being attended, however, on the part of Soliman only by the *segbanbaschi*, or second in command of the *Janissaries*, and by Soliman's commissioner in Hungary, the Venetian Gritti, whose name has been already mentioned. A Turkish *commandant* was left in the place, and the Pacha of Semendria, Mohammed Bey, was sent on in advance towards Vienna to obtain intelligence and clear the roads.

CHAPTER 3

September 1529

Before Soliman quitted Pesth he had issued a proclamation to the effect that:

> Whosoever in Hungary should withhold obedience and sub-
> jection from the Count John of Zips, Wayvode of Transylvania,
> whom the Sultan had named king, had replaced in the sover-
> eignty, and had engaged himself to uphold, should be punished
> and extirpated with fire and sword; but that those who should
> submit themselves should be stoutly protected, and maintained
> in. the possession of their property and privileges.

On the 21st of September, Soliman with his main army crossed the Raab at Altenburg in Hungary, and on the same day his advanced corps of plunderers and destroyers under Michael Oglou, after spreading terror far and wide around them, reached the neighbourhood of Vienna. It may be questioned whether the main objects of the campaign were promoted by the employment of this force. As a scourge to the defenceless portion of an enemy's country, none could be so effective; but though terror may paralyze the resistance of the scattered and the weak, cruelty serves to excite the indignation and organise the resistance of those beyond its immediate reach; and in the case of the *Sackman* cruelty was combined with a reckless treachery, which was laid to the account and affixed to the reputation of the general body of the invaders and their great leader, in some instances hardly with justice.

Contemporary writers have exhausted their powers of language in describing the atrocities perpetrated by these marauders. We find, for example, in a rare pamphlet of the time, (*The Besieging of the City of Vienna in Austria by the cruel Tyrant and Destroyer of Christendom, the*

25

Turkish Emperor, as it lately befell, in the Month of September, 1529"), the following:

At which time did the Sackman spread himself on every side, going before the Turkish army, destroying and burning everything, and carrying off into captivity much people, men and women, and even the children, of whom many they grievously maimed, and, as Turkish prisoners have declared, over 30,000 persons were by them carried off, and as has since been told, such as could not march were cruelly put to death. Thus have they wasted, destroyed, burnt, and plundered all in the land of Austria below Ens, and nearly to the water of Ens, but on the hither side of the Danube for the most part the land has escaped, for by reason of the river the Turk could do there but little harm; the towns also round about Vienna beyond Brück on the Leitha, have remained unconquered and unwasted by the Turk, but the open country wasted and burnt.

The irresistible pressure forward of the main army, the threats of the *Sultan*, and the merciless fury of the Sackman, produced their consequences in the prompt surrender of most of the places which were unprovided with garrisons and adequate defences. In this manner fell Fünfkirchen, Stahlweissenburg, and Pesth, without a blow, into the hands of the enemy. In Gran the inhabitants even refused to admit the garrison sent by Ferdinand for its occupation, and the Archbishop Paul Tomori so far forgot his honour and duty as to procure the surrender both of town and citadel to the *Sultan*, to whose camp the prelate also betook himself. Comorn was abandoned by its garrison. Raab also fell, but not till it had been set on fire by the fugitives. Altenburg in Hungary was betrayed into the hands of the enemy.

Brück on the Leitha, on the contrary, defended itself stoutly; and the *Sultan*, pleased with the constancy and courage of its defenders, willingly accorded them terms in virtue of which they were pledged to do him homage only after the fall of Vienna. Content with this compact, he ceased his attack on the city, marched past under its walls, and strictly forbade all injury to the district in its dependence. Wiener Neustadt also defended itself with spirit, and in one day repelled five attempts to storm its defences in the most heroic manner. Several other places, among them Closterneuburg, and Perchtoldsdorf, and some castles held out with success.

★★★★★★

These instances illustrate the fact that Soliman was ill provided with siege artillery. The Turks at this period, as will be seen in the case of Vienna, relied principally on their skill in mining for the capture of strong places, a method very effective in their hands, but slow.—E.

★★★★★★

Such occasional opposition was scarcely distasteful to Soliman, for whom invariable and cheap success had not its usual attraction. His far-reaching ambition looked to a sovereignty of the West corresponding to that which his ancestors had asserted over the East, and he remarked with complacency the valour of men whom he destined for his future subjects. For the same reason he detested cowardice in the ranks of his opponents, and punished it with the same severity as if it had exhibited itself in his own. In contemplation also of the immensity of his force, the rapidity of his progress, and the unprepared condition of Austria, he held success for certain, and isolated instances of resistance could, as he conceived, only afford useful practice to his troops without affecting the general and inevitable result. In fact, the aspect of the time for Austria was one of gloom and danger.

The main force of the enemy was hard upon the frontier, which had already been crossed at several points by the terrible bands of Michael Oglou; and from the walls of Vienna the horizon was seen reddened with the flames of burning villages, while within the city little or nothing had yet been done for its fortification and defence. It is true that, on the near approach of the danger, Ferdinand had called meetings of the States, as well in Austria as in the other provinces of his hereditary dominions; and had for this object proceeded in person through Styria, Carinthia, Tyrol, and Bohemia. The cause was everywhere taken up with much alacrity. In Austria the tenth man was called out for service; the other provinces undertook to furnish considerable forces; and Bohemia promised, in case of the actual invasion of Austria, to send to her aid every man capable of bearing arms.

The king, however, saw but too well that with all this aid he would be no match in the field for the *Sultan's* force; and he turned his thoughts to the Empire, in which the religious disputes of the time presented serious difficulties in the way of the assistance he required. The danger, however, was pressing enough to allay for the moment even the heats engendered by the Reformation. At the Diet of Spire, which was attended by most of the Electoral and other Princes of the Empire, Ferdinand addressed to them an urgent appeal, in which he made a prominent allusion to the fact that Soliman had declared his determination never to lay down his arms till he had erected a monument to his victories on the bank of the Rhine.

The voice of party was indeed silenced by this appeal to a common interest; but the succour, voted after protracted discussion, was nevertheless scanty, not exceeding 12,000 foot and 4000 horse, as the contingent for the Germanic body. Then followed interminable debates as to the selection of a commander; and the Turks were over the Save and in possession of Pesth before the Germanic contingent was mustered. There were not wanting men hard of belief, pedants of the true German stamp, who maintained that mere apprehension had exaggerated the danger; and finally it was agreed at Ratisbon, to which city the assembly had transferred itself, to send a deputation of two persons to Hungary to investigate the state of affairs on the spot. (These commissioners were civilians. One of them was a lawyer, answering probably to our barrister of six years' standing.—E.) They went; and, having the good fortune to escape the hands of the Turks, returned with evidence sufficient to satisfy the doubts of their sagacious employers.

On the day on which Soliman crossed the Hungarian frontier, a detachment of Imperial cavalry under Paul Bakics encountered a body of the Turkish light troops in the immediate neighbourhood of Vienna, and took a few prisoners. The conquerors showed themselves apt disciples in cruelty of the Turks, and even exceeded their teachers, who with the sabre usually made short work with their captives, whereas the men now taken were racked or tortured before they were bound together with ropes and flung into the Danube. Meanwhile the near approach of the Turks and the delay of all succour raised consternation in Vienna to the highest pitch. The news of the fall of Pesth, which reached it on the 17th September, suggested flight to all who had the means of escape. In defiance of an urgent summons on the part of the authorities, addressed to all capable of bearing arms, many burghers left the city on pretence of bearing their women and children to places of safety, and few of these returned.

These delinquents were called afterwards to severe account, though much excuse was to be found for such conduct on the part of individuals in the shameful neglect of their rulers, who had postponed measures of defence till resistance appeared hopeless. The countless hosts of the invader had crossed the frontier before any force had been collected which could even impede its advance. The royal troops encamped at Altenburg hardly amounted to 5000 men, who on the first appearance of the enemy effected a rapid retreat in order not to be cut off from Vienna. The succours promised by the Empire were not forthcoming, though messenger after messenger was sent to hurry their advance. Even the Bohemian troops approached but by slow marches, under their leader John of Bernstein, and required every exhortation to greater diligence. At length Duke Frederick of the Palatinate, the prince elected as leader of the army of the Empire, arrived on the 24th of September at Lintz with the scanty levies, amounting to a few thousands, which had as yet been collected.

At Lintz he held conference with Ferdinand as to the measures to be pursued, and then hastened forward to effect his entrance into Vienna before the arrival of the Turks. On the 26th, however, he received at Grein the intelligence that the Turks had appeared in force in the neighbourhood of the city. He was at first resolutely determined to cut his way at all hazards, but when he learned that both the bridges over the Danube were in possession of the enemy, being satisfied that by the attempt he could only involve his feeble forces in certain and useless destruction, he determined to halt at Crems for reinforcements. His cousin, however, the brave Pfalzgraf Philip, succeeded in throwing himself into the city, with a small number of Spanish and German troops, three days before it was surrounded by the Turks.

In Vienna the necessary preparations had now been made with almost superhuman exertion, but in such haste and with so little material, that they could only be considered as very inadequate to the emergency. The city itself occupied then the same ground as at present, the defences were old and in great part ruinous, the walls scarcely six feet thick, and the outer palisade so frail and insufficient that the name *Stadtzaun*, or city hedge, which it bears in the municipal records of the time, was literally as well as figuratively appropriate. The citadel was merely the old building which now exists under the name of Schweizer Hof. All the houses which lay too near the wall were levelled to the ground; where the wall was specially weak or out of repair, a new entrenched line of earthen defence was constructed and well palisaded; within the city itself, from the Stuben to the Kärnthner or Carinthian gate, an entirely new wall twenty feet high was constructed with a ditch interior to the old.

The bank of the Danube was also entrenched and palisaded, and from the drawbridge to the Salz gate protected with a rampart capable of resisting artillery. As a precaution against fire the shingles with which the houses were generally roofed were throughout the city removed. The pavement of the streets was taken up to deaden the effect of the enemy's shot, and watchposts established to guard against conflagration. Parties were detached to scour the neighbouring country in search of provisions, and to bring in cattle and forage. Finally, to provide against the possibility of a protracted siege, useless consumers, women, children, old men, and ecclesiastics were, as far as possible, forced to withdraw from the city. Though this latter measure was successful for its special purpose, and prevented any failure of subsistence during the investment of the city, it had the melancholy consequence that many of the fugitives met with massacre or captivity at the hands of the Turkish light troops.

In the neighbourhood of Traismauer, for instance, in the very beginning of September, a body of no less than 5000 were unsparingly massacred by the Sackman. To meet the financial exigency of the time, an extraordinary contribution was levied throughout Austria. A bishop was taxed 5 florins, a mitred prelate 4, an unmitred 3, a count 4, the rest of the noblesse, as also the secular clergy, and all citizens who were accounted to possess 100 florins, 1 florin each; peasants, servants, and others of the poorer classes a kreutzer in the dollar; day labourers 10 pennies, and every communicant 9 pennies (see *Chronicon Mellicense*, part vii). Should these sums appear small, the value of money must be considered at a period when a considerable country-house might be purchased for 50 florins, and when 200 florins were reckoned a competence.

In respect of the active defence, the Pfalzgraf Philip had taken the command in the city. Associated with him was the veteran hero Nicholas, Count of Salm, who had crossed the March field from Upper Hungary with a chosen band of light troops, and on whose proved fidelity and valour Ferdinand principally relied for the defence of the bulwark of Christendom. These qualities had been tried through fifty -six years of service in the field, and recently in the victory of Pavia (1522), in which he had borne a distinguished share, having crossed swords and exchanged wounds with the French king, Francis I. At the age of seventy, he now undertook a heavier responsibility than any he had yet incurred; for though the Pfalzgraf's rank gave him a nominal precedence, the confidence both of the soldiery and the citizens rested chiefly on the veteran leader.

The other commanders were William, Baron of Roggendorf, general of the cavalry, who had distinguished himself in the Italian wars; Marcus Beck, of Leopoldsdorf, commissary general; Ulrich Leyser, master of the ordnance; John Katzianer; Leonhard, Baron of Vels; Hector Eck, of Reischach; and Maximilian Leyser. Of Austrian states-deputies and councillors, the following were in the city:—George von Puechhaim, governor of Lower Austria; Nicholaus Rabenhaupt, chancellor; Rudolph von Hohenfeld, Felician von Pottschach, privy councillors; John von Greissenegg, *commandant* of Vienna, and of the foot militia of the city; Melchior von Lamberg; Trajan von Auersberg; Bernardin Ritschen; Helfreich von Meggun; Erasmus von Obritschen; Raimund von Dornberg; Otto von Achterdingen; John Apfalterer; Siegfried von Kollonitsch; Reinbrecht von Ebersdorf; and Hans von Eibenswald. The Styrian troops were commanded by the gallant Abel von Holleneck; the Bohemian, by Ernst von Brandenstein.

The contingent of the Empire consisted of two regiments, under Kuntz Gotzman and James von Bernan. Luis de Avallos, Melchior de Villanel, Juan de Salinas, and Juan de Aquilera, commanded the Spaniards. The magistrates remaining in the city were Wolfgang Troy, burgomaster; Paul Bernfuss, judge; and the councillors Sebastian Eiseler, Sebastian Schmutz, and Wolfgang Mangold. The limits of this work do not admit a list of subordinate officers. It would include names connected with the first houses of the German and Austrian nobility. Among these were several who had joined the garrison as volunteers. In the camp of the Imperialists at Crems were two young nobles, Rupert, Count of Manderscheid, and Wolf, Count of Oettingen, so zealous in the cause, that after the city had been invested they swam the Danube, and were drawn up over the wall near the Werder gate.

The garrison altogether amounted to 20,000 infantry and 2000 horse; the armed *burghers* to about 1000. The distribution of the troops was as follows:—The Pfalzgraf Philip occupied, with 100 *cuirassiers* and 14 companies of the troops of the Empire, the Stuben quarter from the Rothenthurm to the middle of the curtain towards the Kärntner gate. Thence the line of defence was taken up to the Augustine Convent by Eck von Reischach, with 3000 infantry. Thence to the Burggarten were posted the Styrian troops under Abel von Holleneck. The citadel was held by Leonard von Vels, with 3000 chosen troops.

Thence to the Scottish gate Maximilian Leyser was in command. In the four principal squares of the city were posted cavalry, under William von Roggendorf, ready to advance in any direction. From the Scottish gate to the Werder gate were posted 2000 Austrians and 700 Spaniards, under Rupert von Ebersdorf. The tower in the spot called Elend, was strengthened with a rampart, and mounted with heavy guns to annoy the Turkish flotilla, which covered the Danube as far as Nussdorf. Finally, from the Werder gate to the Rothenthurm, including the Salz gate, were posted 2000 Bohemians under Ernst von Brandenstein and William von Wartenberg, with a detachment of cavalry under John, Count of Hardegg. The artillery mounted on the defences appears to have consisted of between sixty and seventy pieces, of the very various calibres and denominations in use at this period.

A small armament according to our present ideas, if the circuit of the defences and the lightness of some of the pieces be considered, but respectable perhaps for the time, and more than a match for the light pieces of the Turks. The city would probably have been still less provided with this arm of defence, but for the Emperor Maximilian, with whom the fabrication and use of artillery had been a favourite study and pursuit, of which his heirs and country now reaped the benefit, (see Ranke, *Deutsche Geschichte*, vol. iii.) The care of this artillery was committed to seventy-four gunners under the master of the ordnance, Ulrich Leyser.

After all these preparations the defences were very weak, even according to the engineering science of the time. There were no bastions on which the guns could be properly disposed. It is mentioned that several of the pieces which had been adjusted to embrasures or loopholes opened in the wall were found useless in that position, and were removed to the roofs of neighbouring buildings; the ditches were dry, and it was left to the defenders to supply by gallantry and endurance the deficiencies of art and the precautions of prudence.

The hour of trial was at hand; on the 20th September, Altenburg surrendered, after a gallant defence, and its garrison, 300 strong, were made prisoners. These men were interrogated by the Sultan as to the condition of Vienna, the strength of its garrison, &c., and having, as would appear, answered in terms which agreed with his ideas of the truth, were well treated by him, but forced to accompany him on his march. Soon afterwards Brück on the Leitha and Trautmannsdorf fell into his hands by capitulation; and, freed from these petty obstacles, he advanced with his collected might, and with every prospect of achieving the ruin of the empire in the subjection of its capital.

Chapter 4

From September 16 to September 26, 1529

In Vienna it was resolved by a council of war, as it was not possible to face the overwhelming numbers of the enemy in the open field, to neutralize, at least as far as possible, the advantages of any positions in the neighbourhood by the sacrifice of the suburbs, and of all buildings within range of fire from the walls. A more timely adoption of this indispensable measure would have obviated much of the violence and misery which attended its hurried execution. The necessity was one which from the end of August, and after the fall of Pesth, had been obviously inevitable. By the 16th of November the whole neighbourhood was swarming with the bands of Michael Oglou, who spared neither age nor sex; children, old people, and pregnant women were murdered with every circumstance of cruelty, and those who were spared from the sabre were swept into slavery.

A contemporary writer, Peter Stern von Labach, describes these horrors in the following terms:—

> After the taking of Brück on the Leitha and the castle of Traut-mannsdorf, the Sackman and those who went before him, people who have no regular pay, but live by plunder and spoil, to the number of 40,000, spread themselves far and wide over the country, as far as the Ens and into Styria, burning and slaying. Many thousands of people were murdered, or maltreated and dragged into slavery. Children were cut out of their mothers' wombs and stuck on pikes; young women abused to death, and their corpses left on the highway. God rest their souls, and grant vengeance on the bloodhounds who committed this evil.

The peasantry fled either to the depths of the forests, or to the city, and increased by their narratives the consternation there prevailing. By the 20th September every road which led from east and south towards the city was crowded with fugitives endeavouring to save themselves and their moveables.

As however the Eastern horsemen were familiar with all difficulties of ground, and overcame all impediments of morass, or forest, or mountain, few of the fugitives escaped. A few fortified towns and castles only held out. A chronicle of the time asserts that scarcely a third part of the inhabitants of Upper Austria survived the invasion. It was only on the 22nd September, when the enemy was at the gates of Vienna, that the resolution we have mentioned was finally adopted, to sacrifice to the general security the entire suburbs and the many sumptuous buildings which they included. The most valuable of the moveable property was first conveyed into the city, and the work of destruction commenced.

It was soon, however, found that it had commenced too late for its orderly and deliberate execution. It was left to the proprietors to save hastily what they could; the rest was given up for the soldiery to glean, and the torch was applied to all the buildings. Disorders and excesses such as might be expected were the result, and the inhabitants were little better treated by the foreign soldiery than they would have been by the Turk. That many wine-casks should have been broken in the cellars, the owners of which at this period cultivated the vine to a great extent, and much store of provisions and other valuables burnt, and that even the churches should have been desecrated and plundered, can scarcely be matter of censure, except eo far as it may be conjectured that with better discipline on the part of the soldiery, the articles destroyed might in part have been removed; but the wretched people who were conveying the sole remnants of their property to the city were remorselessly plundered, misused, and even murdered on any attempt at resistance.

The example of this unrestrained licence spread its effects even to within the walls. Several houses in the city were broken open and plundered, and even the citadel itself was entered by a band of marauders. A proclamation was speedily issued against these disorders, and put in force by the erection and employment of a gallows at the so-called Lugeck. Eight hundred houses had within four days been burnt. Among the most important of these were—the great City Hospital, dedicated to the Holy Ghost, which stood between the city and the Wien River, the situation of which, till about twenty years ago, was marked by an ancient pillar, bearing an inscription, with the date 1332 (from this building, which also had a fine church, the sick and helpless inmates were transferred first to the convent at the Himmel's Pforte, and next to the desecrated church of the nunnery of St. Clara)—the Franciscan Convent at St. Theobald's, the present corn-market—the churches of St. Anthony and St. Coloman, between the city and the Wien River the great nunnery of St. Nicholas, before the Stuben gate, and that of St. Magdalen, near the Scottish gate—the Closterneuburgerhof, also near the Scottish gate. Finally, in order to deprive the Turks of the advantage of a stronghold, on an eminence near the city, it was unfortunately necessary to destroy the castle on the Kahlenberg (Leopoldsberg), formerly the residence of the Margrave Leopold, who died in the odour of sanctity. The last measure adopted was that of walling up and fortifying all the gates, except the Salz gate, which was left open as a sally-port.

On the 23rd September, while the suburbs were in full conflagration, a strong body of Turks pressed forward as far as St. Mark's, cut to pieces a number of invalids who had scandalously been left there to their fate, and ventured still further on the high road. This occasioned the first sally from the city of five hundred *cuirassiers* under Count Hardegg. These having pressed too far forward, the Turks took advantage of the ruins of some of the burnt houses to attack them in flank while the front was also engaged with superior numbers. The *cuirassiers* fell back in disorder without waiting for a support which was detached to their assistance. They must have had good horses and sharp spurs, for only three were killed, but six, with a cornet, Cornet Christopher von Zedlitz, were taken.

The Turks immediately placed the heads of the three killed on the points of lances, and to make the number of the dead equal to that of the prisoners, they beheaded four of the invalids of St. Mark's, and compelled the prisoners to bear the seven heads to the presence of the *Sultan*, then on his march from Brück on the Leitha, in order to gladden him as soon as possible with the sight of these grisly trophies of his first success over the defenders of Vienna. He interrogated the prisoners as to the strength of the garrison and the present position of Ferdinand, on both which points they gave him true replies. Upon this Soliman released four of the prisoners, presented each with three ducats, and sent them back to Vienna with the following message:—

If the city would surrender on terms, the conditions should be arranged with its commanders without the walls, none of his people should be allowed to enter the city, and the property and persons of the inhabitants should be secured. It was Soliman's sole desire to follow the king till he should find him, and then to retire to his own dominions. Should the city, however, venture to resist, he would not retreat till he had reduced it, and then he would spare neither old nor young, not the child in the mother's womb, and would so utterly destroy the city that men should not know where it stood. He would not rest his head till Vienna and the whole of Christendom were under his subjection, and it was his settled purpose within three days, namely on the feast of St. Michael, to break his fast in Vienna.

The other three prisoners with the cornet he retained about his person. To the latter he showed great favour, caused him to be sumptuously attired in silk and gold, and kept him constantly in his suite. At the close of this narrative will be found the curious and lively account of the prisoner, preserved in the collection of the Baron von Enenkel in the archives of Vienna.

At length, September 29th, the *grand vizier* with the main army appeared before the city. On the 25th, nevertheless, two companies of imperial troops, raised from Nuremberg, effected their entrance through the Salz gate with drums beating and colours flying. They related that between Tuln and Traismauer they had fallen in with a body of 5000 fugitives on foot and 3000 in boats, mostly women, children, and regular clergy, who on the following day had been overtaken and destroyed by the bands of Michael Oglou. On the 26th September, Soliman sent into the city a Bohemian, one of the garrison which had surrendered in Altenburg, with the contemptuous offer that he would send the other Bohemians there taken to strengthen the garrison of Vienna.

The man was sent back accompanied by two Turkish prisoners, each of whom was presented with two *ducats*, with the reply that they had more garrison than enough in Vienna, and that Soliman might keep his Bohemian prisoners. Soon after the arrival of the main army a discharge of arrows, which literally darkened the air, was followed by a first summons to surrender, succeeded by a second and a third. These remaining unanswered, Soliman sent in four prisoners richly dressed, and liberally supplied with presents, with a repetition both of

36

his offer of a favourable capitulation, and of his threats in case of resistance. Officers should be put to death with torture, the site of the city sown with salt and ashes, &c. The stern commanders, however, merely despatched in return a like number of Turkish prisoners, as richly provided with presents and apparel, but without an answer either to his threats or promises.

CHAPTER 5

From September 26 to October 2, 1529

The Turkish Army had scarcely arrived in the neighbourhood of the city, when a forest of tents rose from the ground, presenting so striking a spectacle, that even Austrian contemporary writers are excited to exchange their usual phlegmatic style in describing it for something of the Oriental.

The country within sight of the walls as far as Schwechat and Trautmannsdorf was covered with tents, the number of which was calculated at 30,000, nor could the sharpest vision from St. Stephen's tower overlook the limit of the circle so occupied. The flower of the Turkish force, the *Janissaries*, took possession of the ruins of the suburbs, which afforded them an excellent cover from the fire of the besieged. They also cut loopholes in the walls yet standing, from which they directed a fire of small ordnance and musketry on the walls of the city.

The tent of Soliman rose in superior splendour over all others at Simmering, on the spot and to the extent now occupied by the building called the Neugebäude. Hangings of the richest tissue separated its numerous compartments from each other. Costly carpets, and cushions and divans studded with jewels, formed the furniture. Its numerous pinnacles were terminated by knobs of massive gold. The colour of the chief compartment was green striped with gold. Five hundred archers of the Royal guard kept watch there night and day.

Around it rose in great though inferior splendour, the tents of ministers and favourites; and 12,000 *Janissaries*, the terror of their enemies, and not unfrequently of their masters, were encamped in a circle round this central sanctuary. The Pacha of Roumelia was posted opposite the Stuben gate, and thence down to the Danube, securing the baggage and its attendant train of horses, mules, and camels: the latter, some 20,000 in number, were at pasture in the meadows. The camp of the Vizier Ibrahim extended from Simmering over the Wienerberg as far as Spinnerin, and thence down the declivities as far as Wieden and the high road opposite the Stuben and Kärnthner gates. The Pacha of Bosnia occupied the line of the Wien River, from St. Ulrich and St. Theobald to Penzing. The Pacha of Roumelia communicated with his right by a body of the renegades who had joined the Turkish forces. From St. Veit to near Döbling the second line was formed by the Pachas of Scutari and Semendria; the camp of the Pacha Nesters with many Christian prisoners was formed at Sporkenbühel.

The corps of the Pacha of Belgrade, which extended itself from Schönbrunn to beyond Laxenburg, secured the rear of the besieging force. The guard of the Royal tent was intrusted to the Pacha of Anatolia. The meadows and islands of the Lobau as far as Nussdorf were occupied by the crews of the Turkish flotilla, which had arrived on the 25th of September, with charge to watch the banks and prevent the passage of succours. These mariners, a well-trained and efficient body, were called Nasser or Nassadists, and Martolos, a Turkish corruption of the German Matros. The number of their vessels amounted to 400. Amid the ruins of the suburbs the *Janissaries* and the *asapes* (a species of sappers) dug trenches, from which they plied their arrows and musketry with such assiduity, that no one without extreme danger could show himself on the walls.

Their archers' aim was so accurate that they often sent their missiles through the embrasures and loopholes of the defences. It happened, however, fortunately for the weak garrison, that the greater part of the Turkish heavy artillery had been left behind in Hungary, its further transport having been rendered impossible by heavy rains. For this reason, the besiegers were reduced to limit their operations to mining, and to a discharge of arrows so heavy and incessant, that through the town generally, and especially in the Kärnthner street, no one could walk abroad in safety. The line of actual attack extended from the rampart near the Augustine Convent to the tower situated between the Stuben and Rothenthurm gates, where Eck von Reischach commanded. In face of this line of defence they excavated a labyrinth of deep entrenchments, strengthened with earth and timber, the Kärnthner tower being their principal point of assault.

Their artillery fire, probably from its inefficiency for breaching purposes, was principally directed against the higher buildings of the city, especially St. Stephen's tower; but the arrows flew in all directions. Some of the latter, probably discharged by persons of distinction, were of costly fabric, painted, and even set with pearls, and were kept long afterwards as curiosities. The total force of the besiegers is stated by Peter von Labach and Meldemann at nearly 300,000, of whom, however, only 100,000 were fully armed.

The remainder was employed with the baggage, ill equipped, untrained to arms, and rather a burthen than an assistance to the more regular force. The artillery amounted to about 300 pieces, of which not more than thirty were of respectable calibre. The investment of the city was completed, and the passage of the Danube effectually closed by the Nassadists on the 27th September; and soon afterwards three companies of German and Spanish horse made a sally from the Burg gate.

A skirmish ensued, in which some two hundred Turks and several of their officers were killed. The Spaniards at the Werder gate also opposed with success the landing of a cargo of arms, which had arrived by the Danube from Kahlenberg. From this time forth, to prevent unauthorized alarms, all the bells in the city were silenced, and even the striking of the hour was forbidden, the only exception being in favour of the prime bell of St. Stephen's, which was allowed to strike the quarters. On the 29th—that St. Michael's day on which Soliman had declared his purpose of breakfasting in Vienna—the Vizier Ibrahim rode the circuit of the walls with a numerous suite. He had wisely laid aside the usual costume of his high office, and exchanged its turban of white and gold and flowing robe for a coloured shawl and a simpler soldier's attire. He adopted also the further precaution of keeping pretty well out of gunshot. This ride was perhaps meant as a substitute for that celebration of the saint's day which the *Sultan* had announced, but failed to observe.

The Viennese, who were possessed in the sixteenth century by the jocular propensity which they still retain, did not fail to indulge it at the *Sultan's* expense. Prisoners were released with a message to him that his breakfast had waited for him till the meat was cold, and he must be fain to content himself with such poor entertainment as they could send him from the guns on the wall. To this, however, about midday, they added a vigorous sally, conducted by the brave Eck von Reischach, from the Kärnthner gate; through which also the Spaniard Luis d'Avallos led a company of his people, and killed many of the

Turks, who had been attracted by the grapes of the neighbouring vineyards. The Spaniards only retired at last before superior numbers, with the loss of their cornet, Antonio Comargo.

On the same day, for the first time, a spy ventured out of the city, who twice swam the Danube and returned in safety, but on a third venture was no more heard of. Measures were now adopted for taking an exact account of all provisions in the city, the duration of the siege being uncertain. The troops were then divided into messes of four men; and to each mess a ration was allotted of eight pounds of bread and fifteen measures of wine. It was found necessary to diminish this quantity to some of the foreign *lanzknechts*, who, unaccustomed to the strong Austrian wines, found it sufficient to incapacitate them for duty. Five-eighths of their wine and two pounds of their bread were struck off. From St. Michael's day, continued rains, and frosts, unusual for the season, at night, caused much suffering to the Turks in their light tents, unused as they were to the climate.

The cold continued after the rain abated, and was aggravated by severe storms. The 30th September passed with no other incident than an assault by the Turks on the guard at the drawbridge, which was driven into the city with some loss. On this day a Christian boy and a girl escaped from the Turkish camp into the city. The girl had been appropriated by a rich *pacha*, who had lavished upon her adornment ornaments and apparel. Upon a nocturnal alarm in the camp, which caused a general movement towards the walls, they had left their tent and succeeded, under cover of the darkness, in reaching the city. Much information was obtained from both. On the 1st October, Friday, the principal day of the week with the Turks, the *vizier* with all the *agas* paid their respects to the *Sultan*, who, in consequence of the inclement weather, had taken up his quarters in Ebersdorf.

Three hundred *lanzknechts* made a sally on this day from the Scottish gate, and a conflict ensued without material advantage to either side. Towards noon a man made his appearance near the drawbridge attired as a Turk, who prayed earnestly for admission, saying that he had been brought up in Turkey, but had come of Christian parents, and was determined to revert to their faith. This man was questioned both by ordinary interrogation and by torture, and gave much valuable information as to the strength of the enemy. Of their artillery, he said that he had seen ten of the largest guns, called wall-breakers, each three fathoms long, in a boat on the Danube; that the number of the Nassad boats was 400, manned with 5000 soldiers. He gave also

41

the first accurate information of the mines to the right and left of the Kärnthner gate, a point of intense interest to the defenders of that post, respecting which nothing had previously been ascertained.

The besieged, having now ascertained that one principal mine was directed against the Kärnthner tower, and the other against the convent of St. Clara, betook themselves with the utmost zeal to the excavation of counter-mines at these two points, propping, at the same time, the walls with posts and beams, so that upon any springing of the enemy's mines, the ruins might fall outwards and impede the access to the breach. The General Roggendorf ensured to the informant a subsistence for life in return for his intelligence; we may suppose, also, with some consideration of the manner in which it had been extracted. On the same evening a heavy fire was kept up on both sides, which led to the expectation of an assault, but none ensued. On the 2nd of October, the enemy's mine under the Kärnthner tower was detected and destroyed. A large body of Turks, however, about the same time, pressed forward nearly to the Scottish gate, and retired, after a lively skirmish, with ten prisoners and thirty heads of the slain.

To meet the danger of the enemy's mines, guards were placed in all the cellars near the walls, trenches dug near the fort of the rampart, and drums with peas strewed on thein parchment, or tubs filled with water, placed at the suspected spots, to indicate by their vibration the neighbourhood of the Turkish labourers, and guide thereby the operations of the counter-miners. By these precautions, many of the enemy's galleries were discovered, and either ruined by counter-mines, or penetrated and robbed of their powder. It is here expedient to contradict the tale, current to our own time, that the continual efforts of the Turks had pushed a mine as far as the house on the so-called Freiung, which bears still the name of Heidenschuss, where it is said that a baker's apprentice discovered it and occasioned its destruction. (The distance of this spot from the wall would be about one-third of the extreme breadth of the city.—T.)

This incident is in itself highly improbable, I may almost assert impossible. Not to take into account that it is mentioned in none of the narratives of the time, of which I have fourteen before me, the distance alone would make it next to impossible that so long an operation could have been carried on without detection. It appears also, from the archives of the Scottish foundation in Vienna, that the house in question bore the name Heidenschuss long before the Turkish siege, namely, from the year 1292, when the Tartars overran Austria. Others aver that it belonged to a family of the name of Hayden, which bore in its arms a Tartar discharging an arrow. This is, indeed, disputed; but the antiquity of the name Heidenschuss is certain, and it is equally so that no Turkish mine ever was carried so far as to the spot in question. It is just to mention that the fraternity of bakers, as well as many other corporations, rendered great services in this season of common danger, and it is likely enough that one of that body may have performed the particular service in question in some other locality.

The services of the bakers' guild were acknowledged, after the raising of the siege, by the present of a silver cup, and the privilege of carrying the same in procession round the city every Easter Tuesday. This practice was observed till the year 1811, when the disorders incident to the concourse of people it collected, and the loss of some days' labour which it was apt to occasion, led to its suppression by the authorities of the bakers' corporation.

Chapter 6

From October 3 to October 13, 1529

On the 3rd October, the enemy's fire was much increased, and protracted even far into the night. An assault was therefore confidently expected. The garrison remained under arms night and day. Nothing, however, ensued except considerable damage to the Kärnthner tower and the adjacent bastion, in return for which the kitchen of the Beglerbeg of Roumelia was almost entirely disorganised by a heavy shot from the city. On the following day orders were issued in the Turkish camp for the most active prosecution of the mines. Michael Oglou's people were ordered to convey ladders and bundles of straw to the trenches, and every preparation was made for a general assault. On this day Simon Athinai, surnamed the Learned, a friend and dependant of Zapolya, made his appearance in the camp, to pay his respects to Soliman, who received him with the honours which he was accustomed to show to men of letters.

In the evening a council of war was held in the city, and a strong sally was resolved upon for the following day, principally with the object of discovering and destroying the mines last commenced; and also of driving the *Janissaries* out of the ruins of the suburbs, from which their incessant fire greatly annoyed the garrison. Eight thousand men of all arms and nations were appointed to this service, and the operation was commenced at six in the morning. Its success was by no means such as was expected; though at first it promised the happiest results. The batteries of the enemy were in the first instance carried and left behind; the soldiers, well led by their officers, flung themselves on the enemy with the deadly weapons used in hand-to-hand conflict at this period, such as the morning-star and the battle-axe, and with murderous effect, but as day broke the alarm ran through the Turkish camp and brought heavy numbers to the rescue.

A sudden apprehension of being cut off from the city, suggested by a few voices, degenerated into a panic, and the troops fell into confusion, which ended in a general flight. The voices of their officers, the encouragement from the garrison on the walls, and the example of a brave commander, Wolf Hagen, were unavailing to check the torrent. Hagen himself, with a few brave men who remained about him, was surrounded and beheaded. His body was rescued and brought into the city for honourable burial. There fell also in this disastrous action a German officer of noble blood, George Steinpeiss, and a Spaniard, Garcia Gusman: the brave Hector von Reischach was severely wounded. Five hundred heads and several prisoners remained in the camp of the Turks, who, however, on their part, suffered considerable loss.

The retreat was conducted with such confusion, that many were forced over the parapet of the bridge, and, maimed by the fall, remained at the mercy of the Turks, who pursued so closely up to the walls, that they were only driven back from them at push of pike. At noon there was a fresh alarm that camels were conveying fascines of wood, straw, and vine-sticks to fill up the ditch. The expected assault, however, did not take place. The fire of the Turks recommenced at 5 p.m. and was maintained without cessation, which caused the soldiers to remain at their posts through the night. On the 7th, at 9 a.m., the Turks assaulted two bastions, and sprung a mine at the Kärnthner gate, by which the wall opposite the nunnery of St. Clara was destroyed for a space of thirteen fathoms.

The following night the camp was illuminated with several thousand torches, and a general shouting and alarm took place without further result. It was probably the celebration of some festival. The garrison having been assembled at their posts, Count Salm announced to them that by a trusty messenger, who had swum the Danube at midnight, he had received consolatory tidings from King Ferdinand and the Duke Frederick, who promised to come to their relief within a week. The garrison hailed this intelligence with noisy acclamation, which probably excited as much notice and surprise in the Turkish camp as their illuminations and shoutings had excited in Vienna. Though this cheering assurance raised the hopes of all, yet the difficulties of the defence became every day more urgent, and a proclamation was issued, forbidding, on pain of death, all self-indulgence and neglect of duty.

To illustrate and enforce this edict, two *lanzknechts*, who, over their cups, remained absent from their posts after the alarm had been given, were hanged at the Lugeek as traitors: On the 8th the whole artillery of the Turks played upon the city. The timber bulwark in front of the Kärnthner gate was set on fire, and the walls, deprived of their breastwork, threatened to fall inwards. To avoid this, possibly fatal, catastrophe, trunks of trees and huge beams were brought to their support, and a new breastwork was thrown up with incredible celerity. A similar work was thrown up before the Scottish gate, and mounted with two guns, which did much mischief in the Turkish camp towards Sporkenbühel.

On the 9th October an alarm took place at daybreak, and preparations for a storm were evident in the Turkish camp. At 3 p.m. mines were sprung to the right and left of the Kärnthner gate. The one on the left opened a breach in the wall, wide enough for twenty-four men to advance in order. The assault was nevertheless gallantly repulsed by Salm and Katzianer in three successive instances. Several Spaniards and Germans had been buried or blown into the air by the explosion; others were hurled back into the city without serious injury. The explosions would have been more effective if the besieged had not succeeded in reaching some of the chambers of the mines by countermining, and in carrying off eight tuns of the charge.

During the repeated assaults the heaviest artillery of the city was discharged incessantly upon the Turkish cavalry, and with such good aim, that, to use the words of Peter Stern von Labach, man and horse flew into the air. Upon every retreat of the storming-parties, trumpets from St. Stephen's tower, and warlike music on the place of St. Clara, celebrated the triumph of the besieged. The *Sultan*, dispirited at these repeated failures, adopted a precaution which indicated apprehension on his own part of a sally from the city, for he directed trenches to be dug round the tents of the *Janissaries* and other picked troops. In the city, when quiet was restored, the old wall was rapidly repaired, a new one constructed, the houses which interfered with it levelled, and their materials employed to fill up the wooden breastwork.

On the 10th all was quiet, and the work of repair proceeded. Two mines were discovered and destroyed, and in a small sally of some eighty men five camels were captured.

On the 11th, towards 9 a.m., a mine was sprung between the Kärnthner and Stuben gates, which made an enormous breach, equivalent to an open gateway in the wall. Heavy bodies of men rushed on to the assault: a second mine was sprung at the Stuben gate, and, according to some accounts, the city was positively entered at this quarter by some of the enemy. This, however, is doubtful; but it is certain that a Turkish standard-bearer had mounted the wall, when he was struck down by a musquet shot into the ditch. The assault and defence were continued with equal determination for three hours.

Twelve hundred bodies were heaped up in the breach, and though new assailants seemed to spring from the earth, their efforts failed before the unshaken courage of the defenders. The conflict ceased at midday. The loss of the garrison was far less than that of the Turks; yet, at a general muster of the armed citizens which took place in the evening, 625 were missing from the numbers mustered at the beginning of the siege. The wrath of the *Sultan* was kindled to the highest pitch. He stormed, entreated, promised, and threatened; and on the following day the assault was renewed.

Again two mines exploded in the same quarter as before, and again the ruin of the wall was extensive. The Turks were in the breach sooner almost than their approach could be detected, as they thought, but the wall was scarcely down before its ruins were occupied by a company of Spaniards, with their colours flying and courage undepressed. The storm was fierce, but short; the repulse was again complete, and depression and exhaustion prevailed in the Turkish ranks.

From the towers of the city their officers were seen urging them forward with blows. In several places explosions were observed which did no injury to the walls. Although the attacks were several times repeated, and to a late hour in the evening, as the courage of the defenders rose that of the enemy quailed, and the latter efforts were more and more easily repelled. The loss of the assailants could not be ascertained, as the Turks, according to their custom, carried off their dead. Late in the night, however, a council of war was held in their camp, in which the former tone of confidence was remarkably lowered. The lateness of the season and the difficulty of subsistence were the topics of discussion. The latter difficulty was not indeed a fictitious one, for, under the expectation of a speedy surrender of the city, supplies had been collected on a scale quite inadequate to the present exigency. It was also remembered that three main assaults had been executed, and that three times on each occasion the troops had advanced to the charge.

This magic number had fulfilled the law of Islam, by which, whether in the field or against defences, no more than three attacks are required of the faithful. Notwithstanding these good reasons and fair excuses for immediate withdrawal, the temptation of plunder was so strong, that it was agreed to attempt on the following day, the 14th, one more assault with all their force; but, should this fail, to raise the siege. The *Janissaries*, who were loudest in their complaints, were pacified by a payment of the ordinary assault money, namely, a thousand aspers, or twenty ducats, to each man. The 13th October passed therefore without attack, but the preparations for one were in active progress. Numerous criers perambulated the camp, proclaiming the great assault for the following day, and announcing the following rewards:—To the first man who should mount the wall, promotion from his respective military rank to the next above it, and a sum of 30,000 *aspers* (600 *ducats*). (See note following).

★★★★★★

The vast pecuniary resources of the Turkish Empire at this period, and the profusion with which they were dispensed abroad, offers a striking contrast to the poverty and niggardliness of the House of Austria and the Germanic body. While Soliman was marching upon Pesth the operations of the Austrian flotilla on the Danube were paralyzed for want of 40,000 florins to pay the arrears of the crews. With great difficulty 800 florins were raised for the purpose. See Ranke, *Fursten und Volker*, vol. iii.—E.

★★★★★★

The *Sultan* inspected in person and on horseback the preparations, and expressed his satisfaction. Nor were they idle in the city. While the soldiers stood to their arms, the citizens of both sexes, and of all classes, ages, and professions, spiritual as well as lay, were at work without cessation, removing rubbish, digging new entrenchments, throwing up works, strengthening the ramparts, and filling up the breaches. Many so engaged were wounded by the enemy's various missiles. Their attention was also carefully directed to the enemy's mines, and they succeeded on this day in detecting and carrying off six tuns of powder from one intended for the destruction of the Kärnthner tower. Thus prepared and thus determined, they waited for the dawn of the day which was to decide the fate of the Christian stronghold, so long and so gallantly maintained.

CHAPTER 7

October 14 to November 20, 1529

At daybreak of the 14th October the flower of the Turkish army was arrayed in three powerful bodies for the assault, and towards nine o'clock they advanced, led on by officers of the highest rank. On this occasion, however, the desperate courage and cheerful contempt of death which had usually been conspicuous among the Turkish soldiery were no longer distinguishable. It was to no purpose that their officers, the *vizier* in person at their head, urged them forward with stick and whip and sabre-edge, they refused obedience, saying they preferred to die by the hands of their own officers rather than to face the long muskets of the Spaniards and the German spits, as they called the long swords of the *lanzknechts*.

Towards noon two mines were sprung to the right and left of the Kärnthner gate, but a third, which had been carried under the Burg, was fortunately detected, and its entire charge of twenty barrels of powder fell into the hands of the counter-miners. A breach, nevertheless, twenty-four fathoms wide, was the result of the mines which succeeded, and through this, supported by the fire of all their batteries, repeated attempts were made to storm, but in every instance repulsed as before. These attacks were the last expiring efforts of exhausted men. Two incidents connected with them have been considered worthy of record.

The first is the adventure of two officers, a Portuguese and a German, who had quarrelled over night, and were proceeding to settle their difference with the sword in the morning, having selected the breach or its immediate neighbourhood for their place of meeting. Being interrupted by the Turkish assault, they naturally enough, instead of proceeding with their own foolish and useless purpose, agreed to turn their arms against the Turks. The point of the story seems to be, that after one had lost his left arm and the other the use of his right,

49

they stood by one another, making a perfect soldier between them, till both were killed.

The other incident is one of more historical importance. It is that of the severe and ultimately fatal wound of the brave Count Salm, who, after escaping all the previous dangers of the siege, was hit on the hip towards 2 p.m. by the splintered fragments of a stone, and carried from the breach, which till then he had never quitted. He survived till the spring of the following year, when he died of the effects of this injury at his residence of Salm Hoff, near Marchegg in Lower Austria. King Ferdinand caused a sumptuous monument to be erected to this deserving soldier in the church, then existing, of St. Dorothea, in which was the family vault of the Salms. This church was pulled down in 1783, when the Salm family took possession of the monument, and removed it to their residence at Raitz in Moravia.

On the failure of these last attacks, Soliman abandoned all hope of gaining possession of the city, and the troops received accordingly a general order of retreat. Its execution was attended by an act of atrocity which throws a shadow over the character of the sovereign by whose servants it was perpetrated,—a shadow not the less deep because contrasted with many recorded indications of a noble and generous nature. It may, indeed, possibly be considered as another specimen of unavoidable condescension to the passions of an ill-disciplined soldiery, such as the massacre of the garrison of Pesth, and rather as an exhibition of the weakness than the misuse of despotic rule.

The *Janissaries* broke up from their encampment an hour before midnight, and set on fire their huts, forage, and every combustible article which they could not or would not carry with them. Under this latter head they included the greater portion of the vast swarm of prisoners of all ages and both sexes collected in their quarters. Of these the younger portion alone, boys and girls, were dragged along with their retiring columns, tied together by ropes, and destined to slavery.

The old of both sexes and the children were for the most part flung alive into the flames of the burning camp, and the remainder cut to pieces or impaled. The glare of the conflagration and the shrieks of the sufferers disturbed through the night the rest so dearly earned by the brave defenders of the city, and though their approaching deliverance might be read in the one, it was probably easy to conjecture from the other the horrors by winch that deliverance was accompanied. When this act of cowardly vengeance was accomplished, a parting salvo from all their fire-arms was discharged at the walls; and after all remaining buildings in the suburbs and adjacent villages had been set on fire, the army commenced its retreat.

With the first light of morning came assurance of the city's safety, which was hailed by a general discharge of artillery from the walls, and by warlike music in the public squares, and from St. Stephen's tower. The bells, too, were released from the silence to which they had been condemned since the 29th of September, and a solemn *Te Deum* and high mass were celebrated in St. Stephen's in honour of the Holy Trinity. The *Sultan* questioned his prisoner the Cornet Zedlitz as to the cause of the sounds which reached his ear. The cornet avowed at once his belief that the clamour was that of joy and triumph over the deliverance of the city. The *Sultan* evinced his satisfaction at the frankness of his favourite's reply by dismissing him in safety to the city, bearing on his person the marks of Oriental favour in the shape of silken and gold-embroidered apparel, and accompanied by two of his fellow-prisoners, who thus shared the advantage of the good-will which the soldier had earned by his manly bearing. Soon after this creditable act, the *Sultan* commenced his march in the direction of Brück on the Leitha.

Early the following day the flotilla began to drop down the river, not, however, unmolested by the artillery from the city, which sunk several of the vessels. The *grand vizier* remained for some time with some 60,000 cavalry in the neighbourhood of the Wienerberg, partly to cover the retreat, partly to rally the light troops dispersed on plundering expeditions. It is stated by some writers, further to account for this delay, that he waited for the issue of the machinations of certain of his agents in the city, who had undertaken to set it on fire, and that he hoped even at this late hour by such means to effect his entrance. This supposition is not very consistent with the haughty and elevated character of the man. It is however certain that three suspected individuals were arrested, who gave themselves out for escaped prisoners. They had been at first admitted as such without suspicion; but when it was observed that their purses were well filled with Turkish money, this was thought a sufficient reason for putting them to the torture, by which a confession was extorted that they had been hired for the purpose above described.

They were quartered, and their limbs affixed *in terrorem* on the walls. At the distance of a mile the *Sultan* again halted, and held a divan to receive the felicitations of his great officers on the fortunate termination of the campaign. After these functionaries had kissed his hand, he distributed among them rich rewards. The *vizier* received a jewelled sabre, four costly pelisses, and five purses. (The purse held 500 *piastres*, or 60,000 *aspers*, which, at 50 *aspers* to the *ducat*, makes 6000 *ducats*). The *pachas* received each two *pelisses* and a sum of money. The money distributed as reward to the storming-parties had amounted to 240,000 *ducats*, so that the closing act of the siege cost the *Sultan* at least 250,000 *ducats*. The most curious feature of the transaction is the tone of the bulletins in which the retreat was described. The great Orientalist and historian Von Hammer has given us translations of several. The concluding passage of one of them is to this effect:—

> An unbeliever came out from the fortress and brought intelligence of the submission of the princes and of the people, on whose behalf he prayed for grace and pardon. The *padischah* received his prayer with favour, and granted them pardon. Inasmuch as the German lands were unconnected with the Ottoman realm, that hence it was hard to occupy the frontier places and conduct their affairs, the faithful would not trouble themselves to clear out the fortress, or purify, improve, and put it into repair; but a reward of 1000 *aspers* was dealt out to each of the *Janissaries*; and security being established, the horses' heads were turned towards the throne of Solomon.

Before the *vizier* joined the column of retreat, a messenger was despatched to him with proposals for an exchange of prisoners. The *vizier* presented the messenger with a rich *caftan* of blue silk, and returned the following answer written in bad Italian:—

> Ibrahim Pacha, by the grace of God, First Vizier, Secretary and chief Councillor of the most glorious, great, and invincible Emperor, Sultan Soliman; head and minister of his whole dominions, of his slaves and *sandschaks*, *generalissimo* of his armies. Well-born, magnanimous officers and commanders, receiving your writing, sent by your messenger, we have digested its contents. Know that we are not come to take your city into our possession, but only to seek out your Archduke Ferdinand, whom however we have not found, and hence have waited here so many days, he not appearing. Yesterday moreover we set free three of our prisoners, for which reason you should be fain to do likewise by those in your possession, as we have desired your messenger to explain to you by word of mouth. You may therefore send hither one of your people to seek out your

countrymen, and without fear or anxiety for our good faith, for what happened to those of Pesth was not our fault but their own. Given before Vienna in the middle of October.

The above was written on smooth Italian paper, the signature alone and the signet impression in Turkish characters. The authorities in Vienna presented the bearer of this missive with an upper garment of red damask, and sent him back with the verbal answer that they were the more anxious to deal strictly according to the usages of war, because they looked forward to much future matter for intercourse. If rightly reported, it must be confessed that both reply and rejoinder in this negotiation appear to have somewhat lost sight of the point at issue. The contemporary writer, Labach, asserts that Soliman, *after his withdrawal*, sent a message to the city containing an offer to withdraw on payment to him of 200,000 florins, to which the authorities made answer that the keys of their treasury were missing.

On the 17th of October the *vizier* really commenced his retreat under a heavy snow-storm which lasted from early morning till late into the night. The day's march extended as far as Brück on the Leitha, and was one of great difficulty and attended with much loss of baggage. The garrison exerted itself to take advantage of these circumstances. A sally took place on the same day, under command of John Katzianer, Paul Bakics, and Sigismund von Weichselburg, with eight squadrons of cavalry and four companies of foot, in which many prisoners were made, many Christians rescued, and a rich booty captured in tents and camp furniture, together with some camels.

On the 19th another sally was attended with still happier results. Near the village of Laa on the Wienerberg upwards of 200 Turks were slain, a *pacha* captured, and many children rescued from captivity. The Turkish rear-guard was thus annoyed, till, on the 20th of October, it crossed the Hungarian frontier. The invaders, however, left fearful traces of their incursion over a vast extent of country, and on their line of retreat wreaked to the last their vengeance for the failure of their main purpose on every object animate and inanimate within their reach. To their usual practices of massacre, plunder, and incendiarism, they superadded the destruction of fruit-trees, vineyards, and gardens; and the wretched inhabitants who had saved their lives by flight or concealment, returned to scenes of desolation which required years to repair.

The loss of the invaders during the siege has been very variously stated, at numbers indeed varying from 80,000 to 30,000. The Hungarian historian, Tarff, reduces this to 20,000, and Ortelius to 14,000. The truth probably approaches the lower calculation, as, in the absence of all general encounter in the field, the loss in action fell heavily only on the storming-parties. The return of 1500 killed on the side of the city, though adopted in all the narratives, is manifestly below the truth, for we have seen that as early as the 11th October 636 of the armed citizens were missing.

On the 25th October, the tenth day from the raising of the siege, Soliman entered Pesth, where he was received with all honours by Zapolya. On the 28th, in full *divan*, Zapolya renewed his homage, and was presented with ten caftans and three horses, with bits and chains of gold. His minister, Ludovico Gritti, received 20,000 ducats. On the 30th, Soliman recommenced his march, and pursued it through Peterwaradin to Belgrade, which he reached only on the 20th November, having been much delayed by inundations. Much baggage remained behind in the swamps, and many men and horses perished of starvation. These incidents did not prevent Soliman from writing in a victorious strain to the Venetian Doge, Andreas Gritti.

This letter, dated from Belgrade, was written in Italian, and began with a pompous list of titles of sovereignty, comprising Asia and Europe generally; and descending to particulars, Persia, Arabia, Syria, Mecca and Jerusalem, the whole territory of Egypt, and the shores of the Mediterranean. The letter further related how the Sultan had:

> ... taken from Ferdinand the kingdom of Hungary and invested with the same the Wayvode of Transylvania; how with his Vizier Ibrahim, his *agas* and *pachas*, he had marched over Syria to Pesth, and there placed the crown of Hungary on the head of the Wayvode, and had looked for King Ferdinand in Vienna: but inasmuch as the latter had fled towards Prague, and it was impossible even to ascertain whether he were alive or dead, had again, at the end of twenty days, turned round towards Pesth and there received the homage of his vassal.

The whole is a curious specimen of the perfection which this mode of describing occurrences had attained three centuries before our time. The tone is the same of most of the Turkish narratives of the day, all of which extol to the skies the magnanimity and moderation of the *Sultan*. One only, that of Ferdi, describes with some fidelity the devastation effected by the army. The national animosities of this writer are so violent that he calls Ferdinand by no other name than the "accursed." The conclusion of his narrative runs as follows:—

As it came to the ear of His Majesty that a portion of the Christian Army had shut itself up in the city, and from this it was to be conjectured that the accursed Ferdinand was among them; the victorious army besieged the said fortress for fifteen days, and overthrew the walls in five places by mines, so that the unbelievers prayed for mercy from the faithful. As some of the garrison were taken prisoners, and from these it was ascertained that the accursed was not in the fortress, the Imperial mercy forgave their offence, and listened to their entreaties; but His Majesty, who governs the world, to gain the merits of this holy war, and to ruin the aforesaid accursed, had sent out the *akind-schis*, the runners and burners, in all directions into Germany, so that the whole country was trodden down by the hoofs of the horses, and even the lands north of the Danube wasted with fire by the crews of the vessels.

Cities and hamlets, market-towns and villages, blazed up in the fire of vengeance and destruction. The beautiful land, the treasury of spring and abode of joy, was trodden down by the horsemen and filled with smoke. Houses and palaces were left in ashes. The victorious army dragged away captive the inhabitants, great and small, high and low, men and women, strong and weak. In the bazaars were sold many fair ones with jasmine foreheads, eyebrows arched and thick, and countenances like Peris; and the booty was incalculable. Property, moveable and immoveable, men and cattle, the speaking and the dumb, the rational and the senseless, were destroyed and slaughtered at the edge of the sabre. Thus on the page of time was written the fulfilment of the prophecy of the *Koran*, 'Thus deal we with the wicked.'

On the 28th November, the *Sultan* reached Constantinople, and made his triumphal entry with the portion of his army which had least suffered by the march. The greater part of the exhausted troops remained at Belgrade, Nissa, and Adrianople to recruit their strength and numbers; for the *Sultan* was passionately intent upon retrieving his failure, and prosecuting with new resources his plans for the establishment of an Empire of the West. Years, however, were required to place his forces on a footing for another expedition, the results of which will be hereafter disclosed.

CHAPTER 8

From November 20 to the end of the year 1529

Although for the moment Vienna was relieved from dread of the Turk, other causes of distress and apprehension survived the removal of the main danger, and required equally the application of violent remedies. Not to mention that the open country was l

ong infested with roving parties of Turkish marauders who were little interfered with by a soldiery who had forgotten their own discipline in the excitement of success, in Vienna itself this spirit displayed itself in a fearful insurrection of the troops of the Empire, which threatened the citizens with greater calamities than even those of the siege itself. On the ground that they had repulsed five main attacks, they demanded fivefold pay; and as it was impossible at once to concede this demand, they indicated, not obscurely, an intention to pay themselves by a general plunder of the city.

The authorities attempted in the first instance to appease them with fair words and moral reflections. These only led to increased demands, and at length to distinct threats of a total rejection of military obedience, and of a general assault on persons and property. The invitation of one of their ensigns, Paul Gumpenberger, for every man to rally round his colours who would be content with double pay, had, it is true, the desired effect, so far that several reasonable men broke off from the mass and rescued for the moment the superior officers from their turbulent comrades. On the following day, however, the clamour and the menaces were revived with increased violence. The Pfalzgraf Frederick, who had meanwhile arrived in Vienna, promised them now threefold pay, with which the greater number were satisfied, but it was not till the ringleaders had been executed that tranquillity was entirely restored.

The troops were finally divided and marched off, some to Pressburg, others to Altenburg in Hungary, and with their departure confidence revived and the citizens were enabled to commence the work of restoration and repair both of their defences and of the houses which had suffered by the enemy's fire. The whole of the extensive space occupied by the fortifications now existing, as well as the glacis, both of which at this period were covered with buildings, were now cleared of such, and the repeated and obstinate attempts of the former proprietors to rebuild their dwellings as obstinately resisted. By the same operation the booths, so called, of the suburb vanished for ever, and when, some three years later, the alarm of invasion was revived, the extensive remains still standing of the Burgher hospital, and of many other large buildings and churches between the River Wien and the city, were levelled to the ground.

In exchange for the vast and richly endowed Burgher hospital, the ruins of which had afforded the Turks so excellent a position in front of the Kärnthner gate, the city obtained in 1580 the nunnery of St. Clara, the nuns of which, reduced in numbers by the Reformation, had fled to another establishment of their order at Villach in Carinthia. Those who returned to Vienna after the siege were received in the Pilgrim-house near St. Anne, where they gradually died out, and their former buildings were formally made over to the city, out of which has since grown the great hospital now existing.

ORIGINAL NARRATIVE OF THE ADVENTURES OF THE CORNET CHRISTOPHER VON ZEDLITZ IN THE TURKISH CAMP. FROM THE COLLECTION OF THE BARON VON ENENKEL IN THE STATE ARCHIVES AT VIENNA.

Among such praiseworthy Christian knights, may also justly be celebrated the honourable and noble knight and master, Christopher von Czetliz, who in his honourable knightly deeds against the hereditary enemy of Christendom, the Turk, has learned and known the use and profit of diligent prayer, and how to acquit oneself with the Psalter or Prayer-Book of the good knight and king, David, much better than other careless, idle, godless people, who take no account of psalm or paternoster; for when in years past the Turkish tyrant, Soliman, with a terrible power came from Constantinople upon Hungary, and having marched 280 German miles, without reckoning the bendings of roads and by-ways, sat down before Vienna, as it were at the door of the old and famous German people, so that all Germany behoved to be stirring, then did this noble knight, Christopher, essay himself often and manfully against the enemy.

Firstly, before Comorn; secondly, at the coronation at Stuhlweissenburg, where he distinguished himself among all the other knights there present, and exhibited himself before the king in knightly fashion, in tilting-feats, which no one could repeat after him, and which the chivalry present and His Majesty himself had much content to witness; and the latter soon after ordered him a cornetcy under the Count von Hardegg, when Pesth was recovered from the Turk. When Soliman in 1529 retook Pesth, and marched upon Vienna, Cornet Christopher was in the latter city, attached to the principal in command, when and where he gained much honour in skirmishing, and was moreover made prisoner, as will be related.

In 1530, having been meanwhile knighted by His Majesty, he marched again to Pesth, under Count Hardegg, for the recovery of that city, where he joined himself with one Von Reussenstein, agreeing together to mount to the assault, as they did, and got as far as the breach, where, inasmuch as the others did not follow like men, but remained in the ditch, Cornet Christopher was hardly entreated, a Nimptsch (one of the family of Nimptsch) shot by his side, and he thrown back into the ditch; and this siege passed without success.

In 1532, when the Turk was minded again to march on Vienna, but who for the good fortune of the Emperor Charles, who joined King Ferdinand in person at Vienna, had turned off to Güns, against which he failed in several assaults, Cornet Christopher was at the head of some knights from the principalities of Schweidnitz and Jauer; and when some on our side skirmished with the Turk at Neustadt, he advanced in front of all, and assailed and dismounted a Turk of consideration; not to mention that he was somewhat ailing, and enfeebled by his march, so that so soon as he had found his way back to Breslau, he departed in God, helped surely by a Turkish syrup which he had taken, and which worked the stronger with time.

For when, in the year before mentioned (1529), the Turk assailed Vienna, this noble knight had fallen upon him, and well conducted himself, and in a skirmish had fallen from and parted company with his horse, which had not trusted itself to come back to him, and a cry being raised to save the standard, which was performed by a Fleming, Cornet Christopher had taken post on a small round hillock, where three Turks perceived and assaulted him, but he with his sword stood at bay, and stuck one of their horses in the head, and would have got clear off, but that twelve other Turks assailed him before and behind, and by numbers struck him to the ground; and when he had wounded one of these through the arm, they wrung his sword from him, and endeavoured to loose his armour, but as he was armed with a whole cuirass, no one could strip him, else, without doubt, in their fury they would have sabred and cut him to pieces.

As it was they made him prisoner, and carried him off among them, by the side of their horses, a good quarter of a mile, and then set him in his *cuirass* on a baggage-mule, and carried him on through the night as far as Brück on the Leitha, the head quarter of the Turkish emperor. When they entered the camp there was much concourse to see a figure in full harness, *cuirass*, and head-piece, all screwed up, so that there was nothing but sheer iron to be seen; then one of the bystanders spoke to him in the Croat tongue, and asked him what he could do and compass, having such a load of iron on him; and he answered: "Had I a horse, and were I loose and free, thou wouldst then quickly see what I could do." Being further asked whether he, Von Zedlitz, could touch the ground with his fist, he quickly bent himself down thereto: meanwhile the girth of the baggage-saddle burst, and he fell with a crash to the ground; and when the Turks began to laugh, he (Von Zedlitz) rose nimbly up, and, without a run, jumped in his heavy armour on the tall mule, so that the Turks admired and forbore to laugh.

In this expedition there was about the Emperor Ibrahim (in German *Emerich*) Pacha, an eminent and notable man, the next to Solyman in that day, ruler and minister of everything in the Turkish realm, and who in this war counselled and directed everything. Before him when Von Zedlitz was brought, he gave order that they should take him out of his armour; but among the Turks was no man familiar with knightly equipment, who could deal with the manner of fastening of such a cuirass, then no longer much used and quite unknown to the Turks, and he remained armed till questioned by Solyman himself. To him Count Christopher made answer, that if assured of his life he would undo himself. When Ibrahim Pacha had given him such assurance, he showed the interpreter two little screws at the side, which being loosed, the *cuirass* came to its pieces, to the great wonder of the Turks. When he had laid aside his harness, the Turks, observing a gold chain about him, fell upon him violently to tear it off; but he, seizing it with both hands, tore it in pieces and flung it among them.

They also took from him his seal and ring, and on account of the gold, concluded him to be of great means and condition; but he held himself out for a gentleman of small means, who had won these things in war. As the account of these things spread itself through the camp, much was said of the feats of this man-at-arms, and of his singular dexterity under his strange attire, and everyone was curious to see him, being, moreover, among the first who had been taken prisoners out of the city itself of Vienna. He was, therefore, ordered to exhibit himself in full *cuirass*, armed at all points for fight, and to prove whether in this fashion he could, without vantage, lift himself from the ground.

On the following day, mules and several kicking horses being produced, Count Christopher laid himself on the ground with his *cuirass* screwed, and rising nimbly, without any vantage, sprung on a horse, and this he repeated several times; and then, with running and vaulting, afforded those hellhounds a princely spectacle of knightly exercises, to their great admiration, and specially that of Ibrahim Pacha, who soon after took him to himself, and kept him safe in his own custody. Meanwhile, there came to him certain officers to frighten or to prove him, telling him to hold himself in readiness, for that the *pacha* would do him right that same day.

To these he answered, that as a Christian he was in truth not afraid of death; as one who, in honour of his Redeemer, in obedience to his sovereign, and in defence of his country, had prepared himself by prayer for death at any hour or instant, and hoped and believed most certainly to enjoy eternal joy and happiness through Christ; but, nevertheless, could not credit that such was the order of the *pacha*, for he knew for certain that what the *pacha* had promised he would perform like an honourable soldier. When this reached the *pacha*, the longer he considered the more he admired, not only the knightly feats, but the noble spirit of this hero. When, also, Soliman himself asked him whether, if he (Soliman) should release him, he would still make war upon him, Count Christopher answered, undismayed, that if God and his Redeemer should grant him deliverance, he would while life lasted fight against the Turks more hotly than ever.

Thereupon the *Sultan* replied, "Thou shalt be free, my man, and make war on me as thou wilt for the rest of thy life." Soliman knew perhaps well that he would not live long, for it has been conjectured that the Turks had given him a potion, which in a few years attacked his life and carried him off. The *pacha*, however, kept him in good case while the siege lasted, namely, about a month; and in place of his cuirass, gave him a dress of red velvet Tyrian stuff, which he wore and lay in night and day, and sent him from his own table meats and mixed drinks (probably sherbet), as daily prepared for himself, and even in course of time offered and gave him wine.

******

This specimen of favouritism, won, not by mean arts, but by soldierlike and simple bearing, does honour to both parties. No one in these days would, like the Chronicler, give credit to the tale of slow poison with which his credulity impairs the merit justly due to the Turk. Even were it more consistent than it is with the character of Soliman or his minister, it is obviously irreconcilable with the other facts recorded.—E.

******

The count, for special reasons, gave himself out for a Bohemian, being conversant in the Slave language, which is much in use with the Turks. When it came to the time appointed for the great assault, the *pacha* said to him at table, "This evening will the great Sultan take possession of Vienna, and it will fare ill with your people," and then asked him further, how strong the garrison was; and the count answered, "All that he could tell was, that the garrison within were of that stamp that they would one and all be killed before they would surrender the city."

When the assault took place, the count was left in the *pacha's* tent without any special guard, but loose and free of his person, and able to look about him in the camp; but when, by help of God, the Turks being repulsed broke up their camp, the *pacha* took the count with him the first day's march, but in the morning after put another Turkish robe of velvet on him over the former, which is still preserved by his brothers, Francis and Hans von Zedlitz; and added a present of a hundred aspers, and also a cavalry prisoner whom the Count knew and had begged for, and caused them to be honourably attended and passed safe, so that on the following day they reached Vienna, where the count was honourably received by the princes, counts, gentlemen, and officers there present.

NOTICE OF THE DEVASTATION EFFECTED BY THE TURKS; FROM

ORIGINAL SOURCES.

The general character of the operations of the *sackman* has been sufficiently described. From the foot of the Kahlenberg, from Heiligenstadt and Döbling to the shore of the Leitha, his presence was pro-

61

claimed by the smoke of burning villages, and his march was tracked by wasted fields and vineyards. In the first days of the investment of Vienna the vineyards of Heiligenstadt had been destroyed by the Bosnian light troops; and on the day of the last assault its failure was avenged by the indiscriminate massacre of the inhabitants. At Döbling the pastor, Peter Heindl, was flung on a burning pile of the registers and archives of the district. Hütteldorf, St.Veit, Brunn, and Enzersdorf were burnt.

In Perchtoldsdorf the inhabitants indeed held out in the castle, but everything beyond its walls was destroyed. From the fortress of Lichtenstein, the eldest son of its possessor of that day was dragged into slavery. In Closter-Neuburg the upper town and the ecclesiastical buildings held out, but the lower was destroyed. Baden shared its fate. The destroyers penetrated even into Upper Austria, and thence into Styria, where, however, they on several occasions met with their match, for the people rose upon their scattered bands, and burned alive those whom they overpowered. A detachment also crossed the Danube in thirty vessels, and made' an incursion on the left bank. After having set fire to the village and castle of Schmida, they were surprised and in great part destroyed by a body of 200 cavalry under Count Hardegg.

A number of fugitives were pursued to the shore, and perished in an over-crowded vessel, which went to the bottom. Another body, which, disturbed in its occupation of plunder, had taken refuge in a tower near Korneuburg, were surrounded and cut to pieces by the land-bailiff George von Leuchtenberg, and the Bavarian colonel of cavalry Wolfgang von Weichs. In spite of these isolated acts of vengeance and resistance, upwards of 20,000 Christians were slaughtered or dragged into slavery; and but few of the latter, most of them young persons of either sex and priests, ever returned. It is a remarkable fact, proved from all the original accounts, that the Turks preferred making slaves of the clergy to the putting them to death; possibly, for the pleasure of tormenting them at leisure.

According to a contemporary narrative, upwards of 14,000 of the Akindschis perished in these desultory conflicts. Taking their whole force at the number, usually admitted, of 40,000, the proportion is not improbable.

Book 2: From the End of the First Siege of Vienna to that of the Second. 1530 to 1684

CHAPTER 1

1530 to 1538

The close of the year 1529 had been made memorable in the annals of Christendom by the retreat of Soliman. He had retired not without loss and a degree of exhaustion which promised an interval at least of repose to the countries he had so cruelly ravaged. He was, however, neither satiated with blood nor discouraged by that signal failure of the main object of his expedition which the Turkish historiographers strove in vain to conceal beneath the flowers of Oriental eloquence. So early as in the spring of 1532, he poured down upon Hungary and Styria a force even more numerous than that which had invested Vienna. Some have computed it at 600,000 men, probably an exaggeration; but Ortelius, a writer generally to be depended upon, speaks of 500,000, and of these 300,000 horsemen. The first serious resistance which this immense accumulation of numerical force had to encounter, was opposed to it by the inconsiderable and scarcely fortified town, Güns.

The defence of this place ranks high among the instances in which patience and resolution, arrayed behind very feeble defences, have baffled all the efforts of numbers stimulated by the hope of plunder and a strong sense of the disgrace of failure. Nicholas Jurechich, a Croatian nobleman, was the leader to whom the credit of this defence is due. In the character of ambassador extraordinary from Ferdinand to the Sultan, he had very recently displayed firmness, temper, and sagacity; and now, behind walls which had been mined in thirteen different places, and which presented a practicable breach eight fathoms wide, with a body of troops originally of insignificant numbers and reduced by eleven assaults, he met with unshaken resolution a twelfth desperate attempt of the enemy.

It was all but fatal. The troops were nearly driven from the walls, upon which eight Turkish standards were already planted, when a shout of despair raised by the women and unarmed inhabitants of the place was mistaken by the assailants for the cheer of a reinforcement. The garrison profited by a moment of hesitation, and again succeeded in their noble effort. For twenty-five days they had occupied the whole force of the Turkish Empire in a fruitless attempt,—a period fully sufficient to exhaust the patience of the brave and impetuous but ill-disciplined armies of the faithful.

The *Sultan*, unwilling to waste a further portion of the best season and of his best troops before a place so unimportant in itself, adopted his usual expedient in such cases, magnanimity. He invited the commanders under a safe conduct to his presence, complimented them on their conduct, and making them a present of the town and citadel, a donation founded on a right of property on which they had no inclination to raise a verbal dispute, for the utter exhaustion of their resources of all kinds would have rendered further resistance impossible, withdrew his forces; not however, as was expected, in the direction of Neustadt and Vienna.

He marched, on the contrary, up the course of the Mur, by roads of the most difficult and harassing description; and, establishing himself in Styria, sat down before Gratz, which, after a tedious siege, he took and ransacked, but failed to reduce the citadel. Some writers are of opinion that this diversion of his force, in fact a circuitous retreat, was the work of the Vizier Ibrahim, who had been bribed by Charles V. Nothing has been discovered in the Austrian archives which contain the state secrets of the time, and no passage has been detected by such inquirers as Von Hammer in the pages of Turkish history to favour this supposition. The bribe also must have been a large one which could have influenced the conduct of a man who had the treasure of the seven towers at his disposal. A far more natural cause may be assigned for the movements of the *Sultan*.

The relative position of the two parties was very different from that of 1529. It is true the frontier provinces were, as then, exposed to the first onset of the invader; but the preparations of the House of Austria for defence were further advanced, better organised, and on a more respectable scale than before.

The Emperor Charles in person had put himself at the head of the troops of the Empire, and had well employed the interval of security which the delay of the *Sultan* before the town of Güns had afforded him. With an army rated at 260,000 men, of which however only 126,000 were combatants, namely, 96,000 infantry and 30,000 cavalry, he lay encamped at no great distance from Vienna. In his former campaign Soliman had sought in vain for the accursed Ferdinand, and had made much of his disappointment in the bulletins from his camp and in the pages of his servile historiographers. He was probably not equally desirous of falling in with such an antagonist as Charles, at the head of an untouched force of this magnitude. The sudden direction of his army upon provinces bare of troops, but which contained plunder to be gathered, and villages to be burned, and helpless people to be slaughtered, was a safe and a tempting, though inglorious proceeding.

These were the motives, as far as inquiry can now detect them, which postponed to a subsequent century the great spectacle of actual collision in the field between the main armies of Turkey and the Empire. Austria meanwhile derived from the postponement of so tremendous an issue no immunity from a repetition of the horrors of the last invasion. While the main Turkish army occupied Styria, the bands of Michael Oglou were again let loose upon her plains, re-enacting, up to the walls of Lintz and Vienna, every former atrocity.

If, however, they were allowed for a period thus to extend and pursue their ravages, they came at last within reach, not merely of the partial resistance by which the more adventurous of their parties had before been occasionally cut off, but of the heavy blows of a disciplined enemy. Vienna itself was in a state of defence which fully secured it against any attack from the irregular troops of the Turks; and it is not probable that Soliman at any time had contemplated a renewal of his attempt upon that city with his main army, for he had again left his heavy artillery behind; and all his preparations tended to a pitched battle in the open field.

The Pfalzgraf Frederick was able, therefore, with a strong detachment, to address himself to the deliverance of the open country from the marauders, and took up a position at Enzesfeld, which threatened the communications of Michael Oglou with Styria. The latter commenced a hasty retreat in the direction of Neustadt and Pottenstein; but the principal passes of the mountains beyond were already occupied by the Pfalzgraf; and a strong force of arquebuziers under a skilful officer, Sebastian Scheitl, moved upon his rear by Kaumberg. On the 18th of September, his main column, encumbered with plunder and with 4000 prisoners, was suddenly attacked by this detachment, and driven through Pottenstein towards the defiles in front, which were strongly occupied by the Pfalzgraf.

The savage leader, thus caught in the toils, kept up his character for courage and cruelty to the last. He directed an instant and indiscriminate massacre of his prisoners, setting the example with his own hand; and, dividing his forces into two bodies, scattered one into the pathless forests to the south, and headed the other and main body in a desperate attempt to cut its way to the front by the valley of Stahremberg. He fell among the foremost. His jewelled helmet, appropriately adorned with vultures' wings, was conveyed to Ferdinand, and may still, (1879), be seen in the Ambros Museum at Vienna.

On his fall, the command was assumed by his lieutenant, Osman, who struggled through the defiles only to fall in opener ground upon the troops of the Empire commanded by the Count Lodovic and the Margrave Joachim of Brandenburg. Tired horses and despairing riders fell an easy prey, not only to the troops, but to the peasantry. Attacked by the latter in the neighbourhood of Siebenstein, many were forced over a picturesque precipice, which still bears the name of the "Turkish Fall." Osman himself fell by the hand of Paul Bakics, who bore him from the saddle with his lance, and finished him with his own jewelled dagger, which hung at his saddle-bow.

Of this division of the robber force, nearly 18,000 strong, it is said that not one escaped. Those who were detached through the forests had better fortune. Part, at least of them, effected their junction with Soliman in Styria. In Austria the *Sackman* was seen no more. In Hungary, indeed, and Styria, their excesses continued for some years, but the frontier of Austria proper was henceforth secure. In the Battle of Guirgewo against the Poles in 1596, the last remnant of the Akindschis was destroyed, and the name appears no more in the Turkish annals. On the 2nd of October the Emperor Charles V. and his brother Ferdinand descended the river from Lintz, and were formally received at Vienna on the 3rd. A great review was held, at which Charles, to conciliate the Hungarians, appeared in the costume of that country. Soliman, on receiving intelligence of the fate of Michael Oglou, pursued his retreat with so much precipitancy and confusion, that if Charles had followed him with activity, the fate of Hungary must have been decided.

The affairs of religion, however, were nearer to the heart of Charles than those of Hungary, and the approaching convocation of the Council of Trent attracting him to Italy, the golden opportunity was lost. Zapolya retained possession of his throne, under the protection of 60,000 Turks encamped on the bank of the Drave. In 1538 the peace of Grosswaradin was concluded, in which Ferdinand recognised the usurper as King of Hungary in the portion of that country occupied by him, and as Wayvode of Transylvania, in return for the reversion of that kingdom on Zapolya's death, whose son, should he leave one, was to enjoy only the hereditary succession of his house, the Countship of Zips.

CHAPTER 2

1539 to 1566

In 1539, Zapolya, advanced in age, but anxious to bequeath his powers of mischief to a lineal descendant, contracted a marriage with Isabella of Poland. His wishes were gratified in the following year by the birth of a son; an event which he himself survived only twenty-four days. The ambitious mother, setting at defiance the terms of the treaty of Grosswaradin, asserted the claim of her child to the throne of Hungary, and invoked the protection of the *Sultan*. The secrecy with which the treaty of Grosswaradin had been concluded between Ferdinand and Zapolya had excited the deep indignation of the Sultan; and though, as might be supposed, fully determined to prevent its fulfilment in favour of Ferdinand, he was little inclined to allow the widow and race of Zapolya to profit by its infraction. In June, 1541, he for the ninth time took the field in person; and in August he appeared before Pesth, from which a besieging army of Ferdinand had lately been repulsed with loss.

On the 29th August, the fifteenth anniversary of the battle of Mohacs, the infant Zapolya was brought into his camp, and Pesth admitted a Turkish garrison. Much negotiation passed with the widowed queen; presents and civil speeches abounded on both sides; and finally she received, and counted probably at its real value, the solemn assurance of the Sultan that the capital should be restored to her son on the attainment of his majority. Meanwhile the young Zapolya was acknowledged as Wayvode of Transylvania; but a purely Turkish administration was organised and placed in authority over the whole extent of that portion of the kingdom of Hungary which had been under the real or nominal sovereignty of Zapolya. In a small part of it the House of Austria had all along maintained itself; nor did that power submit to the summary appropriation of the remainder by the enemy of Christendom.

For many a year, and through many a reign, Hungary continued the field of a struggle of race and religion, which the temporary exhaustion of either or both parties could but occasionally interrupt, and in which, during the lifetime of Ferdinand, the Turks had generally the advantage. In 1547, an armistice of five years was purchased by humiliating concessions on the part of Austria. *Punctually* at the expiration of the period hostilities were resumed, and continued without cessation or decisive result to the death of Ferdinand in 1564, and into the reign of his successor Maximilian II. In the prosecution of the struggle, this wise sovereign reaped advantage from the system of toleration which he extended to the powerful Protestant party in Hungary.

The Hungarian campaign of 1566 was distinguished by the famous siege of the small fortress of Szigeth, and the self-immolation of its defender, the Hungarian Leonidas, Nicholas, Count of Zriny. In early life he had distinguished himself at the siege of Vienna; and having pursued a successful career in arms, held under the present emperor the chief command on the right bank of the Danube. Soliman had undertaken the siege of Erlau; and the Pacha of Bosnia was on the march with reinforcements, when he was attacked near Siklos by Zriny, completely defeated, and slain. The *Sultan*, furious at this disaster, raised the siege of Erlau and marched with 100,000 men upon Zriny, who, with scarcely 2500, flung himself into Szigeth, with the resolution never to surrender it; a resolution to which his followers cheerfully bound themselves by an oath. To the utmost exertion of his vast military means of attack, Soliman added not only the seduction of brilliant promises, but the more cogent threat of putting to death the son of Zriny, who had fallen into his hands.

All was in vain. The *Sultan's* letter was used by Zriny as wadding for his own musket; and for seventeen days the town held out against repeated assaults. The enfeebled garrison were then driven to the lower castle, and at last to the upper one. No hope remained of repelling another general assault, for which the Turkish preparations were carried forward with the utmost vigour under the eye of the *Sultan*, who, however, was not destined to witness their issue. On the 6th of September he was found dead in his tent, having thus closed, at the age of seventy-six, by a tranquil and natural death, a reign of forty-five years, which for activity and variety of military enterprise, for expenditure of human life, and for the diffusion of the miseries of warfare, unmitigated by the conventional usages and inventions of later times, could scarcely find its parallel.

His decease afforded no respite to the besieged. The event was kept a rigid secret from the soldiery by the Vizier Ibrahim, who adopted the Oriental precaution of putting to death the physicians in attendance. Zriny did not wait for the final assault. On the 8th September the Turks were pressing forward along a narrow bridge to the castle, when the gate was suddenly flung open, a large mortar loaded with broken iron was discharged into their ranks, according to their own historians killing 600 of them, and close upon its discharge Zriny and his faithful band sallied forth to die. His resolution was evinced by some characteristic preparations. From four swords he chose a favourite weapon which he had worn in the first campaigns of his youth, and, determined not to fall alive into the hands of his enemies, he wore no defensive armour. He fastened to his person the keys of the castle and a purse of a hundred ducats, carefully counted and selected, of the coinage of Hungary. He said:—

> The man who lays me out, shall not complain that he found nothing upon me. When I am dead, let him who may take the keys and the *ducats*. No Turk shall point at me while alive with his finger.

The banner of the Empire was borne before him by Laurence Juranitsch. In this guise, followed by his 600 remaining comrades, he rushed upon the enemy, and by two musket-shots through the body and an arrow in the head obtained the release he sought. With some of his followers the instinct of self-preservation prevailed so far that they retired from the massacre which followed into the castle, where some few were captured alive. It is said also that some were spared in the conflict by the *Janissaries*, who, admiring their courage, placed their own caps on their heads for the purpose of saving them. Three *pachas*, 7000 *Janissaries*, and the scarcely credible number of 28,000 other soldiers, are said to have perished before this place.

The Vizier Ibrahim's life was saved by one of Zriny 's household, who was taken in the castle, which the *vizier* had entered with his troops. This man, to the *vizier's* inquiry after treasure, replied that it had been long expended, but that 3000 lbs. of powder were then under their feet, to which a slow match had been attached. The *vizier* and his mounted officers had just time to escape, but 3000 Turks perished in the explosion which shortly followed. Zriny's head was sent to the Emperor; his body was honourably buried, as some accounts state, by the hands of a Turk who had been his prisoner, and well treated by him. Szigeth never recovered from its destruction, and some inconsiderable ruins alone mark the scene of Zriny's glory.

CHAPTER 3

1566 to 1664

Soliman was succeeded on the throne by Selim II., son of a favourite slave, Roxalana. The male issue of the other inmates of the royal
harem, whether wives or concubines, had been remorselessly sacrificed to secure the undisputed succession of one who proved the first
of his race to set an example of degeneracy from the qualities which
had made his predecessors the terror of Christendom. Under the rule
of Soliman the power and reputation of the Porte had reached a point
of elevation from which it rapidly declined under his sensual and inactive successor, and to which it has never re-ascended. The structure,
indeed, raised by the warrior founders of the Ottoman dynasty, survived, without suffering material injury or diminution, too long for
the peace and safety of Europe; but this permanence was due less to
its own solidity than to the jealousies and dissensions of the Christian
powers, political and religious, but more especially the latter.

Within two years of Selim's accession, in 1568, he concluded with
the Emperor Maximilian an armistice on the basis of their respective
occupation of territory, by which the Turk remained in possession of
Lower Hungary. In 1575 this compact was renewed for eight years.
The younger Zapolya had previously agreed that after his decease
the government of Transylvania should devolve by election upon a
Wayvode, a subject of the crown of Hungary; and on his death, in
1571, Steven von Bathory had been accordingly elected. This prince
subsequently attained the crown of Poland, and in 1589 his cousin,
Sigismund, made over Transylvania to Hungary.

In 1590, in the reign of Rodolph II., son and successor to Maximilian, war again broke out between Austria and Turkey, and was prosecuted with much bitterness, but with alternations of success which
led to no important results. In 1595 the Turks, after two years of dis-

comfiture, recovered themselves so far as to approach the Austrian frontier in force, and seriously to threaten Vienna. The *landsturm* of that city was called out, and the defences were strengthened in all haste; but the force of Turkish invasion spent itself upon Upper Hungary. Several strong places in that, district having been surrendered, as was alleged, by treason and cowardice, Vienna became during several years the scene of bloody executions.

Thus, in 1595, Ferdinand Count Hardegg, and several of his officers, expiated on the scaffold the surrender of Raab. In the same year an engineer, Francis Diano, was executed on a charge of having undertaken to blow up the Rothenthurm bastion on the appearance of a Turkish force. Raab, after three years and a half possession by the Turks, was retaken by the Austrian commanders, Rodolph Schwarzenberg and Nicholas Palfy, an important service which the Emperor Rodolph acknowledged by the erection of columnar monuments, and by the addition of a raven to the escutcheon of the Schwarzenbergs. One of the columns remains to this day in the neighbourhood of Mödling.

In 1600 a mutinous project for the surrender of the fortress Papa was detected and suppressed by summary execution, and fifteen of the leaders were reserved for a more terrible example at Vienna, twelve of whom were quartered and three impaled. It would be tedious and disgusting to pursue the list of similar atrocities perpetrated both at Vienna and in the frontier fortresses. The Austrian authorities would appear to have considered that the devices of Oriental cruelty were the only remedies or preventives for treason and cowardice, and to have overlooked the fact that many of the misdemeanours so savagely punished were attributable to their own maladministration, to the inactivity of the emperor, and to the maltreatment and non-payment of the soldiery.

In 1609 the Archduke Mathias assumed the practical exercise of sovereignty, and on his formal succession to the imperial throne on the death of Rodolph in 1612, he transferred the imperial residence from Prague to Vienna. Under his administration better measures were applied to the existing evils than those which had, by their use and their failure, disgraced the reign of Rodolph. Mathias found himself shortly after his coronation compelled to prepare for a renewal of hostilities with the Turks, who were now in possession of the whole of Hungary and Transylvania, in addition to Moldavia and Wallachia. When, however, he made application to the states of the empire, the

Protestants, by far the majority, excused themselves on the allegation that no powers had been delegated to them to furnish aid to a Turkish war, and they recommended forbearance and delay in dealing with the hereditary enemy of Christendom. Mathias had no resource but to conclude an armistice for twenty years, which the Turks, on their part, exhausted by the long previous struggle, and no longer led by such a ruler as Soliman, were not reluctant to accept.

They retained, however, their conquests. This truce was observed with scrupulous and unshaken fidelity by the Turks under five feeble successors of Selim II., (Murad III., Mohammed III., Achmet I., Mustapha L, Osman II.) By this honourable forbearance, practised under strong temptation of advantage from its infraction and in resistance to the allurements of Christian powers, especially of France, Austria during the thirty years' war enjoyed immunity from attack on the most assailable portion of her frontier. Even Amurath IV., who ascended the throne in 1623, and was the first of Soliman's successors who showed symptoms of a warlike spirit, concluded a fresh truce with Austria, and thus the Turks remained tranquil through the first half of the seventeenth century.

In fact, the moral energy of their race had declined while civilization and attendant power had progressed in Christian Europe, and no exertion could have raised them to their former elevation. Amurath's son and successor Ibrahim, notorious for his vices and cruel actions, was strangled in 1648. He was succeeded by Mohammed IV., a boy seven years of age, during whose minority confusion reigned supreme. His grandmother and mother contended for power, and *Janissaries* and *spahis* fought over the dead bodies of *viziers*, murdered in rapid succession for the spoil, till they met, A.D. 1656, with a master in the energetic Mohammed Kinperli.

Under his administration internal licence was repressed by measures of salutary severity, and when foreign war again broke out it was conducted by him in a manner which revived the terror of the Turkish name. This war had its origin in the troubles of Hungary and Transylvania. The Transylvanians, on the death of their sovereign George Rakoczy, second of that name, elected as his successor a distinguished leader of his army, John Kemeni, who entered into an alliance with the Emperor Leopold I. At the instigation, however, of the Turkish *vizier*, a faction of Hungarian nobles set up a rival candidate, Michael Apafi. Kemeni was defeated and slain in the Battle of Nagy Szollos, fought against a Turkish force in 1662. Apafi seized on the government, cancelled all the measures adopted by Kemeni, and in an assembly of the States outlawed the adherents of Austria. He failed, however, in all his attempts upon the places occupied by German garrisons, and the presence of a so-called auxiliary Turkish force was a scourge rather than a protection to the exhausted country.

In 1663 Apafi was compelled to lead his forces in the train of the Vizier Achmed Kinperli, son of Mohammed, who was marching upon Hungary with the intention and expectation of annihilating the power of Austria. The advance of the Turks was so rapid and unimpeded that Vienna once more trembled at the prospect of a siege. The measures for defence, of destruction, and repair were, as usual in the moment of danger, commenced in haste, and prosecuted with more confusion than real despatch.

The progress of the Turks was favoured by disputes between the civil and military authorities of Austria, and the *vizier* was thus allowed, without opposition, to secure the open country of Transylvania, and to reduce the important fortress of Neuhaüsel. After these successes he marched with his main army on Raab, with the project of exciting alarm for the safety of Styria, and then of suddenly flinging himself upon Vienna. It was, however, the good fortune of the Emperor Leopold to possess at this period the services of the only great commander of the moment, Raymond, Count of Montecuculi, as general of his forces in Hungary. On the 1st of August, 1669, this leader overthrew the Turks, in numbers fourfold greater than his own, with the loss of 17,000 men and all their artillery, in the memorable Battle of St. Gothard. The armistice of Basvar followed close upon this victory. Twenty years were specified for its duration, but the civil and religious troubles of Hungary, and the severities by which Leopold sought to suppress them, led to its earlier infraction.

CHAPTER 4

The Troubled Borders

Montecucdli had derived but little assistance in his campaigns from the good will or aid of the Hungarians. Their disaffection led to the adoption by the Austrian Government of a course of measures at variance with the laws of the realm, and as impolitic as they were illegal, their main objects being to Germanise the nation, and to extirpate the Protestant heresy. The excesses of the German troops were such as to make the Hungarians, especially the Protestants, feel that they would rather gain than lose by the restoration of Mahometan rule. The proselytizing activity of the Jesuits was specially irritating to the non-Catholics, but the discontent was so general, that when the natural consequences broke out in the shape of an extensive and dangerous conspiracy, nearly all its leaders were dignitaries of the realm, and zealous Roman Catholics.

The emperor, whose natural disposition was mild and humane, was goaded to severity by the falsehoods and exaggerations of his advisers. The Hungarians, for instance, were accused of having poisoned the well of the citadel of Vienna. It was found, on examination, to have been tainted by the dead bodies of dogs and cats. The French ambassador, Grantonville, was exciting the emperor to measures for the extirpation of heresy, and the destruction of the Hungarian constitution and nationality, while, at the same time, he was holding secret communication with the heads of the Hungarian nobility—Counts Nadasky, Zriny, and Rakoczy, and encouraging their reunion.

At the head of the malcontents were the brave Palatine Francis Wesseleny, and Nicholas Zriny, a great grandson of the defender of Szygeth. At a meeting at Neusohl it was agreed to apply for Turkish assistance. The designs, however, of this formidable league were thwarted by the untimely deaths of the two above-mentioned leaders.

Zriny perished by a wound from the tusk of a wild boar, and Wesseleny was carried off in the prime of life by a sudden fever. The ranks of the conspirators could furnish no man worthy, from talent and influence, to replace the loss so unexpectedly incurred at this critical juncture; and the enterprise, falling into inferior hands, was commenced without plan and prosecuted without energy. The young Prince Rakoczy, and Peter Zriny, brother to the deceased, were the inefficient substitutes elected for its guidance. The latter had gained over to the cause his brother-in-law Francis Frangipani, a young and ardent man, incited by motives of revenge for an injury received from a German officer. The governor also of Styria, Count Tettenbach, a man related by marriage with the Hungarian leaders of the conspiracy, joined its ranks. He undertook to arm his peasants and foresters to the number of some thousands, to impart all official intelligence which should reach him, as governor, to the party, and to put them in possession of the town and citadel of Gratz.

Frangipani undertook to provide a naval force in the Adriatic, and to gain over the Uskok and Greek population of Croatia. The chief meetings of the parties took place at the castle of Pottendorf, on the Hungarian frontier, a residence of the Count Nadasky, in a summer-house, the roof of which was adorned with a rose in stucco, from which the common expression "*sub rosa*" derives its origin. The moment of execution for the designs of the conspirators was near at hand, when the danger, of incalculable magnitude to the Austrian government, was averted by an accidental disclosure. Tettenbach, too confident of success, had thrown into prison for some petty theft a servant initiated into the plot. This man, in the accidental absence of the count, was submitted, in the usual course of law, to the torture, and to save his life confessed all he knew.

The officers who administered the province in the absence of Tettenbach lost no time in forwarding the weighty intelligence to Vienna. Tettenbach on his return to Gratz was arrested. His papers contained ample evidence of his designs, which was confirmed by the discovery of arms for 6000 men in the cellars of his residence. The imperial minister, Prince Lobkowitz, offered a generous forgiveness to Zriny, bat sent a force to occupy his residence of Czakathurn. Zriny betrayed a fatal vacillation of purpose, observing in the first instance and afterwards violating the conditions of his pardon. He was finally, together with Frangipani, arrested, and confined at Czakathurn. Effecting their escape, they conceived the project of presenting themselves and offering their submission at Vienna.

Their project was betrayed to the emperor by a friend named Keri, with whom they had taken refuge. He was instructed to encourage them to persevere in their design, but should they depart from it, and proceed to join Rakoczy, to arrest them. Keri preferred, for the purpose of magnifying his own services, to act at once on the latter part of the instruction. He arrested and conveyed them to Neustadt. Rakoczy, who had taken as yet no open measures, fled to his mother, who by her influence with the Jesuits procured his pardon. Charles Duke of Lorraine besieged the fortress Murany, occupied by the widow of Wesseleny, Maria Szetsi. She surrendered it without resistance, and died some years after, a prisoner at Vienna.

The papers found at Murany compromised many leading men, and especially Nadasky, the Judex Curiae of Hungary, who bore the name of the Hungarian Croesus, coin to the amount of five millions being found in his treasury at Pottendorf. He also was conveyed a prisoner to Vienna. Of the remaining conspirators Stephen Tekeli was the most formidable. He died during the siege of his fortress of Arva by the imperialists. His daughters were dragged to prison at Vienna; but his son Emerich, afterwards so famous, escaped to Transylvania, and, joining the Turks, became an active adviser and promoter of every design of that power hostile to Austria.

An extraordinary commission was instituted at Vienna for the trial of the accused. Its acts were submitted to the Imperial Chamber at Spire, and to the universities of Ingoldstadt, Tubingen, and Leipzick, and these learned and merciless bodies unanimously condemned the prisoners to suffer all the refinements of cruelty which the practice of the age assigned to the crime of treason in the highest degree. The Imperial Privy Council advised the loss of the right hand and beheading, which the emperor mitigated to simple beheading, accompanied by degradation from the rank of noble and confiscation of property.

The ceremony of the degradation of Nadasky took place with the accustomed form of words, "No longer Count Nadasky, but thou traitor." He was then brought to the town-house by the captain of the city guard in a close carriage. The Pope, Clement X., had interceded for his life and that of Zriny, but in vain. On the 30th of April, 1674, at an early hour, the gates of the city were closed; the Burgher guard under arms; chains drawn across the streets; the principal public places occupied by regular troops, foot and horse.

In the Burgher hall, near the Register office, the scaffolding hung with red was prepared, and the executioner, John Moser, in attendance, the black staff in his right hand, the sword in his left. The spectators sat round, all dressed in black. A Turkish *chiaus* or officer of the *Sultan's* guard was present in a private tribune. Nadasky's head fell at one blow. The body was laid on a bier and exhibited till evening in the court of the town-house. It was then conveyed to the Augustines, and subsequently to the convent founded by the victim at Lockenhaus, in Hungary, where it is said to remain to this day uncorrupted. The sword and chair used in the execution are now in the Burgher arsenal. On the same day Frangipani and Zriny were also executed. Tettenbach's fate was deferred till December, when he also was beheaded at Gratz.

CHAPTER 5

1672 to 1680

The suppression of the dangerous conspiracy above described—however on many grounds we may sympathise with its authors—can hardly be considered in itself other than as an event favourable to the interests of Christian Europe. Unfortunately, however, the Austrian Government, not satisfied with the severity exercised on the leading conspirators, wreaked its impolitic and unjustifiable revenge upon the kingdom of Hungary at large. It was treated as a conquered country. The Protestant churches were closed; the preachers who declined to subscribe to conditions incompatible with the exercise of their functions were arrested, banished, and in some instances condemned to the galleys. Resistance and civil war ensued, more fertile in atrocities even than war with the Turk. The adherents of either party, as usual in cases of intestine strife, adopted popular designations long remembered for the misfortunes with which they were associated.

The national partisans were called *Kuruzzen*, probably a corruption of *Kreuzer*, or cross-bearer; and the German *lanzknecht* was modified into the term *Labanz*. Each impaled, or flayed, or roasted the other on every opportunity. The *Kuruzzen* not unfrequently passed the Austrian frontier, reviving, wherever they appeared, recollections of the atrocities of the *Sackman*. The name to this day is coupled with that of the Turks in Lower Austria. Then, as at subsequent periods, the insurgents received aid and encouragement from France, and in 1679 they were even joined by a force levied in Poland, and officered by Frenchmen. The young Tekeli also came forward to wreak his vengeance upon Austria. He defeated the Imperialists in several encounters, and even led his forces, joined by hordes of Tartar cavalry, to the walls of Neustadt, over the March field, and far into Moravia. A pestilence which broke out in this year could hardly persuade man to resign to the powers of nature the task of decimating his species; and it was not till the mortality of disease had reached an awful pitch that the spirit of mutual destruction came to a pause.

In 1681 a *diet* was convened at Œdenburg with views of reconciliation, and attended by the emperor in person. A *palatine* was elected, old privileges and institutions, the power of the Ban, and the frontier militia were revived, the licence of arbitrary taxation restrained, a general amnesty conceded, and the laws of the empire re-established, under which religious freedom was to be enjoyed by the professors of the Helvetic or Augsburg forms of Protestantism. The disruption, however, had gone too far to allow of a speedy and solid re-union of parties. The spirit of ambition and revenge in the bosom of Tekeli was not to be appeased even by the concession of his marriage with the widow of Rakoczy, which conveyed into his hands the important fortress of Munkacs.

The deputies of the Austrian Government also betrayed unfortunate and unreasonable indications of a lurking tendency to revengeful measures. The Hungarians, on the other hand, considered merely as their due the concessions obtained from the emperor. At last the parties agreed so far as to determine upon sending an embassy to Constantinople, with the purpose of obtaining a prolongation of the twenty years' truce, which was about to expire. Count Albert Caprara was the envoy selected. He left Vienna in February, 1682, with a large suite and rich presents, and instructions to spare no pains for the avoidance of a Turkish war. The utter fruitlessness of his mission was apparent to him from the date of his arrival at Constantinople. He found the war party in that city, with the Vizier Kara Mustapha at its head, eager to avail themselves of the distractions of Hungary, which Tekeli's emissaries could hardly exaggerate in their reports. Troops were sent before his face to the assistance of the rebels, and the conditions of peace demanded by the Porte were such as to extinguish all hope of an accommodation.

An annual tribute of 50,000 dollars was demanded in the first instance, the surrender of the territory between the Theiss and the Waag to the Turks, and of several places of strength to Tekeli. The latter was also to be recognized as Prince of Upper Hungary, and of equal rank with the Prince of Transylvania. Finally, the restitution of all the confiscated estates of the conspirators was insisted upon. Troops poured in from Asia and Egypt to support these pretensions, and swell the European forces collecting under the eye of the ambassador; and the demands of the Turks rose with the tidings they now received of the progress of the arms of Tekeli, till at last they claimed the fortresses of Raab, Komorn, and Szathmar, and an indemnification for their war expenses of six million dollars.

The ambassador saw the futility of further attempts at negotiation. His firm but temperate reply to the Vizier Kara Mustapha procured him the treatment of a prisoner of state. His couriers were detained, and he was reduced to despatch the tidings of Turkish insolence and preparation by secret messengers, and by the way of Venice to Vienna. He himself was compelled to accompany the Turkish army of invasion on its march. There was but too much ground for the Turkish confidence. The undefended condition of the Austrian frontier, the general inadequacy of the military preparations of that power, were known and appreciated at Constantinople; but it also happened that three Arabian astrologers had predicted the reduction of Vienna, the fall of the West Romish Empire, and moreover the further advance of the armies of the faithful to Rome and to the Rhine.

Even without respect to such prophecies as these, the moment was propitious for reducing to entire subjection the long disputed kingdom of Hungary; and the influence of Kara Mustapha, eager for war, prevailed against the serious opposition of the *ulema*, of the mother Sultana, Valide, and even against the inclination of the unwarlike Sultan Mohammed himself. The *vizier*, while he dazzled the latter with splendid visions of ulterior conquest, was influenced in secret by ambition on his own account. He destined for himself the plunder of Vienna, and he considered his own advancement to the throne of Hungary, at least as a tributary to the Porte, a reasonable and attainable reward for his anticipated success as leader of the army of the faithful. His influence with the *Sultan*, exerted to the utmost, gained the ascendancy over that of the *Sultana*. He contrived to win over the chief of his spiritual opponents.

The soldiery, including that formidable body the *Janissaries*, were naturally of the faction which promised them plunder and blood. The strong party which appealed by various methods against the injustice of the war was silenced by harsh measures; and by the autumn of 1682 the army was in motion under the immediate command of the *vizier*, and accompanied by the *mufti* and the principal dignitaries of the empire. It was halted, and encamped for the winter, at Adrianople, to refresh the contingents which had marched from the more distant Asiatic provinces, and to prepare for effective operations in the spring.

Here also it was joined by the *Sultan*, the pomp and expenditure of whose progress, and especially the hundred carriages devoted to the female portion of his retinue, moved the soldiery to rough comparisons with the practice of Murad IV., who took the field with one wife and two pages.

The army had to contend with those autumnal rains which more than once had impeded under Soliman the progress of similar expeditions. The superstition of the people interpreted these incidents of climate into omens of failure; but the *vizier*, though his own tent was swept away by an inundation which, on the first night after the troops were halted, ravaged the camp, was unshaken in his purpose, and the horse-tails continued planted before the royal residence in the direction of Hungary. The tedium of winter quarters was relieved by a royal chase, for which 30,000 peasants were collected to drive the game. The result, if the beaters themselves are not reckoned, was small—one wild boar, six roes, and thirty hares—but a much larger number of the beaters perished from exhaustion. Where the *Sultan* met with their corpses he observed that they had probably spoken ill of him, and had met with their reward—a safe and satisfactory assumption.

In the following spring, while the army was mustered in presence of the *Sultan*, a still more violent storm occurred, which among other exploits of its fury carried off the turban from the head of the sovereign. Undeterred by this omen, the *Sultan* accompanied the march of his army as far as Belgrade, where on the 12th May he received the ambassadors of Tekeli. Here, however, he also received intelligence of an event which, could his Arabian soothsayers have predicted its results, might still have made him pause in the prosecution of his purpose. This was no less than the signature of an alliance between the Emperor and John Sobieski, King of Poland.

On the following day he committed the green standard of the Prophet, and with it the chief command, to the *vizier*, who undertook the further conduct of the campaign uncontrolled by the presence of a master who had not the taste of his earlier ancestors for the fatigues of the march or the dangers of the field. The strength of the regular force with which he took the field is known with accuracy from the muster-roll which was found in his tent in the lines at Vienna. We thus find the total strength of the regular troops amounting to 275,000 men. The attendants on baggage, commissariat, camels, horses, &c., were never numbered, and would be difficult to calculate. If we add the force which afterwards joined the Turks under Tekeli, including

12,000 Tartars, 13,000 *Janissaries*, and 2000 *Spahis*, and amounting in all to 60,000 fighting men, we cannot estimate the numbers which poured into Hungary at less than 400,000.

The approach of the Turkish Army, following upon his own successes, excited the pride of Tekeli to the utmost. He assumed the title of Duke of Hungary, and threatened with banishment and even with death all who should fail to appear at a Diet which he summoned to assemble at Kaschau. He struck coins, now become rare, with his own likeness, and the legend, "*Emericus Comes Tekly in Kaesmarki, Dux Ungariae*," and on the obverse a naked sword with the words "*Pro Deo et Patriâ.*" Several French officers and engineers served in his forces, in pursuance of the unworthy policy of Louis XIV., whose jealousy of the House of Hapsburg rejected no means, however disgraceful, and no ally, however discreditable; and overlooked all the evil consequences to Christendom of the success of the schemes he thus supported. The last proposals for peace conveyed from the Austrian court to Tekeli, by the Baron Sapomara, were haughtily rejected.

At Essek, where he was received with royal honours by the *vizier*, he accepted at the hands of the latter his investiture as Prince of the kingdom of Hungary, which he acknowledged subject to the Porte. With all his pomp, and after all his exploits, he was but what J. Zapolya had been before him, a scourge in the hands of Providence to a miserable country, a tool and catspaw to the *Sultan* and the *Sultan's* slaves.

CHAPTER 6

1682 to 1683

On the 8th December, 1682, the servants of Count Caprara had reached Vienna with tidings of the enormous preparations of the Turks. The reports from Hungary were also unfavourable, and the necessity for immediate measures of defence was palpable as it was urgent. The first requisite, money, was sought for in an impost of a hundredth part of the means of the higher and lower nobility, and of the clergy, usually exempt from such burthens, but considered liable in the case of invasion by the enemy of Christendom. It was, however, to Poland that Austria now looked with the deepest anxiety, though it must have been with profound reluctance, and at first with little expectation of success, that the emperor could turn to that quarter for assistance.

The fate of Hungary at the least, and of the Austrian capital, hung, however, on the success of Austrian diplomacy with the great soldier, John Sobieski, who now filled the throne of Poland. His neutrality alone would have left both to a certain fate, and even that neutrality was hardly to be depended upon; for at a recent period French officers in the service of Tekeli had been allowed to commence the levy of a force in Poland for the support of that dangerous ally of the Turks. Mohacs had been lost by the defection of Zapolya. John Sobieski as a leader was as much superior to Zapolya as the 20,000 Sarmatian horse which he and he alone could bring into the field were superior to Zapolya's Transylvanian cavalry.

A long course of slights received and interests thwarted had alienated him from the throne of Austria, and cemented the connexion which his education, his marriage, and his political interests had hitherto maintained with France. To remove these obstacles, it was necessary in the first instance for the hereditary sovereign of the House of Hapsburg to concede to the Elective King of Poland the title of

Majesty. This was an act of derogation which nothing but hard necessity could have wrung from a sovereign so faithful to the traditions of Austrian etiquette as Leopold. It was easier to hold out hopes, which he never intended to realise, of more substantial advantages, of a marriage between Prince James, the heir of Sobieski, and an Austrian archduchess, and of the establishment of themselves and their descendants on an hereditary throne. The devices, however, of diplomacy would probably have been unavailing to overthrow the influence of France, which was unceasingly exerted against that of Vienna, but for an accident of the time.

Porta salutis
Quâ minimè reris Graiâ pandetur ab urbe.

The intrigues of the French court were defeated by those of a Frenchwoman. Sobieski had espoused, in 1665, ten years before his accession to the throne, Marie Casimire de la Grange, daughter of Henri de la Grange, Marquis d'Arquien. She had early acquired an influence over her husband, which she exerted in a manner almost uniformly detrimental to his peace, his interests, and those of his kingdom; and the wife of 41 continued now to exercise over the consort of 53 the dangerous fascination of a mistress. It pleased that Providence, which so frequently works out its greatest designs by contemptible instruments, to disappoint this woman in an intrigue which she had set on foot at Versailles for the elevation of her father to a French dukedom.

On her announcement of an intended journey to France, question had been raised in this quarter also as to that title of Majesty which has been mentioned as affecting her husband's relations with Austria. These, and such as these, were the influences which are said at this critical moment to have caused the scale to descend in favour of Austria, to have outweighed the uxorious Sobieski's recollections of his education in France, to have saved Vienna and rescued Hungary from Mahometan rule. That other and sounder considerations had not their influence upon Sobieski's decision, it would be preposterous to suppose. Sincere and earnest to the verge of bigotry in his attachment to the Romish form of Christianity, he could not look with indifference to the probable success of the Turkish arms in Hungary and Austria. He had received, however, assurances from Turkey that in the event of his continued neutrality the Polish frontier should be kept free from invasion.

To that neutrality he was in strictness bound by the fidelity with which the Ottoman Porte had observed the engagements of her last pacification with Poland—a fidelity which all historians agree has usually characterized the proceedings of the Porte, and which stands out in strong and frequent contrast with the practice of Christian States. Relying on the faith of treaties, Mohammed IV. had left the important fortress of Kaminiec and the frontier of Podolia unguarded; and if Sobieski had sought for an excuse to avoid alliance with Austria, he might have found it in the obligations of the Treaty of Zurawno, which had been so faithfully observed by the Turks. Rome, however, was at hand to dispense with these obligations towards the *infidel.*

Advisers meanwhile were not wanting to suggest that by continuing awhile a spectator of a struggle which must produce exhaustion on either side, and by striking in at the proper time and in the proper quarter, Sobieski might best find occasion to recover from the Turk the much coveted fortress of Kaminiec. It was under such circumstances that the good genius of Christendom stepped in in the disguise of an intriguing Frenchwoman. Influenced for once in a right and sound direction by his wife, and inspired by the memories of former victories, among others of that great Battle of Choczim, in which he had seen the turbans floating thick as autumnal leaves on the Dniester, he flung his powerful frame into the saddle and his great soul into the cause, and gladly forgot, in the congenial occupation of collecting and recruiting his reduced and scattered army, the perpetual intrigues of his court and household.

By the treaty now concluded the two sovereigns contracted a mutual obligation to assist each other against the Turk, bringing into the field respectively 60,000 and 40,000 men. The emperor conceded a questionable claim to the salt-mines of Wieliezka, and the more important point of a pretension to the eventual succession to the crown of Poland in favour of his son. He was well advised to exact that the treaty should be ratified by the solemn sanction of an oath administered by a Cardinal Legate. There is no doubt that the sense entertained by Sobieski of the obligation of this oath had a serious influence on his subsequent conduct. By a precaution to which Pascal, had he been alive, might have referred as illustrative of the practices which spring from the school of Loyola, the two parties to this oath bound themselves not to resort to the Pope for any dispensation from its observance.

How far it was logical and consistent thus to limit the Pope's power, and confine its valid operation to one dispensation, it is not for

Protestants to decide. The Abbé Coyer quotes this as a secret article. Possibly at the moment the parties were ashamed of it; but it is extant in the copy of the treaty printed in Dumont's *Corps Universel Diplomatique*, 1731. It was agreed that, should either sovereign take the field in person, the chief command should be vested in him. This article was doubtless intended to effect the purpose, which it accomplished, of turning to practical account the acknowledged military talents of Sobieski, and the terror which his name excited among the Turks.

No provision is made in the treaty for the contingency of the appearance of both sovereigns in the field. Leopold was no soldier; and though he at one time threatened a visit to the army, from which he was judiciously dissuaded by his confessor, it is not probable that he ever contemplated an appearance on the field of battle. An anecdote however is current that, after the great success before Vienna, he reproached his minister, Sinzendorf, for having advised his absence from the field, with so much bitterness, that the latter died of the infliction. If this had been believed at the time, it is not probable that Sobieski would have failed to report so piquant an anecdote in his correspondence with his wife.

In Poland as well as in Austria time was required to bring into the field the forces promised on all hands; and in the meantime the Austrian frontier was uncovered, for the Imperial army under command of the brave and experienced Duke Charles of Lorraine, stationed in the neighbourhood of Presburg, scarcely amounted to 33,000 men. From this scanty force garrisons were to be drawn for Raab, Komorn, Leopoldstadt, and Presburg two flying corps to be furnished against the first advance of the enemy on the Raab and the Mur, and with the overplus the Austrian monarchy was to be upheld till the promised succours should appear. Austria was fortunate in the leader upon whom these difficult and complicated duties devolved. Trained to arms against the Turks under Montecuculi, and against Condé under William of Nassau, Charles Leopold, Duke of Lorraine, had matured his military talents, in independent command, against the armies of France, through several scientific campaigns on the Rhine and in Flanders.

He was now in a situation which required him to call forth all the resources acquired in such schools as these, and which demanded a cautious and patient application of strategical and tactical lore to retrieve the disadvantages of vast disparity of numbers and great local difficulties of position. To make any serious stand against the first rush of the invaders with the small force at his command was impossible, and his first duty was to save from destruction an army outflanked and nearly surrounded, upon the extrication of winch the ultimate preservation of the capital depended. It was manifest, under these circumstances, that Vienna must again bide the brunt of the storm.

The shape of the city was nearly what it had been in 1529, and what it still continues, but the defences had been improved under Ferdinand III. and Leopold I. The entire population of the neighbouring country were now summoned by Imperial edict to labour on the outworks, and to fell trees for palisades. On the fortifications themselves 3000 labourers were daily employed, and the families in the suburbs were called upon to furnish a man from each house for two months for the same object. Elevated spots within range of the walls, and the nearer houses, as in 1529, were levelled, and upwards of 30,000 palisades of solid oak prepared and disposed. On the 20th March the labourers mustered from all sides, and the work of fortification went on from that date with regularity, but slowly, from the insufficient supply of tools and materials. By another edict every citizen was summoned under heavy penalties to furnish himself with provisions, for a year's consumption, within the space of a month. Those clearly unable to do so were directed to quit the city.

While these measures were in progress hostilities had commenced in Upper Hungary. The Pacha of Neuhaüel received orders under pain of the bowstring to make himself master of the Schütt island of the Danube. He attempted in the middle of February to pass the river for this purpose on the ice, but it broke, and he was compelled to retire with a loss of 90 men. On the 8th of March he repeated the attempt with 2000 men. but after a partial success, was driven back into the fortress with loss by the Imperialist, Colonel Castelli. Other places, however, of small note fell into the hands of the Turks, and the tide of war rolled steadily on towards Vienna. On the 6th of May the Emperor reviewed the army near Kitsee, but it had as yet received no material accession to its strength. Hungary, although at a Diet held in Oedenburg it had promised a levy *en masse*, had as yet scarcely furnished 3000 men. under the Palatine Esterhazy, a number insufficient to protect the shores of the Raab and the Danube from the predatory excursions of the Turkish garrison of Pesth.

The emperor, accompanied by such of the princes of the empire as were present, inspected the army, distributed 500,000 florins among the troops, and caused the Pope's indulgence to be read to them by the Primate of Hungary, the Archbishop of Gran. In a council of war, in which it is probable the Lorraine was overruled by the influence of the court, it was determined to adopt the course, difficult if not impossible, of taking the initiative of hostilities in Hungary, on the reliance that the main army of the Turks could not be in presence before July, and in the hope of encouraging the troops by some preliminary success. It was first proposed to lay siege to Gran; but as it was found impossible to close the passage of its supplies by the Danube, and 20,000 men were moving from Pesth to its relief, this enterprise was abandoned, and the army encamped on the 3rd of June before Neuhaüsel.

The *pacha* made answer to a summons that the Imperialists should learn to what kind of men the *Sultan* confided his fortresses, and he was as good as his word. The Imperialists had carried the suburbs and attacked the body of the place when they were driven back by a successful sally with the loss of two young volunteers of distinction, the Counts Taxis and Kazianer. The report also reached them of the approach of the Turkish main army, and of the wide-spread irruption of its forerunners, the Tartar cavalry, which threatened their line of retreat. On the 10th June this siege without an object was raised, and the army withdrew along the Danube, but not without loss from sallies of the enemy. Garrisons were hastily flung into Raab, Komorn, and Leopoldstadt, sufficient for their defence should the enemy leave them in his rear. The army, reduced by this draft on its numbers to about 12,000 foot and 11,000 horse, took up the best position it could find between the Raab and Raduitz, and there awaited the approach of the enemy.

CHAPTER 7

From June 30 to July 13, 1683

The *vizier* during the above transactions had led the main army by way of Belgrade as far as Essek, where, as before related, his meeting with Tekeli took place. In the discussions of a council of war held at this place, several *pachas* and Tekeli himself declared their opinions strongly against undertaking a siege of Vienna, at least in the current year. They recommended, not without substantial military grounds, the previous reduction of the strong places in Hungary still held by the Imperialists, and the establishment of a base for further operations in the complete subjugation of that kingdom. The *vizier*, obstinate in his own view, and irritated by the strength of the opposition, concealed his determination, and, appearing to acquiesce in the advice of Tekeli, gave orders for an advance upon Raab, which was invested and summoned on the 30th of June.

The governor returned a reply to the summons by which, whether by collusion or accident, he played into the hands of the *vizier*. It stated the impossibility of a present surrender: the *vizier* would do well to pursue his march on Vienna: after the fall o that city Raab should be surrendered without resistance. In a council of war, the aged Ibrahim Pacha, Governor of Pesth, strongly advocated the reduction of Raab and the other fortresses of Hungary. A king, he said, once placed a heap of gold on the middle of a carpet, and offered it to anyone who could take it up without treading on the carpet. A wise man rolled up the carpet from the corner, and thus obtained possession of the gold. Hungary was the carpet, and if rolled up in like manner the gold might be reached in the autumn, or at latest in the following spring.

This apologue only drew down the insolent wrath of the Vizier upon the venerable councillor, and Raab was left unmolested in the rear of the advancing army, which the Tartar hordes preceded in all directions. With the exception of a few places, which, surrendering themselves to Tekeli, were spared from destruction, the old system of havoc was everywhere pursued. The works of man were everywhere destroyed, and the population slaughtered, or dragged into captivity. The Imperial army soon beheld the flames of burning villages rising in the rear of its position. Not a moment was to be lost in effecting its retreat: the infantry had scarcely time to fling itself into the Schütt island, and thence, gaining the left bank, to pursue its retreat over the March field to Vienna. The cavalry, under the immediate command of the Duke of Lorraine, retired by Altenburg and Kitsee.

Its advanced guard was, on the 7th of July, surprised near Petronel by an attack of 15,000 Tartars, and the whole body was thrown into a confusion which, but for the presence and exertions of its commander, might have been fatal. He was ably seconded by the Margrave Louis of Baden, the Duke of Sachsen Lauenberg, and others, and, order once restored, the enemy was repulsed without difficulty. About 200 men fell on the side of the Turks; the Austrians lost only sixty, but among them were a young prince of Aremberg and Louis of Savoy, elder brother of the future conqueror of the Turks, Eugene. The first fell by the Turkish sabre; the latter was crushed beneath his horse. The baggage of the Dukes of Sachsen Lauenberg and Croy, and of General Caprara, containing their plate, with which it was the fashion of the day for generals to encumber themselves, fell into the hands of the Tartars.

The tidings of this action produced their immediate effects on either party. The *vizier*, on the day after receiving them, crossed the Raab. He took care to disseminate through his ranks exaggerated reports of the discomfiture and confusion of the Imperialists, and of the unprovided condition of Vienna; and while he stimulated the Janissaries by the prospect of an easy triumph and boundless plunder, he silenced the opposition of the timid and the wise by the promulgation of the *Sultan's Hatti Scheriff*, which invested him with sole and unlimited power of command. Some time, however, had been lost in deliberation, and in going through the formality of the investment of Raab, and these moments were precious to the defenders of Vienna. The usual tendency to exaggerate evil tidings had strongly displayed itself in that city.

The skirmish of Petronel had been magnified into the total defeat and hasty flight of the Imperial army. Those who had been the first to leave the field, and therefore knew least of the actual result, were the authors of this intelligence; and it derived dismal probability from the flames which reddened the nightly horizon in many directions and at no great distance. The villages, for instance, of Schwechat and Fischamend gave this evidence of the presence of the Turkish horse.

The Emperor Leopold was not one of those rare instances of military talent on the throne which appear once perhaps in a century in the shape of Gustavus Adolphus, John Sobieski, or Charles XII. Such men by their presence would have made a capital impregnable. Leopold would have been but an encumbrance during a siege; and he adopted the wiser course of removing himself and his court to a sufficient distance from the scene of danger. Before, however, he had decided on this step, events had left him little time to lose; and it had become matter of serious deliberation which road he should take to avoid the risk of falling into the hands of the Tartar cavalry. The direct road to Lintz was adjudged by his council no longer free from this danger, and it was determined that he should make his way thither by the left bank of the Danube.

On the evening of the 7th, therefore, the long file of the Imperial carriages issuing from the Rothenthurm gate crossed the Leopoldstadt island and the Tabor bridge, and reached that evening the village of Chor Neuburg, some fifteen miles from Vienna, which had been previously occupied by a small detachment of musketeers under an Irish officer, whose name, probably O'Haggerty, has been Germanized into Von Haffti. Thence he pursued his journey to Lintz, but not without serious risk. It is said that but for the prompt and able interference of the French envoy, the Marquis de Sepville, who caused a part of the bridge at Crems to be removed, the Emperor and his entire suite would have fallen into the hands of the Tartars. It would be a curious matter of inquiry how far this important service was approved of at Versailles.

It is evident that the first route proposed would have consigned the head of the empire, his consort, far advanced in pregnancy, and the empress mother, to the hands of the Tartars. Even Lintz was considered insecure; and the Royal party continued its discreditable flight till it found refuge beyond the frontier of its own dominion in the Bavarian fortress of Passau. From nine in the evening till two of the following morning the carriages of the wealthier fugitives, who followed the example of the court, filed over the Tabor bridge, lighted on their route by the flames of the Carmelite convent on the Kahlenberg. They left the city in a state of well-grounded alarm and discontent bordering upon revolt. The public feeling was strongly evinced against the Jesuits, who were not unjustly accused of having instigated the naturally mild disposition of the emperor to courses which had alienated the affections of the Protestants, and driven them into the arms of an *infidel* enemy.

The city also, thus left to itself, was at this moment nearly without a garrison. Besides the usual *burgher* guard, a mere police force, the regiment of Kaiserstein, about 1000 strong, were the only troops within the walls. The palisades were not fixed; the bastions were unprovided with artillery or gabions. The number of those who left the city on the 6th and 7th of July amounted to 60,000, of whom a large proportion, whose means of conveyance failed them on the way, and all those who took the road of Styria, fell into the hands of the enemy. The Turks are said to have used bloodhounds to hunt down those who fled to the woods. So large an emigration reduced to a fearful extent the number of citizens capable of bearing arms. The courage, however, of this remnant was somewhat restored on the 8th by the appearance of the cavalry, who filed through the city with much military clangour and display, and encamped in the meadows near the Tabor.

This substantial contradiction of the rumour previously circulated of the total destruction of the imperial army was well calculated to produce a reaction on the public mind; but a still happier impression was made by the arrival on the same day of Ernest Rudiger, Count Stahremberg, another pupil of the Montecuculi school, to whom, on the score of his successful defence of Moravia against the incursions of Tekeli in 1681, the emperor now confided the command and defence of the city. He lost no time in setting all hands to work on the fortifications; but at first little more could be done than to complete the fixing of the palisades, for the scarcely credible fact is on record that the necessary works for the main defence of the city could not be prosecuted for want of the common and essential tools.

The annals of the city are silent as to the parties responsible for this monstrous neglect; but it is certain that if the Turks had not lingered before Raab, or if by greater expedition on the march they had arrived before Vienna a few hours sooner than they did, that city must have fallen without a blow, and with all its treasures, into the hands of the destroyer.

It was not till the following day after Stahremberg's arrival that, by the unwearied exertions of the Imperial Chancellor Benedict Geizer, the contents of the secret archives and the treasury were conveyed away by the Danube under circumstances of imminent peril. The population of all classes, the richest citizens, and even women and ecclesiastics, now laboured unremittingly at the fortifications. The burgomaster, Von Liebenberg, set the example, doing active service with a wheelbarrow. The wood stored for building or fuel without the walls was conveyed into the town; every householder was enjoined to have water ready on his roof, and all persons whose usual employment would be in abeyance during the siege were armed and taken into the regular service of the state. They formed a body of 1200.

The most important works were conducted between the 7th and the 12th July, and towards the end of that period almost under the eye of the enemy, who on the 10th had crossed the Austrian frontier at Hungarian Altenburg, destroying everything as he advanced. At Klosterneuburg a number of boats were collected for the construction of a floating bridge there in case of necessity, and the arsenals were well stored with ammunition brought by water from Crems. On the 12th the nearer vicinity of the enemy was evinced by the contracting circle of blazing villages. From the Hungarian frontier to the neighbourhood of the Kahlenberg every unfortified place bore lurid token of Turkish occupation—Baden, Mödling, Ebenfurt, Inzersdorf, Pellendorf, Laxenburg, Laa. Neustadt alone held out by the strength of its walls and the gallantry of its inmates. Perchtolsdorf emulated this example in the first instance, but its ulterior fate demands separate and particular narration.

The Tartar bands in the course of this day ventured as far as St. Marks, and to the present Theresianum. All that man can do to blast the results of human labour and defeat the powers of production inherent in a fruitful soil was performed by this tribe of human locusts. One spot alone was held sacred by them: this was the imperial villa at Sommering, occupying and nearly co-extensive with the site of Soliman's tent at the former siege. From respect to his memory this building was spared and converted into a magazine. These scenes of desolation were not confined to Lower Austria.

The marauders followed the course of the Danube into the Upper Province, and even in Bavaria and Suabia the terror of their rumoured approach was such that many of the inhabitants fled with their moveable effects to Switzerland and over the Rhine. On the 13th July, towards 8 a.m., several bodies of Turkish horse showed themselves on the Wienerberg, whence they spread themselves towards Schönbrunn, Hietzing, Ottakrin, Hernals, and Währing as far as Döbling and Nussdorf. Towards 2 p.m. another numerous body showed itself from St. Marks, which took possession of the whole ground from the so-called Gatterholzel to the Hundsthurm. The first fire from the city was opened on these troops, which caused them to retire behind the enclosures of the numerous vineyards of this neighbourhood.

At this, the last available moment, the commandant gave the order, which an hour's delay would have made impossible of execution, to set fire to the suburbs, the inhabitants of which had on the previous day removed their property into the city. The conflagration was general and effective for its purpose: many costly buildings, public as well as private, were its victims, and many valuable contents still remaining in them shared their fate. A high wind sprung up at the same time, and as much timber was still accumulated near the palisades and up to the walls of the city, it required all the exertions of the *commandant* and the city authorities to prevent the city itself from sharing the disaster which was intended for its preservation.

Stahremberg has been by some blamed for postponing so long the destruction of the suburbs. Others would have been found to blame him if, while a hope or a possibility remained of an abandonment of their undertaking by the Turks, he had given so many costly public edifices, so many abodes of luxury and comfort, so much wealth, to the flames. To the last moment that hope was probably entertained—that possibility might reasonably be held to exist. The disputes in the Turkish council were no secret, and perhaps were exaggerated in the imperfect reports which reached Vienna. The movement on Vienna might be an empty menace; even if serious, it might be frustrated by a counter advance of the forces of the Empire.

If these or other possible contingencies had occurred, what complaints of ruined proprietors would have assailed him—what a stigma of useless barbarity would chroniclers have attached to the name since become so famous! The circumstances were very different in 1529. The suburban buildings of that day were of far less extent and value, but approached much nearer to the city; and the necessity of their demolition was much more palpable, inasmuch as after the fall of Pesth the advance of such a leader as Soliman was a matter of far greater certainty than that of the *vizier* in this instance; the more so because in the former case there was no regular force whatever to oppose the invasion—in the present, an army of some strength, well disciplined, and ably commanded, was in the path of the invader.

The ultimate event certainly justified the wary advice of the old

Pacha of Pesth, but it was rather in the execution of his plan than in its conception that the *vizier* can now be held to have failed. If Vienna had fallen, we should have heard little of the rashness of the rapid and daring march by which so great a blow had been struck, and the operation would have been possibly considered as an anticipation of the system of Napoleon by a semi-barbarian but kindred genius. As such indeed it is now considered by some military critics.

CHAPTER 8

From the 13th to the 19th July

In the evening of the 13th, the infantry of the Imperial army destined for the garrison of Vienna marched into the city; and now all the gates, even including that of the Rothenthurm, by which these troops had entered, were built up and barricaded. On the same day two summonses in the Latin language were thrown over the counterscarp. They remained unanswered. The following were the military arrangements for the defence:—Stahremberg's principal subordinates in command were the Generals Daun and Serini; the Brigadiers Souches and Scheffenberg; the Marquis of Obizzi, commander of the city guard; Colonels the Duke of Wirtemberg, the Baron von Beck; Counts Dupigny and Heister—all men of experience and proved courage. (Sigbert Count von Heister, one of the best soldiers of his day. At the beginning of the siege his hat was shot through by a Turkish arrow. Arrow and hat are preserved in the Ambros collection at Vienna.)

The affairs of the city were managed by a separate and secret college of Imperial Councillors of State, of which the President was Count Cappliers. The other members were Count Molart, Marshal of Austria; the Baron von Belchamin; Hartmann von Hüttendorf, and the Secretaries Haekl and Fux. Among those who volunteered their services in any capacity, the worthy Bishop of Neustadt, Leopold Count von Kollonitsch, demands special mention. The Bishop of Vienna, Emerich Sinellius, had accompanied the Emperor to Passau, and had thus left the affairs of his see to be administered by one who by his discharge of spiritual functions, by his expenditure on works of charity, and by his attendance on the sick and wounded, earned a reputation as sound and as honourable as could be obtained by others in the battery or the breach.

Nor was his ministry confined to these sacred functions. He had served as a Knight of Malta in his youth against the Turks, and his military experience now became scarcely of less value than his spiritual labours. He was among the most active at the side of Stahremberg; was his companion daily at the posts of greatest danger, encouraging the combatants by his example, tending the wounded, and administering the rites of religion to the dying. The systematic arrangements for the extinction of fires, for the collection and distribution of provisions, and for the prevention of extortion during the siege, were all due to this remarkable man. In the crowded hospital, where the mien of death is most hideous, he was to be found dispensing hopes of heaven to those who had no longer hope on earth. Women, children, and old men, usually the burthens of a besieged place, were by him organised and disciplined for services which would have otherwise drawn off defenders from the walls.

Through his exertions also a subscription was set on foot, which, backed by his own liberal contributions, and those of other leading men, such as Prince Ferdinand of Schwarzenberg, who contributed 50,000 florins and 3000 *eimers* of wine, reached the sum of 600,000 florins. The example of this prelate was emulated by Maximilian, Count of Trautmansdorf; Charles, Count of Fünfkirchen; Godfrey, Count of Salaburg; Count Vignoncourt; Matthew, Count of Colalto; Frederick, Baron of Kielmansegg, who besides his services in action assisted the defence by the invention of a powder-mill, and of a hand-grenade. To the above names are to be added those of Zetteritz, Rünnlingen and Rosstauscher.

The garrison consisted of 13,000 regular troops from the regiments of Stahremberg (now of the Archduke Louis, No. 8); Mansfield (now Duke of Lucca, No. 24); Souches (now Archduke Rainer, No. 11); Bock (now Grand Duke of Baden, No. 59); Scherfenberg; of the half regiments Pfalz Newburg (now Hohenegg, No. 20); Thungen (now Wellington, No. 42); Heister, and nine companies of Dupigny's horse; finally, of the usual city-guard, 1200 strong. In addition to these, all men capable of bearing arms were called out and divided into companies. These amounted to 2382, and were commanded first by the *burgomaster*, John Andrew von Liebenberg, and after his death by fever, by his successor, Daniel Focky. Ambros Frank, a member of the inferior town-council, formed a free corps 255 strong, principally composed of tavern-keepers. In the university, 700 students armed themselves and were distributed into three companies under the command of the Rector Magnifiens, Laurence Grüner.

The merchants and wholesale dealers formed a company of 250 men. The officials and servants of the Imperial household formed a corps of nearly 1000 men, commanded by Maximilian, Count of Trautmansdorf. Finally, many guilds and corporations formed themselves into companies either separate or conjoined. Thus, for example, the butchers with the brewers, 294 strong. The bakers, 150. The shoemakers, 288. The remaining handicraftsmen, 300 in number, were distributed into two companies; some others were employed in the arsenals. The guilds furnished in all 1293 men. The number under arms altogether amounted to about 20,000. The remaining population was not less than 60,000 souls.

At sunrise of the 14th July the main force of the enemy showed itself on the heights of the Wienerberg. It was difficult for the most practised eye to distinguish particular objects from amidst the multitudinous crowd of men, horses, camels, and carriages. The mass extended itself from the Lauer wood to near the Hundsthurm, by Gumpendorf, Penzing, Ottakrin, Hernals, Währing and Döbling, towards Nussdorf and the Danube, in a circuit of some 25,000 paces. The camp was marked out in the form of a half-moon. In a few hours 25,000 tents had risen from the ground.

That of the *vizier* was pitched on the high ground in the present suburb of St. Ulric, behind the walls of the houses which had been burned. It rivalled in beauty and splendour of decoration Soliman's famous pavilion of 1529, being of green silk worked with gold and silver, and adorned within with pearls, precious stones, and carpets, and contained in a central sanctuary the sacred standard of the Prophet. Within its precincts were baths, fountains, and flower-gardens, and even a menagerie.

In respect of its numerous alleys and compartments, it was likened to a town of canvas. The value of it with its contents was estimated at a million dollars. Under St. Ulric, towards the Burg gate, the *aga* of the *Janissaries* had arrayed his forces: the precincts of St. Ulric itself were occupied by the Tartars under Kara Mehemed.

The other *pachas* were stationed opposite the Kärnthner and Stuben gates, and the city was threatened from five distinct quarters, though it was soon easy to perceive that the main attack would be directed against the Burg and the Löbel bastions. The first care of the Turks was to plunder and destroy the few buildings which had escaped destruction in the suburbs.

The church of the Servites in the Rossau was the only edifice that escaped, and this exception was due to a singular incident. Its distance from the town had preserved it from the general conflagration. The Turks are said to have taken the Patriarchs depicted on the ceiling, with their long beards and Oriental costume, for followers of Mahomet, and under this misapprehension to have spared the church. Such is the solution of the fact to be found in all the accounts of the time, but it is probable that there was no misapprehension in the case. The Mussulman holds the Jewish Patriarchs in as much respect as does the Christian, and has even adopted their names, for Ibrahim is nothing but Abraham, Musa Moses, &c. &c. It is not therefore necessary to suppose that the Turks entertained the absurd notion imputed to them that a Christian temple could have been decorated with portraits of Mahometan saints.

CHAPTER 9

From the 9th to the 17th July

The fate of the inhabitants of the small town of Perchtoldsdorf forms a sad episode in the annals of the Turkish invasion. So early as the 9th July the Tartar horse had appeared in its neighbourhood. The inhabitants, after the example of their forefathers of 1529, converted the church tower and the churchyard with its surrounding wall into a fortress, and repulsed without difficulty the first attack of the marauders. The attack was repeated on the following day, but with the same result; the garrison was increased in numbers by many fugitives from other places, and the inhabitants, after some days of repose, began to believe that, as in 1529, the crisis would pass over without serious consequences.

The bailiff of the market was one Adam Streninger; the other authorities were the parish priest and his coadjutor. On the 14th, when the investment of Vienna had been brought to bear by the main army of the Turks, their next care was to secure the strong places within a certain distance of the city. With this view a strong detachment was directed at sunrise of the 14th upon Perchtoldsdorf, which began to throw incendiary missiles into the place, and speedily set fire to it in various quarters. Some citizens ventured upon a daring sally, but the small body, not more than thirty in number, were cut down to a man. The overwhelming superiority of the enemy's numbers and the failure of their own ammunition compelled the inhabitants entirely to abandon the town and to betake themselves to their fortified church and its precincts.

The town was given to the flames, which raged from 2 p.m. through the following night, which was passed by the little garrison in the contemplation of this dismal scene, and in the expectation of an attack at sunrise, which they had no hope of being able to repel. The

Turks, however, preferred craft and perfidy to force, and contented themselves with a blockade of the stronghold, which was moreover rendered scarcely tenable by the heat and smoke of the burning houses adjacent. This state of things lasted till the afternoon, when a horseman rode up the main street, dressed in the doublet of a German Reiter, but otherwise in Turkish attire, and bearing a flag of truce, which he waved towards the church, and in the Hungarian language summoned the citizens to surrender, distinctly promising them security of life and property on condition of an immediate submission. Such terms, under the circumstances, were far too favourable to be refused.

A man and a woman who spoke Hungarian made known their acceptance to the envoy, and a white flag was hung out from the tower in token of surrender. On the morning of the 17th a *pacha* with a strong attendance arrived from the camp, and seating himself on a red carpet near the house of the bailiff, opposite the church, announced through an interpreter the following conditions to the besieged. First, two citizens were to come out to the Turks, and two of the latter to be admitted into the fortress; secondly, as a symbol that the place had not before been yielded to an enemy, the keys were to be delivered to the *pacha* by a maiden with loosened hair and a garland on her head; thirdly, a contribution of 6000 florins was to be levied on the inhabitants. This latter demand appears to have protracted the negotiation for some hours, but finally half the sum demanded was paid into the *pacha's* hands, and the remainder was promised for the 29th August, the day of St. John the Baptist.

These terms arranged, the citizens left their stronghold, the daughter of the bailiff, a girl of seventeen years, at their head, arrayed according to the fanciful conditions above stated. She bore the keys of the place on a cushion, and presented them trembling to the *pacha*, who now required that the whole body of men capable of bearing arms should be drawn up in the market-place, for the purpose, as he pretended, of judging what number of troops might be required for the preservation of order in the town. This requisition excited some misgiving among the townsmen, but there was no retreat, and they prepared to carry it into effect. As they issued from their stronghold bodies of Turkish troops closed about them and took from them their weapons, observing that men who had surrendered had no longer use for such.

Some who hesitated to deliver them were deprived of them by force, and others who, from apprehension, paused in the gateway, were dragged out by the hair. The Turks loaded some carriages in attendance with the arms, and conveyed them away. The men, some 2000 in number, were drawn up in ranks in the place opposite the priest's house, and surrounded with cavalry. At a signal from the *pacha*, a troop of the latter dismounted and commenced a diligent search of the persons of the prisoners for money or concealed weapons. The entrance gate was at the same time strongly guarded.

Some of the townsmen taking alarm at these proceedings, with the bailiff at their head, endeavoured to regain the church. The Turks pursued them with drawn sabres, and the bailiff was cut down on the threshold. The *pacha* now rose, flung down the table before him, and gave the signal for a general massacre, setting the example with his own hand by cutting down the trembling girl at his side. The slaughter raged for two hours without intermission: 3500 persons were put to the sword in the strictest sense of the word, and in a space so confined that the expression, "torrents of blood," so often a figure of speech, was fully applicable to this case. The women and children, who still remained in the asylum of the church, together with the priest and his coadjutor, were dragged into slavery and never heard of more.

A local tradition avers that one solitary individual returned after a lapse of fifteen years, but as from maltreatment he had lost speech and hearing, he was unable to communicate the story of his escape. Another prevalent report, that two townsmen escaped by concealment in the roof of the church, is less probable, because the Turks immediately set fire to that building.

It is certain, however, that three persons did escape, but in a different manner. One of them, Hans Schimmer by name, a tailor's apprentice and an ancestor of the writer of this narrative, wisely fled before the catastrophe to Maria Zell; another, Jacob Holzer, is supposed to have escaped in the first confusion; the third, Balthasar Frank, it is said, hid himself till nightfall in the well of the tower, and then found means to abscond. This last story, however, is less well authenticated than the two former. From the number of the slaughtered, it is evident that many of the inhabitants of the places adjacent had taken refuge in this devoted town, for the ordinary male population never reached that number, and those who were carried off as slaves are also to be counted. It is probable that among the victims were people of condition, for in the course of some excavations which lately took place in the mound of their sepulture, some rings of value, enamelled, and even set with precious stones, were discovered.

CHAPTER 10

From July 15 to July 30

The 15th July, the day from which may be dated the commencement of the active siege of Vienna, was distinguished by an accident
which might well have brought that operation to a close by the destruction of the city. At two o'clock p.m., sometime after the Turkish
batteries had opened, a fire broke out in the Scottish Convent, which,
after destroying that establishment, rapidly spread to the Renngasse
and the neighbourhood of the Imperial arsenal, which contained
some 1800 barrels of powder. Two windows of this building were
actually at one moment on fire. The exertions, however, of the *commandant* and the citizens were proportionate to the emergency, the
windows were built up with great haste, and under a heat which made
the operation very difficult.

This immediate danger averted, a propitious change of wind assisted the final extinction, but several palaces and other extensive buildings had been destroyed, and for three days the smouldering ruins
threatened danger and demanded attention. Nothing certain was ever
known of the origin of the fire. At a period of so much alarm and excitement, it was scarcely possible that under this uncertainty the public
would be satisfied to ascribe it to any of the many accidents which
may give rise to a conflagration in a besieged town. Popular suspicion
fell upon the Hungarian malcontents, and many acts of cruelty were
the result of this surmise. Men wearing the Hungarian dress were
massacred in the streets, but others also fell victims to the spirit of
frantic and undiscriminating cruelty which panic generally engenders.

A poor half-witted man, whose eccentricities had often afforded
amusement at the tables of the wealthy Viennese, chose in his folly
to discharge a pistol in the direction of the fire: he was seized by the
populace and torn to pieces. Even an Imperial officer, in whose resi-

dence some rocket sticks were discovered, was flung into prison after terrible maltreatment. It required great exertion on the part of the authorities to repress this phrenzy, and to bring back the population to that regular discharge of duties on which rested the sole chance of salvation to the entire community.

On this same day, the 15th, the trenches were opened against the Burg and Löbel bastions, and many Christian prisoners were compelled to labour in them. On the part of the town the palisades were completed along the counterscarp, the ditches were furnished with traverses, and with the necessary passages of communication, and on the bastions arrangements effected for placing in battery about 300 pieces of cannon. Countermines were now also commenced, in conducting which the Venetian Bartholomeo Camuccini and a Captain Hafner specially distinguished themselves, being the only persons in the city skilled in this branch of engineering.

On the 16th the Commandant Stahremberg, who with unwearied activity visited every quarter of the defences, was wounded in the head by the explosion of a shell. His exertions were scarcely interrupted by this accident, for before he was sufficiently recovered to walk, he caused himself to be carried in a chair to every quarter which required his presence. The stone seat is shown to this day, high up in the spire of St. Stephen's, from which for many an anxious hour he overlooked the camp of the Turks, and watched the movements of their corps and the progress of their engineers. The fire of the Turks was henceforth sustained with scarcely any interruption, and it has been calculated that during the siege upwards of 100,000 shells were thrown into the city. If this calculation approach the truth, it is difficult to account for the smallness of the amount of damage they are known to have produced.

The buildings indeed of Vienna were then, as now, of very solid construction, and all the usual precautions against vertical fire, the placing of beams, earth, &c., on the roofs and upper stories, had been resorted to. The chronicles of the transaction have however recorded several instances of the inefficiency of the Turkish missiles. It is said that one of the first shells which fell in the city, near St. Michael's, was extinguished by a child of three years old before it could burst; another which fell into a full congregation at St. Stephen's, did no injury beyond carrying off the foot of an old woman; a third fell upon an open barrel of powder, and did no mischief. The fragments of these missiles were occasionally collected, and after being, according to a custom of the day, blessed by a priest, were redischarged at the enemy. The various contrivances of the besiegers for incendiary purposes, arrows wrapped with combustible materials, fireballs, &c.,—proved equally ineffective. To meet indeed this particular danger, the wooden shingles with which the houses were generally roofed were removed; a theatre, magnificent and costly, but constructed with wood, which then stood on the Burg Place, was pulled down; and, to deaden the rebound of shot or shell, the pavement was everywhere taken up. The vaults of the great churches were in general found to supply the best and safest magazines for powder: windows, and superfluous entrances of the churches so used were walled up. All wells were placed under strict superintendence, and every precaution taken for a due supply of water for extinction of fire.

Up to this moment the insular suburb, Leopoldstadt, had remained the only quarter of the suburbs still uninjured and free from the presence of the enemy. General Schulz occupied it with a detachment of cavalry, and was directed to hold it as long as possible. As early, however, as the 16th July, the Princes of Wallachia and Moldavia had thrown two bridges over the arms of the Danube on either side of this suburb, and the Imperialists, from want of artillery, had been unable to interrupt this operation. Early on the 27th the Turks crossed the stream in great numbers, favoured by the lowness of the water at this season; and after a conflict of several hours, General Schulz was compelled to yield to numbers, and to withdraw his troops to the left bank of the Danube. The great bridge of the Danube was now broken up, and Leopoldstadt fully abandoned to the enemy.

The city was now invested on all sides; every communication and every channel of supply cut off. The lot of Leopoldstadt was a severe one. The authorities had given the inhabitants a. premature and inconsiderate assurance that the island would be permanently held and defended by the Imperial troops; and, relying on this prospect, they had forborne to remove their property to any place of safety. It thus happened that not only the buildings, but nearly every object they contained, formed part of the funeral pile which, wherever the Turkish force set foot, was lighted to give token of their occupation. Among the more sumptuous of the edifices destroyed was the Imperial villa called the Old Favorita (now the Augarten). The Turks opened trenches immediately on the island, and established batteries both on the Danube bank and near the church of the Brothers of Mercy, from which they much annoyed the lower part of the city, and especially the Convent of St. Lawrence.

Every possible measure was adopted for the defence of this quarter of the city; the Rothenthurm gate was closed and barricaded, flanking works were constructed, and the windows of adjacent buildings built up, loopholes only for musketry being left. On the 2nd August the Turks made all their preparations for an assault on this side. They sent from Closterneuburg and Nussdorf all their boats down the small arm of the Danube, which, being caught in their descent by the piers of the bridge which had been removed, so clustered together as to form in themselves a sort of bridge.

In the course of the night, however, the boatmen of the city contrived to set the vessels again afloat. This important service was performed under a heavy fire from the island, and cost a good many lives in its execution. On the side of the Burg, meanwhile, the works of the besiegers above and below ground, the battery and the mine, were rapidly pushed forward. The approaches, when inspected after the siege, excited the admiration of the German engineers, for the skill and labour which had been bestowed on them. The trenches were twice the height of a man in depth, and near the city were roofed with timber and sods. Apartments were excavated for the principal officers, and those for the *vizier* and *pachas* sumptuously carpeted and cushioned.

To check this dangerous progress a sally took place from the town on the 19th of July, the first of the siege, under command of Guido Count von Stahremberg, nephew and aide-de-camp to the *commandant*, and Samson von Stambach, by which some of the trenches were filled up, and several of the enemy killed or taken. The latter were immediately exchanged, on which occasion the *grand vizier* presented the drummer who attended the flag of truce with three ducats. These sallies were often repeated, and gave occasion to the students particularly to distinguish themselves by their gallantry and intelligence. Many herds of cattle were captured in some of them, and driven into the city, affording, under the circumstances of blockade and hourly increasing scarcity, a most welcome aid to its resources. The principal object of the Turkish fire was the Burg, which was riddled with shot-holes: next to this, St. Stephen's tower, and the houses from the Carinthian to the Mölk bastion. The further ravelin of the Löbel bastion was so smashed with shot that no one could show himself upon it and live, and the besieged were advised to withdraw its armament, and distribute the pieces elsewhere.

On the 23rd of July took place the first assault. Two mines which had been carried under the counterscarp of the Burg and the Löbel bastion were exploded at the same instant, burying 15 of the garrison in the ruins, and tearing up twenty palisades. The Turks rushed over the ruins to the assault, but were quickly and completely repulsed. The second assault, July 25, was directed against the face of the Burg ravelin. It followed as usual the explosion of a mine, and was led by the *Janissaries*, who, after three successive repulses, retired with a loss of 200 men. The besieged, however, had to lament the loss of some valuable officers, among them of their chief engineer, Rimpler, who died within two days of wounds received in this affair. He is said to have been one of the greatest engineers of his day: he had distinguished himself at the siege of Philipsburg, under the Margrave Herman of Baden, and had written works on subjects of his profession which still retain their value.

On the 27th, an assault took place, in the course of which some of the *Janissaries* surmounted the palisades, but only to perish in the ditch. The Turks lost 300 men. On the side of the besieged, the major, Baron von Gallenfeld, perished by a poisoned arrow. On the 20th there came in a Turkish flag of truce, bearing a request on the part of the *vizier* for an armistice for the purpose of burying his dead, and also a summons fraught with the usual threats of vengeance and extermination. Stahremberg replied, that in the city they were enjoying excellent health, and having no dead to bury could not listen to the proposal for an armistice; as to surrender, they had made up their minds on that head, and were prepared to defend the city while they lived.

A proclamation was now issued offering a reward of 100 ducats to anyone who would swim the Danube with letters for the Duke of Lorraine: for the moment, however, no candidate presented himself. July 20th a mine was exploded under the Löbel bastion, 20 of the garrison perished, but no assault ensued, and the besieged had leisure to repair the damage. On the 29th the palisades of the Burg gate ravelin were shattered by a mine. By this time the underground operations of the Turks had so far advanced as to give them access to the ditch. Although every attempt of the Turks to pass the ditch was repulsed in hand-to-hand fight, yet the known progress of their engineering operations gave reason for expecting an early and general assault of a more formidable nature than the former, and the watchful Stahremberg neglected no preparation to meet it.

The arsenals furnished forth at his order quantities of the devices for laming an advancing enemy, known by various names in various services; in our military language, caltrops; these were distributed at the expected points of attack, and additional lines of palisades were fixed in the inner defences. The sound of bells from church or convent was forbidden, with the single exception of the great bell of St. Stephen, reserved for signal of assault upon the walls, at which the forces, regular and irregular, of the garrison were instructed to hasten to their respective posts. From early in the month of August the Turks scarcely allowed & day to pass without the explosion of one or more mines.

On the 3rd, after several severe checks, they succeeded in effecting a lodgement on the crown of the counterscarp of the Löbel bastion, from which, though several *Janissaries* perished by the springing of a countermine, it was found impossible to expel them. They followed up this advantage by measures for filling up the ditch, which were, however, continually foiled by the diligence of the garrison in removing the materials. On the 6th a Turkish mine blew up a Colonel Leslie and his pages. On the 8th, a sally commanded by General Souches did much mischief to the approaches of the besiegers. On the 9th and 10th similar operations were conducted with still greater effect, and the enemy was dislodged from the counterscarp. On the last occasion three soldiers of the garrison were blown into the air and descended in safety to the earth complaining of nothing but severe thirst.

At midday of the 12th, the salient angle of the Burg ravelin was blown up with an explosion which shook half the city. An assault followed, which, after two hours' desperate fighting, ended in the retreat of the Turks with a loss of 2500 men. The damage was quickly made good. On the 16th, the Turks, after three repulses, succeeded in effecting and maintaining a lodgement in the ditch facing the Löbel bastion, which enabled them to establish near and destructive batteries on the counterscarp, against the Burg and the Löbel bastion.

The two commanders, Stahremberg and the *vizier*, were alike indefatigable in their personal superintendence of their respective operations. The latter was carried every third day in a litter, made shot proof by plates of iron, into the approaches, inspecting the works, punishing the idle, and menacing the timid with his drawn sabre. He had also in the trenches his own peculiar posts sunk deep in the ground, and made bomb proof with planks and sand-bags. His favourite position, however, for general observation and direction was the tower of the church of St. Ulric, from which he overlooked the city, as Stahremberg did the camp from his memorable stone chair in the sculptured spire of St. Stephen.

Towards the middle of August an envoy from the *Sultan* reached the camp, charged ostensibly with the conveyance of rich presents of honour to the *vizier*, furs and jewelled aigrettes, but secretly commissioned to ascertain and report upon the progress of the siege. He remained a fortnight, and returned with a most unfavourable report. On the 15th August the Imperial Ambassador, Caprara, arrived in the Turkish camp after a long compulsory detention at Pesth. He was escorted by a *tschauch*, or officer of the body guard, and 300 men. He fell in on his dismal march with many of his unhappy countrymen, a few only of whom he was able, at an exorbitant price, to ransom from hopeless slavery.

Among these was a girl ten years of age, of noble birth and singular beauty, whose name however has not reached us. On his arrival in the camp, the *vizier*, by special order of the *Sultan*, released him at Tuln, into the hands of the Imperialists. It has been said that he brought a proposal from the *vizier* to abandon the siege of Vienna, and negotiate a peace on the sole condition of the surrender of the fortress of Raab. If this report be founded, as Wagner in his *Historia Leopoldi Magni* supposes, it would show how far the projects of the *vizier* had been checked by the noble resistance of the garrison. If this or any proposal was intrusted to Caprara, it remained unanswered.

Chapter 11

From August 1 to August 2

As far as feats of arms were concerned, the garrison had as yet maintained its own with undaunted resolution and with a success unimpaired by any material discomfiture; but by the middle of August the inevitable consequences of so close an investment of a large town began to show themselves in the shapes of sickness and scarcity. The use of dried and salted meat produced a dysentery, which was often mortal both among the soldiery and the townspeople. Other forms of disease were attributable to the use of beer ill -brewed and hastily consumed, and to the accumulation of impurities in the streets. Among the victims were the Burgomaster Liebenberg, the Bishop's Vicar of Vienna, the Provost of St. Stephen's, the Rector of the University, and many other officials and ecclesiastics.

The *commandant* himself was attacked by the epidemic, but, for the good fortune of Christendom, recovered. The disease yielded at length, a result due in great measure to the exertions of the admirable Kollonitsch, who visited the hospitals daily; and to the sanitary regulations of the authorities, who carried a stricter supervision into the proceedings of the bakers and the brewers, particularly into the brewery which supplied the Burg Hospital. The provisions specially productive of the dysentery, such as herrings, which were much sought after by the soldiers, were confiscated. The sick townspeople were carefully separated from the healthy, and conveyed into temporary hospitals.

The sick and wounded of the soldiers were distributed among the convents, and the city provided for their use 500 measures of wine and 4500 ells of linen. Cesspools were dug to supply the place of the ordinary outlets and transport of the filth of the city; the kennels were irrigated, and proper officers appointed under the direction of

Kollonitsch to carry these systematic measures into effect, and made responsible for their execution. The *vizier*, whose confidence, possibly somewhat abated by the course of military events, had been revived by the reports of the condition of the garrison, is said to have vowed vengeance against the prelate who had thus assumed the noble attitude of the Prophet between the people and the plague; and to have destined his head as a present to the *Sultan*. He did not foresee from whose shoulders such a peace-offering would ultimately be culled.

Coupled with these sanitary regulations, others were put in force to prevent premature exhaustion of the means of subsistence in the city, which fortunately were so ample as only to require good economy to make them sufficient. Twenty hand-mills and five horse-mills were established under regulation of the authorities for the supply of flour. Lists of prices of the principal articles of subsistence are given in the records of the time, which, in themselves, would convey little information to readers not familiar with the measures in use, and with the current prices of the day, but which indicate considerable abundance as still existing at this period of the siege, and which also show that prices were quadrupled before the siege was raised.

The price of wine, in particular, appears to have been low even in comparison with the ordinary prices of the time and locality. The great cellars of the city were reported to contain 169,000 *eimers*, of which 32,000 belonged to the three colleges of the Jesuits, and other ecclesiastical establishments possessed a large portion of the remainder. The stock of the numerous private traders, and the wine-growers of the neighbourhood was not, it would appear, included in this return. The military measures of defence, meanwhile, were carried on, as was well needed, with unabated vigour. The Captain, Elias Kühn, a Silesian gentleman, gained great credit by his services as an engineer. The citizens showed the greatest alacrity. While 1300 of their body were required for daily service at various posts, they furnished, in addition, from thirty to forty waggons for the daily transport of every necessary article to the works, and many of their horses were sacrificed in this service.

In contemplation of the last extremity, chains were furnished from the arsenals to be drawn across the streets. The rings for these are still to be seen in the walls in various parts of the city. To watch the motions of the enemy, two Jesuits were constantly stationed on the tower of Saint Stephen provided with telescopes, who furnished written reports of their observations to the *commandant*. The latter took up his residence in the outer court of the Burg, in the immediate neighbourhood of the principal point of attack, and on his own punctual and conspicuous performance of his duties, established his claim to exact the same from others, and to punish or rebuke every instance of neglect or failure. A lieutenant in command of the watch at the most dangerous part of the Löbel bastion neglected to prevent the enemy from forming by night a timber defence against sallies.

A court-martial sentenced him to death. The *commandant* pardoned him on condition that he would conduct a sally with 29 men and destroy the defences so thrown up. He succeeded, but perished in the execution. Two soldiers, who, upon some dispute as to their pay, rose upon and maltreated an officer, were compelled to throw dice for the life of one, and the loser underwent the penalty. A population so numerous could not but comprise some faint hearts. An order was issued that anyone who, from cowardice, should absent himself from his appointed duty should be hanged from his own window. A commission was appointed to undertake a search for delinquents through the four quarters of the city. We hear of no executions in consequence, but the menace is said to have produced a considerable and welcome accession of able-bodied defenders to the walls, who were encouraged to their duty by a bounty of three *rix*-dollars and ample rations of bread and wine.

During the entire siege, indeed, the fighting men were liberally provided for, and clergy as well as laity opened their cellars for their refreshment. The besiegers meanwhile pushed forward their works with unwearied activity. It is, however, unaccountable that their leaders, who usually showed so much eagerness to possess themselves of every commanding position in the neighbourhood of a besieged fortress, should have neglected to establish themselves on the adjacent heights of the Kahlenberg. These acclivities presented not only a cover to the motions of an army advancing to raise the siege, but a post of the utmost importance if once occupied, and the assemblage of the army of the Empire at Crems could be no secret to the Turks. The latter nevertheless contented themselves with the useless destruction of the Camalduline Convent and the desecration of the tomb of the Margrave in its chapel, and then abandoned the position without leaving either garrison or corps of observation, an error which was certainly the main cause of the ultimate catastrophe.

For several days the offer had been promulgated of a considerable reward to the man who would brave the adventure of endeavouring to make his way with dispatches to the camp of the Duke of Lorraine, when on the 6th of August a trooper of Count Gotz's regiment made his appearance in the city, having swum the various arms of the Danube, and bearing a letter well secured in wax. The hearts of the besieged were thus gladdened with the tidings of the assemblage and daily increase of the Christian Army, and with the assurance of early relief. The safe arrival of this messenger was announced to the yet distant army by a discharge of rockets. The messenger was less fortunate in his attempt to return. He was taken by the Turks and brought before the *vizier*. The dispatch with which he was intrusted being written in cypher, he was closely interrogated as to its contents and as to the condition of the city. He cunningly invented a tale of despair, and described the defenders of the place as depressed in spirits, exhausted in resources, and on the verge of surrender. The invention saved his life.

The *vizier* proclaimed these tidings through the camp, and caused the cypher dispatch to be shot back into the city attached to an arrow, with an appendix to the purport that it was needless to write in cypher, for the wretched condition of those who had sent it was well known to the world, and was but the just punishment of men who had awakened the wrath of the *Sultan*. Soon after this transaction Christopher von Kunitz, a servant of Caprara, who had been detained in the Turkish camp, found means to escape into the city. He brought an account that the *vizier* fully expected to have Vienna in his power within a few days, and that many of the Magnates of Hungary, considering the cause of Austria as desperate, had come into the camp to do homage to the *vizier*. He gave also a dismal confirmation of the ravage of the surrounding country, of which the Viennese had partial evidence in their own observation.

On the 9th of August, Michael Gregorowitz, a Greek by birth, once a lieutenant in the Heister regiment, leaving the city in a Turkish disguise, crossed the Danube with dispatches for the Duke of Lorraine. A fire signal from the crest of the Bisamberg conveyed the intelligence of the safe accomplishment of his enterprise, and he was rewarded with promotion to the rank of Captain. He did not, however, succeed in effecting his return. The condition of affairs in the city began to be serious: the enemy made daily progress in his approaches, and no more volunteers came forward for the dangerous task of conveying intelligence to the army of the increasing pressure.

At last George Francis Kolschitzki, a partisan officer whose name deserves honourable record for the importance of his services, and the courage and dexterity with which they were executed, stepped forward. A Pole by birth, and previously an interpreter in the service of the Oriental merchants' company, he had become a citizen of the Leopoldstadt, and had served since the siege began in a free corps. Intimately conversant with the Turkish language and customs, he willingly offered himself for the dangerous office of passing through the very camp of the Turks to convey intelligence to the Imperial army. On the 13th of August, accompanied by a servant of similar qualifications, he was let out through a sally-port in the Rothenthurm, and escorted by an *aide-de-camp* of the *commandant* as far as the palisades. He had scarcely advanced a hundred yards, when he became aware of a considerable body of horse which advanced at a rapid pace towards the place of his exit.

Being as yet too near the city to escape suspicion, he hastily turned to the left and concealed himself in the cellar of a ruined house of the suburb near Altlerchenfeld, where he kept close till the tramp of the passing cavalry had died away. He then pursued his course, and, singing a Turkish song, traversed at an idle pace and with an unembarrassed air the streets of Turkish tents. His cheerful mien and his familiar strain took the fancy of an *aga*, who invited him into his tent, treated him with coffee, listened to more songs and to his tale of having followed the army as a volunteer, and cautioned him against wandering too far and falling into Christian hands. Kolschitzki thanked him for the advice, passed on in safety through the camp to beyond its verge, and then as unconcernedly made for the Kahlenberg and the Danube. Upon one of its islands he saw a body of people, who, misled by his Turkish attire, fired upon him and his companion.

These were some inhabitants of Nussdorf, headed by the bailiff of that place, who had made this island their temporary refuge and home. Kolschitzki explained to them in German the circumstances of his mission, and entreated them to afford him an immediate passage over the river. This being obtained, he reached without further difficulty the bivouac of the Imperial army, then on its march between Angern and Stillfried. After delivering and receiving dispatches, the adventurous pair set out on their return, and after some hairbreadth escapes from the Turkish sentries, passed the palisades and re-entered the city by the Scottish gate, bearing a letter from the duke to the following purport:—

116

He had received with deep emotion the intelligence of the loss of so many brave officers and soldiers, and of the sad condition of the city consequent both on this loss in action and on the epidemic. He retained his hopes that the defenders of a place so important would never relax in their noble efforts for its preservation. A considerable army was already collected for its relief. Reinforcements were daily arriving from Bavaria, Franconia, and Saxony, and the Duke was only waiting the arrival of the numerous forces of Poland, commanded by their king in person, which was to be expected by the end of August at the latest, to put the united mass in motion for the raising of the siege.

As an appendix to these assurances was added the consolatory intelligence of the surrender of Presburgh to the Imperialists, and of the defeat of Tekeli in two actions. The safe return of the bearer of this dispatch was announced as usual by rockets as night signals, and in the day by a column of smoke from St. Stephen's spire. On the 21st August the daring Kolschitzki was on the point of repeating his adventurous undertaking, when a deserter, who had been recaptured, and was standing under the gallows with the halter adjusted, confessed that he had furnished to the Turks an accurate description of Mochizuki's person. He was himself deterred by this warning, but his gallant companion, George Michailowich, found means twice to repeat the exploit, with the same safety and success as in the first instance. On his second return he displayed a remarkable presence of mind and vigour of arm. Having all but reached the palisades, he was joined by a Turkish horseman, who entered into familiar conversation with him.

As it was, however, impossible for him to follow further his path towards the city, in such company, by a sudden blow he struck his unwelcome companion's head from his shoulders, and springing on the riderless horse, made his way to the gate. He did not, however, after this success, tempt his fortune again. He brought on this occasion an autograph letter from the emperor, full of compliments and promises, which was publicly read in the *Rathhaus*. (Kolschitzki's services would appear to have made a deep impression on the public mind. Several narratives of his adventures were published at the time; and his portrait, in his Turkish costume, figures in the frontispiece of most of them.—E.)

In contrast to so many examples of patriotism and self-exposure, there were not wanting instances of treason. A youth of sixteen, who had twice ventured into the Turkish camp and brought back intelligence which proved to be unfounded, was arrested and put to the question. He had been apprentice to a distiller, or vender of strong liquors (in the vulgar tongue of Vienna, called a water-burner). In his confession, extorted by torture, he stated that the severity of his master had driven him from his employment, and, having no other refuge, he had found means to escape to the camp. Promises of reward had induced him to undertake to procure for the Turks accurate information of the weak points of the defences, the strength of the. garrison, the state of its supplies, &c. He at the same time accused a man of the cavalry stables as having instigated him to these courses.

Being, however, confronted with this man, he totally failed in maintaining the charge. He was executed with the sword. The audacity of a younger traitor, a boy ten years of age, was still more extraordinary. He was arrested on the 10th August, while entering the city at a slow pace. When questioned as to the cause of his having ventured into the Turkish camp, he alleged that his parents, having been inhabitants of the suburb, had been detained by the Turks; that his father was compelled to work in the trenches, and his mother to sew sandbags for the sappers.

While they were conducting him for his subsistence and safe custody to the Burger Hospital, the unfortunate urchin was met by his mother, who flew at him with reproaches for his long absence, and from her it was soon ascertained that she had never been in the Turkish camp, and that the boy's father was dead. After this unlucky meeting the boy, taken before the authorities, confessed that he had carried to the enemy intelligence that several guns on the defences had been rendered unserviceable; that the wheaten loaves were no longer so white nor so heavy as they had been, that the commissariat bread was become black and scarcely eatable; that many soldiers had died of such victual, and that the garrison had lost all courage for fighting.

After endeavouring, with cunning beyond his years, but in vain, to fix on others the guilt of having instigated his treason, this precocious criminal, for whom whipping would have answered every legitimate purpose of punishment, was beheaded. Two soldiers, taken in the act of deserting, suffered with him. The practice of straying beyond the lines for the real, or alleged, purpose of seeking for plunder, in the ruins of the suburb, had become frequent, and it was thought necessary to check proceedings so favourable to desertion and treason by this example, and by severe edicts.

CHAPTER 12

23rd August to 8th September

On the 23rd of August, the enemy, after repeated assaults, had all but gained possession of the Burg ravelin, and had set on fire the palisades in face of the portion of that work still held by the garrison. This the soldiers, carrying water to it in their steel caps, succeeded in extinguishing, and the further advance of the Turks was checked. An assault ensued, in which the combatants mingled hand to hand. The Ottoman sabre, as on other similar occasions, failed in close conflict with the ponderous weapons wielded by the German arm the halberd, the scythe, (see note following), the morning star, and the battle-axe, aided by the pitch and water cauldron; and the Turks retired with a loss of 200 men.

★★★★★★

Count Daun is said to have first suggested the use of the scythe affixed to a long staff for the defence of the breaches at this siege. Under the name of the Lochaber axe it had long been used by the Scots. In the recent wars of liberty in Poland it has acquired much celebrity, and many stories are told of its terrible effects in the hands of the peasantry. Of the weapon called the morning star, a species of club with spikes, 600 were furnished from the arsenal.—E.)

★★★★★★

In various of the adjacent open spaces of the city great fires were kept up to supply the last-mentioned ingredients, which were cooked in huge cauldrons, and transported in smaller vessels, principally by women and children, to the walls. Many Turks were greeted with the contents as they mounted the breach, and finished by a second application as they lay scalded and blinded in the ditch below. Six hundred and sixty-nine cwt. of pitch were used during the siege; but a large part of this was doubtless applied for the purpose of lighting up the ditch, and discovering the nightly operations of the Turkish sappers immediately below the rampart. On this day the Turks were seen from the walls to transport a considerable force of cavalry to the left bank of the Danube, the men in boats, the horses swimming beside them.

This strong detachment was sent to reinforce the Pacha of Peter-waradin, who had crossed the river near Presburg to attack the Duke of Lorraine, who was keeping the field near the Bisamberg with his cavalry. Few of this united Turkish force returned to tell the tale of the thorough defeat they received at the hands of Lorraine, who drove them into the Danube with a loss of twenty-five standards. A Polish contingent, under Prince Lubomirski, assisted at this victory, and much distinguished itself. Its services on this occasion were the first fruits of the Polish alliance. Lubomirski's junction with the Imperialists was an independent movement, and in the first instance excited some jealousy in the mind of Sobieski.

August 25, a gallant sally took place for the purpose of checking the operations of the Turkish miners against the Löbel bastion, and driving them from the ditch. The young Duke of Wirtemberg, who was overlooking this operation from the wall, seeing his troops hard pressed, in spite of all remonstrance, descended at the head of a re-inforcement in person to the fray, and drove the Turks as far as their first battery. With equal courage he conducted the retreat. The sally was brilliant and successful, but cost the besieged 200 men and several officers. The duke himself was wounded in the calf of the leg by an arrow, and thereby disabled for the rest of the siege. For several successive days the Burg ravelin continued to be the scene of murderous assault and successful resistance, of which it would be tedious to narrate particulars.

Both parties, meanwhile, began to feel sensibly the effects of the long endurance of the siege. In the Mahometan ranks, and especially among the *Janissaries*, a prejudice of the nature of a superstition assigned forty days as the limit to which an operation of this nature could be extended. They considered it, at least, as a prerogative of their body to mutiny against an extension of that period. In the city, on the other hand, the condition of affairs had assumed a gloomy complexion. The casualties of war and disease had materially thinned the ranks of the garrison, and the mine and the battery, especially the former, had made gaps of ruin in the defences which no exertion of the besieged could fully repair, and which it became daily more difficult to maintain against the rush of numbers.

Many of their guns had been rendered unserviceable; but the want of skilled artillery officers and men, with whom the city from the first had been ill provided, was still more severely felt. The engineer, Rimpler, had fallen; the colonel Werner, who commanded the ordnance, and who had effected his entrance into the city on the 17th July, lay wounded and disabled; and before the close of the siege, but two regular artillery officers remained fit for service. The outworks from the Burg, almost to the Scottish gate, were nothing but a mass of rubbish. The Löbel bastion in particular, and the adjacent houses in the street of that name, had specially suffered; but still more so the dwelling which still bears the name of the Turks' House. Scarcity also was making rapid strides; and if the casualties of war diminished the number of consumers, falling as they did principally on the fighting men they also made it impossible to repeat the sallies which in the early part of the siege had sometimes swept into the city the cattle of the Turkish commissariat.

The Turks, while their large force enabled them to close hermetically every channel of supply to the city, guarded their own communications with the utmost vigilance. Forage for the live cattle and sheep still in the city had also failed, and the supplies of the public shambles at the Lichtensteg and the Rothenthurm, were as lean and dry as they were dear and scanty. The small store of dried provision which remained was reserved for the soldiery, and the citizens at large were exposed to severe privation. The streets leading to the shambles were crowded with females, who often had to return home with empty baskets. The price of a pound of beef had risen in the proportion of 1 to 9, and sometimes 12. Articles of daily subsistence to families of middle rank had now become the luxuries of the rich. An egg cost half a dollar, pork eight silver *groschen* the pound; veal and poultry no longer existed.

Under these circumstances, cats no longer enjoyed the immunity due, in times of peace and plenty, to their domestic virtues, and the chase of this animal in cellars and over roofs became not merely a pastime of the young and mischievous, but the occupation of serious and hungry men. The Viennese love for a jest is discernible in the appellation of *dachshase*, or roof hare, bestowed on this new object of the chase.

The perilous condition of the city was announced to its yet distant friends by discharges of rockets through the nights of the 24th, 28th, and 30th. They were answered by fire-signals from the crest of the Bisamberg; but it was not from the left bank of the Danube that succour was to be expected, and no cheering sign yet broke the darkness in the direction of the Kahlenberg. The besieged looked forward with deep anxiety to the 29th August, the anniversary of the decapitation of St. John, one held peculiarly sacred and fortunate by the Turks. In Soliman's reign it was the day of the fall of Rhodes, of Belgrade, of Pesth, and of that fight of Mohacs of which three centuries have not effaced the recollection. A general assault was reasonably to be expected on this awful anniversary; but it passed over with no other occurrence than the ordinary explosion of some mines, and a cannonade principally directed at St. Stephen's.

The scanty portion of the Burg ravelin yet held by the besieged had now become untenable. Its communication with the curtain behind was all but cut off, and a reluctant order was at length, on the 3rd September, issued to the officer in command to withdraw his men, which was as reluctantly obeyed, the artillery having been previously removed, and the palisades burnt. It had been actively assailed for twenty-nine days, had withstood fifteen main assaults and the explosion of ten powerful mines, and had been the grave of many thousands of the Turks. Its defence, which was closed in. the last moment of withdrawal by the death of the officer in command of the day, a Captain Müller, has been considered by military writers as one of the finest on record. The *grand vizier* gave it a name which implied that the arts of hell and magic had been applied to its defence. During the French occupation of 1809, this outwork, worthy of being preserved as a monument, was blown up, and altogether levelled by order of Napoleon.

The Turks took immediate advantage of their acquisition to plant on it two guns and two mortars, from which they opened a heavy fire on the main defences. The danger was now become most imminent, arid called for the application of every resource, and the exertion of every faculty, to meet it. Every gate except the Stuben, still reserved as a sally-port, was barricaded afresh with masonry and timber; the chains were drawn across the streets, especially those which led to the Löbel; new batteries were erected; and internal defences so accumulated one behind the other, that, at every ten paces, there rose a breastwork thronged with men and bristling with palisades. In the interior even of the city, at the entrance of the Ballplatz, and near the hotel then occupied by the Spanish ambassador (now the Chancery), were bulwarks, strengthened with beams, and fenced by ditches; and orders were issued to break away the iron gratings of the windows, in order, if necessary, to apply these also to the defence of the streets.

In every cellar of the neighbouring houses were placed vessels of water, and drums with pease strewn on their parchment, to give warning, by their vibratory motion, of the approach of the Turkish miners. The subterranean warfare was carried on with much effect by the Austrian counter-miners, who frequently succeeded in burying or suffocating the Turkish labourers, and carried off many hundredweights of powder from their chambers. The tenacity of the Turks in prosecuting this mode of attack is shown by the loss they experienced: 16,000 of their miners perished during the siege. On one occasion a fourier or quartermaster of the Beck regiment having detected the end of a mine, sprung like Curtius into the abyss, and encountering five Turks, killed three, and drove the other two to flight.

The neighbourhood of the Burg bastion was the scene of the principal of these exploits, and under that fortification occurred also the discovery, more interesting to antiquarians than soldiers, of an ancient stair of sixty-six steps. As the excavations in this quarter soon descended into water, the operations of the enemy were the less to be dreaded, and the vigilance of the besieged was relaxed, but the cellars near the Burg were nevertheless still garrisoned by night, and it was thought necessary to extend this precaution shortly to other parts of the city. The armed force of the city, both regular and irregular, was now so reduced in numbers by repeated assaults and sallies, that the remnant began to pine for the long promised relief.

The Burg ravelin being now in the hands of the enemy, the Burg itself, as well as the Löbel bastion, were hourly threatened with the same fate, the more so that the curtain which connected them was so ruined as scarcely to afford a shelter to the troops which manned it. Almost every house in the city was thronged with invalids; and while the energies of the besieged sunk under such pressure, it was to be expected that the courage and hopes of the assailants would rise in proportion. This was not, however, the case. While through the livelong night whole clusters of rockets were discharged together at frequent intervals as signals of increasing distress and danger, and as invocations for succour, there was trouble also in the camp. On the 24th August a mutinous spirit had displayed itself among the Janissaries.

The term of 40 days, to which, for love of the *Sultan* and the *vizier*, they had added three, was expired, and they demanded to be released from further duty in the trenches. The exhortations and prophecies of the Vani Effendi, a popular preacher, had persuaded them to await the famous anniversary of St. John, and the effect of the extensive mines which had been pushed under the works of the citadel. These mines, however, had failed; it became difficult to keep the secret of that failure from the troops, and the day of St. John had passed, as we have seen, without any signal occurrence. The troops, too, under command of the Pacha of Aleppo had even left the trenches, and it required the influence of the *grand vizier* in person to bring them back to their duty by promises and fearful threats. He was driven at this crisis to the temporary expedient of promulgating a report of the sudden death of the Emperor Leopold.

The *vizier* went so far as to order a general discharge of cannon and musketry throughout the camp, a proceeding which puzzled for a while but did not succeed in, alarming the garrison, for the alleged cause of rejoicing did not obtain a moment's credence in the city. The adoption of such expedients by the *vizier*, and his general mode of conducting the military operations at this period, are explained, in the opinion of many, on the theory of his desire to obtain possession of the city by capitulation and not by storm.

At a period when the result of a simultaneous attack, from the ruined state of the defences, could no longer have been doubtful, he preferred, it is said, to send his troops against the breach in isolated detachments, unequal to cope with the resistance which the garrison, however weakened, was still able to oppose to them. Having destined the valuables of the imperial residence for his own treasury, he was unwilling to expose them to the indiscriminate plunder of a final assault. He was anxious also to preserve from destruction the city itself as the future seat of government for a dynasty of the West, of which he intended to be himself the founder.

Writers contemporary and subsequent have concurred in assigning these motives and this policy to Kara Mustapha, and in looking upon him as a Moslem Wallenstein, prepared, in reliance on the devotion of the army, to brave the displeasure of his sovereign, and possibly to throw off his allegiance. It was only towards the end of the siege and under the prospect of failure that these views underwent alteration, and that he became disposed to force an entrance at any sacrifice. By this time, however, the spirit of his troops was so depressed that, as we learn from Demetrius Kantemir's history of the Ottoman Empire, they often exclaimed, as if addressing the armies of Lorraine and Sobieski:

Ye unfaithful, if you will not come yourselves, Let us see at least the crests of your caps over the hills; for these once seen, the siege will be over and we shall be released.

The demonstration of such a spirit as this left the *vizier* no longer a choice as to his measures. Though he was still incredulous as to the junction of the Polish forces, and still more so as to the appearance of their terrible commander in the field, the gathering strength of the Imperialists and their preparations for a forward movement could be no secret even to one so negligent in procuring intelligence from that important quarter, and he determined upon a conclusive effort. On the 4th September aa explosion took place towards the eastern end of the Burg bastion, the more violent because of the solidity of that work's construction: 4000 Turks, directed by the *vizier* in person, rushed forward to the assault. From every alarm-post the besieged hastened to the point of attack, and among the foremost was Stahremberg, accompanied by his whole staff, prepared and probably expecting to die in the breach, which to a breadth of more than five fathoms had been opened by the explosion.

The rubbish had fallen outwards, filling the ditch and facilitating the advance of the Turks, who, armed with sabre and target, and bearing baskets of earth on their backs, were thronging up the ascent. The shout of *Allah* was heard nearer and nearer, and some bold hands had already planted the horsetails on the crest of the rampart, when the fire of the besieged filled the ditch with the bodies of the bravest. The fight raged for two hours, and the Turks once more retired with a loss of 500 men. The garrison, however, could ill spare a loss of 117 men and two captains. The fighting had no sooner ceased than every available material was used to repair the breach.

Besides the usual appliances of timber, sand-bags, and ox-hides, mattresses and reed mats were pressed into this service. The heavy wooden wine-presses were broken up and the rafters taken from the roofs for the same purpose, and ramparts of planks, in engineering phraseology mantelets, fitted with wheels, were prepared and brought down to the scene of danger. The other portions of the defences were intersected with fresh traverses, and armed with additional guns. A corps 400 strong was raised from parties who had been hitherto exempted from military duty, clerks and artisans in the most indispensable departments of industry. The nightly discharges of rockets from St. Stephen's were thicker and more frequent than before. The city was in its last agonies.

On the 6th, an explosion brought down a length of five fathoms of the wall, 24 feet thick, of the Löbel bastion, making a breach less defensible than that in the Burg bastion, because the parapets of the wall which remained had been previously destroyed. The fury of the assault which followed, and the tenacity of the resistance, may be measured by the Turkish loss of 1500 men. Two standards were at one moment planted on the rampart. A house in the Löbelstrasse opposite the spot where this took place is still called the Turks' house, and bears a date and a painting of a Turk's head commemorative of the occurrence. On the evening of this day, five rockets were observed to rise from the Kahlenberg. (See note following).

★★★★★★

I give this incident as I find it in the work from which, these pages are borrowed, and in other accounts, but I am at a loss to account for the alleged date of its occurrence. The army of the Christian allies had not completed its passage of the river, and was mustering in the camp of Tuln, and I can find no account of any reconnaissance being pushed forward at this date. The statements, however, of the fact are numerous and positive.—E.

★★★★★★

That short-lived apparition was sufficient to scatter the clouds of despondency which had so long been gathering over the city. The lighthouse which identifies the promontory, or the star which marks the Pole, never sparkled on the eye of the anxious mariner with more of comfort and assurance than that fiery sign conveyed to the watchman on the rampart, or the Jesuit on the spire. It indicated not only that the Imperial army had crossed the river, but that its outposts had crowned the heights and occupied the passes which commanded its only access to the relief of the city, heights and passes which nothing but judicial blindness could have prevented the Turks from occupying in force. Still the salvation of the city hung on a thread.

As the imperial army approached, the incentive to attack rose in intensity in the same proportion with the motive to resistance, and it was to be expected that the struggle would be waged to the last with increased energy. Every device of war was exhausted by Stahremberg to provide that no inch of advance should be gained by the enemy unpurchased by streams of his blood. All the ominous preparations for a street fight were redoubled. The houses nearest the breach were converted into batteries; every avenue to it from the interior thronged with soldiers. The city force was mustered at its alarm-posts, waiting for the bell of St. Stephen's to proclaim the moment of the assault. It never came. The Turks, though they continued to mine under the city, pushing one of their galleries as far as the church of the Minorites, never again showed themselves above ground beyond the mouths of their parallels. On the 8th September there was strange movement in their camp. Camels were loaded, horses were saddled. More rockets rose from the Kahlenberg.

CHAPTER 13

The Relief Force

To preserve the narrative of the siege unbroken down to the critical period at which it has now arrived, it has been necessary to withhold our attention from the proceedings of the Duke of Lorraine and the army of the Empire. We left them in the early part of July unable to cope with the tenfold numbers of the Turkish host, and compelled to await at safe distance, and scarcely in a threatening attitude, the accession of German levies and of the promised succour of the Poles. The former mustered with somewhat of the slowness and circumspection which have in all ages characterized the motions of the Germanic body. Distance retarded the junction of the Poles, whose contingents had in many instances to march from the Ukraine. The first care then of Lorraine, was to bring together the troops of the Empire, and Crems, with its bridge over the Danube, was the main position chosen for that purpose.

In the first instance, indeed, the duke had proposed to make a stand in the Leopoldstadt, and by means of *têtes-du-pont* at the several bridges of the arms of the river, to keep up a direct communication with the city, virtually, in fact, to make his force a part of the garrison. The danger of such an expedient, however, became instantly palpable. The summer was a dry one, and the small arm of the river nearest the city was fordable in several places. To place 10,000 cavalry in a position so acceptable to the attack of the whole Turkish Army, and which also from its relative level was commanded from the whole extent of the opposite banks, would have been certain destruction. The army of Tekeli, also, coming over the Marchfield, threatened the rear of the Imperialists, and gave them much anxiety.

The duke therefore selected a series of positions the best calculated to prevent the enemy from occupying the left bank of the Danube, and shifted his head-quarters as circumstances indicated, between Jed-lesee and Stockerau, till he finally fixed them at Crems. His next care was to arm and garrison as extensively as possible the fortified and tenable places of Lower Austria. He confided Crems to the care of the generals Dunnewald and Leslie, Tuln to the Baron d'Orlique; and even Closterneuburg, scarcely five English miles from Vienna, which had beaten off an attack of the Turks, under its commandant, Marcel Ort-ner, was supplied with a garrison. Count Herberstein covered with a corps the avenues to Styria, already threatened by the enemy.

Neustadt was sufficiently garrisoned; and in several instances from these strongholds successful sallies were directed against the maraud-ing bands of the enemy. Measures, late indeed, but energetic, were also adopted for the internal defence of the Austrian provinces. Otho, Count of Traun, in Lower, and Wolf, Count of Weissenthurn, in Upper Austria, directed these with much judgment and activity. The forest passes were guarded with abattis; the fords, especially those of Ybbs and Ens, with palisaded works; and the peasantry summoned and or-ganised for the defence of the castles and convents. Many more in-stances of courage and conduct occurred in the defence of places than it would be possible here to particularise.

The inhabitants of Closterneuburg, commanded by the Sacris-tan of their convent, Marcellin Ortner, on three occasions beat off the assault of many thousand Turks. Gregory Müller, Abbot of Mölk, exchanged the crosier for the sword, and at the head of the armed *burghers*, by the skilful use of this irregular force, kept the Turks at a distance, though they had encamped on the Steinfeld between St. Pol-ten and Wilhelmsburg, and had burnt the suburbs of St. Polten. 2000, however, of the vassals of that rich abbey were dragged into captivity, 120 houses on its estates were burnt, and 5000 head of cattle carried off.

After the retreat of the Turks from before Vienna, the people of St. Polten found a number of deserted children, of whom they kindly took and kept charge, without ever discovering their parents. The de-fence of the abbey of Lilienfeld forms a brilliant episode in the his-tory of the time. Many of the inhabitants of the adjacent districts, and among them a large portion of the gentry, had taken refuge from the Tartar cavalry in this place. On the nearer approach, however, of the dreaded marauders, the greater part of these fugitives continued their retreat, and sought a more assured refuge in Salzburg or the Tyrol.

Not so the brave abbot, Matthew Kolbries. He rallied round him his clergy and vassals, fortified his convent, and prepared to defend it to the last. He did a great deal more than this; for though deserted by all but a small body of devoted adherents, after repelling several assaults, instead of leaving his enemy to rally at leisure, he fell upon him in a series of well-planned sallies and ambuscades, which by their success elevated the courage of his adherents to the highest pitch of daring. Following up these first successes, he fell by surprise on a column of the Tartars near Mariazell, destroyed them almost to a man, and brought back in triumph 200 rescued Christians, a mule load of money, and forty heads of Tartars, whose bodies he had left for example exposed on the roads.

Three Turkish prisoners of distinction were ransomed at from 2000 to 3000 *ducats* each. The casual accession of a Bavarian officer and five troopers to his small force enabled him to introduce into it something of military science and discipline. Military genius was evidently not wanting to the man who, at the age of sixty-three, could perform such exploits. Some Polish troops, who also joined him, gave him more trouble by their indiscipline than assistance by their military experience. With this motley band, however, he struck some more severe blows on the parties of the enemy; and by holding Lilienfeld till the *vizier* was compelled to withdraw his light troops from the country, and thus guarding the main pass into Styria, he saved that province from all the horrors of Tartar invasion.

The value of that exemption may be gathered from the calculations made by contemporary writers of authority, of the number of those who were carried off into slavery from Austria, which amounts to 6000 men, 11,000 women, 19,000 girls, and 56,000 children. Among the girls were 200 of noble extraction. The example of the Abbot of Lilienfeld, though eminently conspicuous, is not the only one which shows how much might have been done to check the brave and rapacious, but undisciplined, horsemen of the East, if the Austrian gentry had not, in a moment of general consternation and depression, emigrated so largely to the Tyrol and other places of safety. Many tales are related of troops of marauders put to flight by the firm countenance of individual men, and even women.

No one of these stories can, perhaps, be so strictly relied upon as to justify its insertion in the page of serious history; and it is certain that in other instances the Tartar cavalry, by their skill in horsemanship and individual daring, were found formidable antagonists. Troops, however, whose occupation is plunder, and engaged in a difficult country, are

130

never safe from such a man as the Abbot of Lilienfeld, and a few more such would at least have caused them to concentrate their numbers, and to include a far less extent of country within their ranges. On the 13th August, the Bavarian forces, 13,000 in number, were ferried over the Danube near Mölk. They were received with salvos of artillery and military music from the fortified abbey. The Margrave of Bareuth crossed the river on the following day with 6000 men. The presence of this respectable force on the right bank of the Danube freed the upper provinces from that of the invaders.

CHAPTER 14

From the end of July to September 11

The corps of Tekeli had meanwhile prosecuted its operations in Upper Hungary. As he was approaching Tyrnau, the Duke of Lorraine reinforced the citadel of Presburg with some regiments of cavalry, and put the remainder of his army in motion across the Marchfield. Learning that the town of Presburg was already occupied, and the citadel threatened by the adherents of Tekeli, and also that 20,000 Turks and 20,000 Hungarians were encamped in the neighbourhood, he pushed on towards the city. He succeeded in flinging an additional force into the fortress, and, after some resistance, drove the enemy out of the suburbs and town. The citizens, excusing their defection on the ground of compulsion, renewed their fealty to the emperor.

The advanced guard of the Polish Army, under Prince Lubomirski, had meanwhile arrived, and with their assistance the duke on the following day gained a victory which cleared the left bank of the Danube, and re-established the communication with Comorn and Raab. The hostile camp fell entirely into the victors' hands. The Turks and Tekeli threw mutual blame upon each other. To whichever it was due, their united forces, after ravaging the Marchfield, were overtaken by Lorraine near Stammerdorf, and again completely defeated. The Pacha of Erlau with 1200 men were left dead on the field, many more perished in attempting to swim the Danube, 22 standards were taken, and a body of 600 Hungarians deserted to the enemy. Meanwhile the troops of the Empire were flocking in from all quarters.

The Bavarians have been already mentioned. The Elector of Saxony, John George III., marched out of Dresden on the 22nd July with 12,000 men and 18 guns, and reached Crems on the 28th August. Sobieski writes to his wife in great admiration of the Saxon troops, as well dressed, complete in numbers, and well disciplined:

We may say of the Germans what has been said of the horse, they do not know their own strength.

The King of Poland left Cracow early in August. The Emperor had undergone the humiliation of imploring the personal presence of a sovereign whose policy and interests he had always thwarted, even should he arrive without his army. This homage to his military talents was doubtless grateful, but John Sobieski needed no stimulus when the Turk was in the field. While the French ambassador was exerting all his influence to detain him, and writing to Louis XIV. that he was too corpulent for active service, he took leave of his wife, and, after making his will, set out, accompanied by his son, a boy sixteen years of age, in advance of his army. His march lay through a country exposed to the incursions of Tartars and Hungarians, but he performed it on horseback with an escort of some 2000 cavalry, and reached the head-quarters of Lorraine in safety. He found them at Tuln, on the right bank of the river, the force weak in numbers, and still employed in the construction of the bridge which the Emperor in his letters had announced as finished.

Many of the German troops had not yet arrived. Lorraine spake with anxiety of the condition of affairs. Sobieski replied:

Be of good cheer, which of us at the head of 200,000 men would have allowed this bridge to be constructed within five leagues of his camp? The *vizier* is a man of no capacity.

The Polish Army, under Field Marshal Jablonowski, reached the bank of the Danube opposite Tuln early in September. It amounted to about 26,000 men of all arms, but with a very small proportion of infantry. After passing them in review, the leaders held a council of war, in which Lorraine suggested that the march for the relief of the city should be directed over the Kahlenberg. The King gave an immediate assent, observing, that he had left his royal dignity at Warsaw, and was prepared to act with the Duke as with a friend and brother. On the other hand, no jealousies would seem to have interfered to prevent an immediate and frank acknowledgment of the authority of Sobieski as commander-in-chief of the assembled forces.

It is not to be forgotten that the Duke of Lorraine had been competitor with Sobieski for the crown of Poland. Sobieski's letters contain some graphic details of their first meeting, which seems to have passed off at table with more joviality than was consistent with the ordinary habits of Lorraine, who was free from the German vice of drinking, but who on this occasion, beginning with the lighter vintage of Moselle, passed on to the stronger wines of Hungary. Sobieski describes him as modest and taciturn, strongly marked with the smallpox, *le nez trez aquilin, et presque en peroquet*; stooping, plain, and negligent in his attire. *Avec tout ça, il n'a pas la mine d'un marchand mais d'un homme comme il faut, et même d'un homme de distinction. C'est un homme avec qui je m'accorderais facilement.*

It was further decided that the Poles should cross the river at Tuln and the Germans at Crems, so as to effect their junction at the former place on the 5th September. The junction did not however take place till the 7th. Three thousand Poles were detached towards the March field to keep the Hungarians in check. The Christian Army now consisted of 85,000 men, Austrians, Poles, Bavarians, Saxons, Swabians, and Franconians, with 186 pieces of artillery. Of this number, some 7000 were detached for the occupation of various posts, leaving about 77,000 effectives for field operations against the Turks. This force, small in numbers if we consider the greatness of the stake at issue, counted among its leaders four sovereigns and twenty-two other princes of sovereign houses.

The electoral houses of Germany were worthily represented by Saxony and Bavaria. John George III., Elector of Saxony, had seen much service in the cause of Austria, and had been the first of the German princes to give a frank adhesion to her cause. Sobieski describes him as speaking neither Latin nor French, and little German; not addicted to harangues or compliments, *étourdi*, drunken, simple, and good-natured. The man thus satirically painted was however a sturdy specimen of the German race, and could deal hard blows in the field. Maximilian Emanuel, of Bavaria, conspicuous in after years for the misfortunes entailed upon him by his alliance with France against Austria, and the principal victim of Marlborough's success at Blenheim, came forward now at the age of twenty -one, to save from destruction the sovereign who, after rewarding him with the hand of a daughter, lived to expel him for a while from his dominions. He had the good sense now to consign the conduct of his troops to experienced hands, and served himself as a volunteer.

Among the others were the Dukes of Sachsen Lauenburg, Eisenach, and Weissenfels, of Brunswick-Lüneburg, Wirtemberg and Holstein, Pfalzneuburg and Croy, the Margrave of Baireuth and Louis of Baden afterwards so famous; the Landgrave of Hesse, the Princes of Waldeck, Hohenzollern, Anhalt, and Salm; last and youngest, Eugene of Savoy. The Prince of Waldeck commanded the troops of the Circles.

The literature of modern Europe, rich as it is in the correspondence of eminent persons of both sexes, perhaps contains no collection of letters of such engrossing interest as those written at this period by John Sobieski to his wife, which have lately found an eminent translator and commentator in the Count Plater. The familiar correspondence of such a man as Sobieski, even if devoted to ordinary occurrences and insignificant events, would derive an interest from the character and fame of the writer which few such collections could claim. In the case of these, however, the circumstances of the time combine with the character of the man to enhance that interest to the highest degree. They are the letters of an absent lover, pledged to punctual and familiar correspondence, and consequently rich in minute details. They are the military dispatches of one of the greatest soldiers who ever lived, penned in moments snatched from hard-earned repose, often when the night-lamp of his tent was growing pale before the twilight of morning, and dealing with the hourly progress of one of the greatest military transactions in history.

Some passages of these documents escaped at the time, and have been quoted by all writers on the subjects concerned, from Voltaire and Madame de Sévigné to the gazette writers of the day; but these passages, principally relating to the great and notorious result, are not of greater interest, and are of less historical value, than the remainder more lately rescued from the obscurity of the Polish language which was the medium of his most familiar intercourse with his absent wife. It is a singular trait of ability in this mischievous woman, especially when we consider the habitual distaste of her countrymen and countrywomen for the acquisition of foreign languages, that she should have so completely mastered the difficulties of a Sclavonic dialect as to speak and write it with fluency and correctness. It is embarrassing to quote from these letters, because there is scarcely a passage in them which does not present the temptation.

The series commences from the 29th August, the first evening after taking leave of his wife at Cracow. This and the five following letters carry him through the fatigues of the march, the tedious ceremonies of his reception at Olmutz and other halting-places; and the seventh, of the 9th September, is written from Tuln, the great rendezvous, and one of the points of passage for the collected forces of Poland and Germany.

At every step the interest thickens; fresh intelligence is announced of the desperate condition of the city; the figures of men then, or afterwards, famous in history, are briefly and graphically introduced to our notice; observations on the busy present, and speculations on the doubtful future, are interwoven with lively sketches of character and costume. At Tuln commenced the main difficulties of the great operation on which the eyes of Europe were concentred, difficulties which nothing but the gross negligence of the Turks could have enabled the allies to surmount.

The Tartar cavalry, properly directed, might alone have rendered impossible the three days' march, by forest paths, through a country destitute of provisions, and scarcely practicable for artillery or carriages, which intervened between the banks of the river and the heights of the Kahlenberg. Baggage and commissariat were of necessity left behind, in the neighbourhood of Tuln. It was necessary to weaken the fighting strength of the army by a strong guard to protect these depots from the Tartars, and by heavy escorts for the transport of provisions from this base of operation.

It was hardly to be expected that the heights of the Kahlenberg themselves would be found unguarded; and to explore the condition of this crowning post, the key to the main operation, was in itself a task of the utmost hazard and delicacy. It was performed on the night of the 10th by the king and the other principal commanders in person, and this service separated him so far and so long from his army then struggling up the precipices and through the forests behind, that the greatest alarm was excited for his safety. The crest of the Kahlenberg, with its castle and chapel, were found unoccupied; but the Turks, too late aware of its importance, were moving towards it in the course of the 11th, when, by great exertion, the first troops which came to hand, five Saxon battalions of the left wing, with three guns, were brought up to the summit.

The Turks, finding themselves anticipated, retired without a serious struggle, and the Saxon guns opening upon their rear, gave signal to the city of its approaching salvation. The king and the other commanders rejoined their several corps about mid-day of the 11th, and the principal difficulties of the march having been now overcome, the army was enabled to arrange itself in nearly the order which was preserved through the following day of battle. (See Appendix).

This operation was conducted without disturbance from the enemy, except on the extreme left, where General Leslie experienced some opposition in the establishment of a battery. The report of this skirmish roused Sobieski, not from slumber, which, as he states, was rendered unattainable by the thunder of the Turkish batteries against the city, but from the occupation of writing a long and detailed letter to his wife. Disturbed in this enjoyment, the indefatigable man, described by the French ambassador as too corpulent to ride, was again in the saddle at three a.m. He appears to have ridden along the whole position, from his tent on the extreme right to the Leopoldsberg on the left. This exertion had the advantage of bringing him once more into personal communication with Lorraine before that final issue which took place on the following day, contrary indeed to the expectation or intention of either, for neither contemplated at this moment the possibility of bringing so vast an operation as the relief of the city within the compass of a single day.

Nothing seems to have given Sobieski so much annoyance at this period as the non-appearance of some Cossack levies, which his agents had been despatched to raise. He writes of them in their absence in a strain which might have been used by a Russian commander of our own day, and which shows that the admirable qualities of the real Cossack for the duty of light troops, especially against the Turk, had fully displayed themselves in the seventeenth century. It is certain that down to the latest period, the Vizier had no belief, or even suspicion, that Sobieski had taken the field in person, or that any strong Polish force had joined the army. The reported appearance of Polish troops was accounted for by the known arrival of Lubomirski's partisan corps.

The muster-roll of the Turkish Army found in the tent of the Vizier gives in round numbers a total of 160,000 men, and historians have been ready enough to adopt a cypher, which would give a difference of 80,000 men as against the victorious party. As this document, however, includes all detachments and garrisons, and also many commanders and men who were certainly no longer in existence, the Pacha of Erlau, for instance, who, with most of his troops, had perished, as has been related, in the affair of Stammersdorf, it is as needless to dwell upon the fallacy of such an assumption of numbers, as it would be difficult to arrive at anything like accuracy with any other. If we accept the statement of Kantemir, that, on the night before the battle, nearly a fourth of the Turkish army disbanded itself, we can hardly calculate the force remaining in the camp at more than 100,000, for whom, exhausted and dispirited as they were, 80,000 untouched regular troops were more than an equal match.

When the advance of the Christian Army became no longer doubtful, the *vizier* called his *pachas* about him to deliberate upon the mode in which to meet the impending attack. The aged Pacha of Pesth, who has been mentioned as adverse from the first to the march upon Vienna, advised the *vizier* to raise the siege without delay, to collect the whole army, and, cutting down the neighbouring forests, to palisade and entrench themselves and abide the attack. On the repulse of the first onset, to launch the cavalry on both flanks of the enemy, and thus decide his defeat. The majority of the council was in favour of this proposal.

The *vizier* was obstinate in rejecting it, alleging, not unjustly, that if the siege were once raised, the city would instantly avail itself of the opportunity to repair its defences, and put itself into condition to defy a renewed attempt. It would be difficult, if the *Janissaries* were once withdrawn from the trenches, to persuade them to return to their toil, even after the achievement of a victory in the field. His opinion then was that a sufficient force should be left in the approaches to carry on the siege operations without interruption, and that the remainder should advance against the enemy, whose inferior numbers would be easily crushed. The *pachas* made some further remonstrances, but were forced to give way to the unlimited authority of their chief. On the 11th September all the Turkish troops in the Leopoldstadt were withdrawn, and the greater part of the cavalry were moved forward towards the Kahlenberg, near the base of which, and on the Wienerberg, they threw up entrenchments; and, disposing themselves in the shape of a crescent, they awaited the appearance of the Imperialists.

Between Weinhaus and Gerstorf are still to be seen the traces of a considerable work, which bears the name of the Turkenschauz, the site of one of their principal batteries. So long previous as the 9th September, the *vizier*, in his first alarm at the approach of the enemy, had determined to collect his force on the Wienerberg, and a field-tent had been pitched for him near the so-called Spinnerkreuz. On the following day, however, he changed his intention and plan, and moving the main portion of his force towards the Kahlenberg, drew it up upon the heights between Grinzing and Heiligenstadt.

On the evening of the same day, the 10th, the advanced guard of the Christian Army arrived on the Kahlenberg, and the first sound of its guns, as above described, was heard in Vienna, as they opened from the heights on the columns of the Turks. The effect was one of mingled joy and anxiety. The issue of the struggle was evidently at hand, but that issue was still uncertain, and the night was one of ago-nising suspense. The population not immediately employed in mili-tary duty, was divided through the day between the churches and the roofs of towers and houses; the first engaged in earnest supplication to Heaven, the latter in surveying the movements of the Turkish camp, and watching for the first gleam of the Christian weapons as they is-sued from the wooded heights.

The *commandant*, as evening closed in, despatched a messenger, who swam the Danube with a letter for the Duke of Lorraine. Its words were few. "No time to be lost!—no time indeed to be lost!" This message was acknowledged by a cluster of rockets from Her-mansdorf. Orders were now issued by Count Stahremberg to all the troops, regular and irregular, to hold themselves in readiness for a sally during the expected battle of the morrow, or for joining the Christian army, and driving the Turks out of the approaches. The night of the 11th of September closed in upon this troubled scene. The man whose doom is sealed will often sleep till morning calls him to the scaffold. Such heavy sleep as his, the offspring of nervous excitement and ex-haustion, perhaps, was granted to the citizen of Vienna; but even this may be doubted, for the criminal is assured of his fate. The doom of Vienna was yet uncertain.

CHAPTER 15

September 12

At sunrise of the 12th September, the crest of the Kahlenberg was concealed by one of those autumnal mists which give promise of a genial, perhaps a sultry day, and which, clinging to the wooded flanks of the acclivity, grew denser as it descended, till it rested heavily on the shores and the stream itself of the river below. From that summit the usual fiery signals of distress had been watched through the night by many an eye as they rose incessantly from the tower of St. Stephen, and now the fretted spire of that edifice, so long the target of the ineffectual fire of the Turkish artillerists, was faintly distinguished rising from a sea of mist. As the hour wore on, and the exhalation dispersed, a scene was disclosed which must have made those who witnessed it from the Kahlenberg tighten their saddle-girths or look to their priming.

A practised eye glancing over the fortifications of the city could discern from the Burg to the Scottish gate an interruption of their continuity, a shapeless interval of rubbish and of ruin, which seemed as if a battalion might enter it abreast. In face of this desolation a labyrinth of lines extended itself, differing in design from the rectilinear zigzag of a modern approach, and formed of short curves overlapping each other, to use a comparison of some writers of the time, like the scales of a fish. In these, the Turkish lines, the miner yet crawled to his task, and the storming parties were still arrayed by order of the *vizier*, ready for a renewal of the assault so often repeated in vain.

The camp behind had been evacuated by the fighting men; the horse-tails had been plucked from before the tents of the *pachas*, but their harems still tenanted the canvass city; masses of Christian captives awaited there their doom in chains; camels and drivers and camp followers still peopled the long streets of tents in all the confusion of fear and suspense. Nearer to the base of the hilly range of the Kahlenberg and the Leopoldsberg, the still imposing numbers of the Turkish Army were drawn up in battle array ready to dispute the egress of the Christian columns from the passes, and prevent their deployment on the plain. To the westward, on the reverse flank of the range, the Christian troops might be seen toiling up the ascent.

As they drew up on the crest of the Leopoldsberg they formed a half circle round the chapel of the Margrave, and when the bell for matins tolled, the clang of arms and the noises of the march were silenced. On a space kept clear round the chapel a standard with a white cross on a red ground was unfurled, as if to bid defiance to the blood red flag planted in front of the tent of Kara Mustapha. One shout of acclamation and defiance broke out from the modern crusaders as this emblem of a holy war was displayed, and all again was hushed as the gates of the castle were flung open, and a procession of the Princes of the Empire and the other leaders of the Christian host moved forward to the chapel. It was headed by one whose tonsured crown and venerable beard betokened the monastic profession.

The soldiers crossed themselves as he passed, and knelt to receive the blessing which he gave them with outstretched hands. This was the famous Capuchin Marco Aviano, friend and confessor to the emperor, whose acknowledged piety and exemplary life had earned for him the general reputation of prophetic inspiration, he had been the inseparable companion of the Christian Army in its hours of difficulty and danger, and was now here to assist at the consummation of his prayers for its success. Among the stately warriors who composed his train, three principally attracted the gaze of the curious. The first in rank and station was a man somewhat past the prime of life, strong limbed and of imposing stature, but quick and lively in speech and gesture, his head partly shaved in the fashion of his semi-Eastern country, his hair, eyes, and beard, dark-coloured.

His majestic bearing bespoke the soldier king, the scourge and dread of the Moslem, the conqueror of Choczim, John Sobieski. His own attire is said to have been plain, but we gather from his letters that in his retinue he displayed a Sclavonic taste for magnificence which strongly contrasted with the economial arrangements of Lorraine, and even of the two Electors. Painters, and others studious of accuracy, may be glad to know that on this occasion the colour of his dress was sky blue, and that he rode a bay horse. An attendant bearing a shield, with his arms emblazoned, always preceded him, and his place in battle was marked by another who carried a plume on his lance point, a signal more conspicuous, though less inseparable, than the famous white plume of Henry IV.

On his left was his youthful son Prince James, armed with a breast-plate and helmet, and, in addition to an ordinary sword, with a short and broad-bladed sabre, a national weapon of former ages; on his right was the illustrious and heroic ancestor of the present reigning house of Austria, Charles of Lorraine. Behind these moved many of the principal members of those sovereign houses of Germany whose names and titles have been already specified. At the side of Louis of Baden walked a youth of slender frame and moderate stature, but with that intelligence in his eye which pierced in after years the cloud of many a doubtful field, and swayed the fortunes of empires. This was the young Eugene of Savoy, who drew his maiden sword in the quarrel in which his brother had lately perished. (*Eugene of Savoy* by Eugene of Savoy & Alexander Innes Shand is also published Leonaur).

The service of high mass was performed in the chapel by Aviano, the king assisting at the altar, while the distant thunder of the Turkish batteries formed strange accompaniment to the Christian choir. The Princes then received the sacrament, and the religious ceremony was closed by a general benediction of the troops by Aviano. The king then stepped forward and conferred knighthood on his son, with the usual ceremonies, commending to him as an example for his future course the great commander then present, the Duke of Lorraine. He then addressed his troops in their own language to the following effect:—

Warriors and friends! Yonder in the plain are our enemies, in numbers greater indeed than at Choczim, where we trod them under foot. We have to fight them on a foreign soil, but we fight for our own country, and under the walls of Vienna we are defending those of Warsaw and Cracow. We have to save to-day, not a single city, but the whole of Christendom, of which that city of Vienna is the bulwark. The war is a holy one. There is a blessing on our arms, and a crown of glory for him who falls. You fight not for your earthly sovereign, but for the King of kings. His power has led you unopposed up the difficult access to these heights, and has thus placed half the victory in your hands. The *infidels* see you now above their heads; and with hopes blasted and courage depressed, are creeping among valleys destined for their graves. I have but one command to give,—follow me. The time is come for the young to win their spurs.

Military music and the shouts of thousands greeted this pertinent harangue, and as it closed, five cannon shots gave the signal for the general advance. A sharp fire of musketry from the small hamlet of Kahlenberg near Nussdorf soon announced that the left wing, under the immediate command of the Duke of Lorraine, had felt the enemy, and it increased as his attack developed itself towards Heiligenstadt and Döbling. The centre, commanded by the Elector of Bavaria and the Prince of Waldeck, moved upon Währing and Weinhaus. The right wing, under the King of Poland, issued from the woods near Dornbach. There is no doubt that the general disposal of the confederated forces was entirely arranged by the King. His rank alone would have entitled him to a nominal precedency, which, even in the case of an ordinary sovereign, it would have been convenient to admit; for, previously to his arrival in the camp, disputes had already arisen between Saxony and Bavaria, and Vienna might have been taken twice over before such disputes between German sovereigns could have been settled.

The respect however in which John Sobieski's military talents were held, his vast experience of the Turkish manner of fighting, and the dread which his presence was known to inspire amongst that people, were such as to obtain a ready and real acquiescence in his slightest suggestions, so long as the difficulty lasted and the danger was imminent. His order of battle was a deep one. To avoid so great an extension of front as would have compelled him to throw his right flank beyond the little river Wien instead of keeping that stream on his right, he adopted a formation in three lines, the third acting as a reserve. The troops were strictly directed to preserve their ranks on the approach of the enemy, and halt to receive his fire and return their own; then to advance steadily, and make good the ground so gained—the infantry gradually developing itself to the right and left, and allowing the cavalry to fill up the intervals, and take its full share in the further advance, charging as opportunity should offer.

The first operation of Kara Mustapha was worthy of one in whom the cruelty was united with the ignorance of the savage—it was the slaughter of the defenceless captives of all ages and either sex, with whom, to the number it is said of 30,000, his camp was crowded. It was obeyed to the letter; and even the inmates of the soldiers' *harems*, women far different in morals from the *courtezans* of the Christian camp, are said to have perished. The command of the right wing, which occupied strong and broken ground opposite the Duke of Lorraine, was intrusted to the Pacha of Mesopotamia. The *vizier* himself commanded in the centre opposite Währing, and the left wing opposite Hernals was commanded by the old Pacha of Pesth.

The cavalry were in advance towards the base of the Kahlenberg. The hollow ways between Nussdorf and Heiligenstadt were strongly entrenched and fiercely defended. It was, as has been noticed, the original intention of the king to content himself on this day with the descent of the acclivity and the establishment of the army in favourable order and position for a general action on the morrow, and he had agreed upon this course with Lorraine, but the fierceness of the struggle on the left of the allies drew his forces gradually to its support, and brought on a more immediate decision. To descend the wooded acclivities without deranging the scientific order of battle devised and adopted was an operation only less tedious and difficult than the ascent of the preceding days, and it was to be performed in the presence of an enemy for courage and numbers not to be despised.

The left wing was engaged for some hours before the Bavarians in the centre or the Poles on the right could deploy. The defence of the broken ground near Nussdorf and Heiligenstadt on the part of the Turks was obstinate, but having occupied in haste and too late their present position at the foot of the heights, they had not brought up their artillery, and their dismounted cavalry, of which the troops here engaged were principally composed, were not a match for the Imperialists, who drove the enemy steadily before them from ravine to ravine, and carried the two villages. It is probable that Lorraine, adhering to the original scheme of action, might have contented himself with this success for the day, and it is not certain at what period of the action a contrary and bolder determination first suggested itself to either the king or himself.

The duke is said to have consulted at a critical period the Saxon Field-Marshal Geltz, who, observing the progress of the Bavarians and Poles towards the centre and right, gave it for his opinion that the Duke might sleep that night if he would in Vienna. Eugene of Savoy was employed during the action in conveying a message from Lorraine to the king. We may indulge ourselves with the conjecture that he was charged with this decision, one worthy of such a messenger. Accounts differ as to the hour at which the action became general by the deployment of the Bavarians and Poles. Some put it as late as two p.m. It is said, however, that towards eleven o'clock the Imperialists on the left were slackening their advance to make good the ground they had gained, and to wait for the appearance of their friends, when the gilded cuirasses of the Polish cavalry flashed out from the defiles of the Wenersberg, and the shout of "Live Sobieski" ran along the lines.

The heat was oppressive, and the king halted and dismounted his people for a hasty repast. This concluded, the whole line advanced, and the battle soon raged in every part of an amphitheatre admirably adapted by nature for such a transaction. The Turks had profited by the lull to bring up heavy reinforcements, and the *vizier* flung himself on the Poles in very superior numbers. In an early part of the encounter, a body of Polish *Hulans* compromised itself by a rash advance, and was for a time surrounded. It was extricated by the prompt and judicious assistance of Waldeck and his Bavarians, but lost many officers of distinction, and among them, a Potocki, the treasurer Modrjewski, and the Colonel Ahasuerus.

The second line was brought up by Sobieski, and the Turks were driven before their desperate valour through ravines and villages, and the fortified position of Hernals, back upon the glacis of their camp. The city of tents with all its treasures was almost within their grasp; but it is said that even with such a spectacle before him, Sobieski's caution all but induced him to pause till the morrow. The approach to the camp was protected by a ravine, the ground in front was undulating and strengthened with works, and occupied by a strong force and a powerful artillery. The King was in face of the centre of this position; his right covered by Jablanowski against the attacks of the Tartar cavalry.

It was five o'clock; his infantry was not yet at hand; the only artillery which had kept pace with the speed of his advance consisted of two or three light pieces which the veteran commander of his artillery, Konski, had brought up by force of arm and levers. Sobieski pointed these at the field tent of crimson silk, from which the *vizier* was giving his orders. The ammunition carriages were, however, far behind, and a few charges carried by hand were soon exhausted. A French officer, it is said, rammed home the last cartridge with his gloves, his wig, and a packet of French newspapers.

At this moment of hesitation, the infantry came up. They were led by the Count Maligni, the king's brother-in-law, against a height which commanded the quarters of the *vizier*. The attack was successful, and the king determined on the instant to pursue his fortune. As he led his troops in a direct line for the *vizier's* tent, his terrible presence was recognised by the *infidel*. "By *Allah* the king is really among us," exclaimed the Khan of the Crimea, Selim Gieray. The mass retreated in confusion. Those who awaited the attack went down before those lances of the Polish cavalry of which it was said by a Polish noble to one of their kings, that if the heavens were to fall they would sustain them on their points. The Pachas of Aleppo and Silistria perished in the fray. The panic became universal and the rout complete. The *vizier*, hurried along with the stream, weeping and cursing by turns—had neither time to deliberate nor power to command.

By six o'clock his gorgeous tent was in possession of Sobieski. His charger, too heavily caparisoned for rapid flight, was still held by a slave at the entrance. One of the golden stirrups was instantly sent off by the conqueror to the queen as a token of the defeat and flight of its late owner. On the left, meanwhile, the progress of Lorraine, though less rapid from the difficulties of the ground and the tenacity of the resistance, had been equally victorious. The great Turkish redoubt, of which the traces yet remain, held out against repeated assaults till near five o'clock, when Louis of Baden, at the head of a regiment of Saxon dragoons, dismounted for the purpose, and two Austrian regiments of infantry, carried the work. The Turks now gave way at every point, and poured into their camp in the wildest confusion.

The Margrave Louis, at the head of a squadron of dragoons, was the first to open a communication with the city from the counterscarp of the Scottish gate. Stahremberg ordered an immediate sally against the approaches of the enemy, from which they had maintained through the day as heavy a fire as on any previous day of the siege, though no assault had been attempted by the strong body of *Janissaries* left in them for that purpose. These men, abandoned now without orders to their fate, endeavoured to turn the guns of the batteries upon the Imperialists. The attempt, however, in the general confusion which ensued, was vain, and the main body of the *Janissaries*, unable or unwilling to retreat, was cut to pieces in the course of the night. The camp meanwhile fell into the undisputed possession of the Poles.

Previous precaution, or a few moments' halt at St. Ulric, enabled the *vizier* to save the sacred standard of the Prophet. One of the many standards captured was sent by Sobieski to the Pope under the supposition that it was the famous Palladium in question, but this proved to be a mistake. It is probable also that the mass of the treasure, which is supposed to have been very great in the *vizier's* exchequer, had been removed; and we learn from the King of Poland's letters that considerable sums of coin were hastily divided among the *vizier's* attendants at the last moment, and carried off. No great amount of coin or bullion was found in the tents. Every other item in the long catalogue of the treasures and luxuries which the *vizier* had accumulated round his person fell into the hands of the Poles. The Turks continued their flight without intermission in the direction of Raab, where the force still employed in the blockade of that fortress afforded them a rallying point.

It was, however, impossible for the Christian leaders to assure themselves at so late an hour of the full extent of the enemy's discomfiture, or even to consider themselves secure against a night attack. Great exertions were therefore made both by the king and the duke to keep their troops well in hand through the night. The king, whose advance had led him to the very centre of the camp, found it necessary to resort to threats of summary and capital punishment to prevent his whole army from dispersing itself at once to gather the rich harvest of the Turkish tents. These threats were, as may be imagined, only partially effectual. Tents guarded in front were cut open from behind, and discipline as usual gave way before the attraction of spoil.

The Germans had no such immediate opportunities for plunder. Two regiments only of Austrian dragoons were despatched in pursuit as far as the Fischa stream. The slaughter of this great battle was not great in proportion to the numbers engaged and the results obtained. The loss of the Turks has been computed at 25,000 men. Among these was that body of *Janissaries*, who were forgotten, and left without orders in the trenches, and were cut to pieces during the night. The king describes the Turks as defending themselves desperately even in full flight. In this point of view, he says, they made the finest retreat in the world. That of the Christians has been stated at 1000 killed and 3000 wounded, which is probably far less than the truth, for the Poles alone lost 100 officers, among them some of their first nobles. In the centre the loss of the Bavarians was probably trifling, but on the left the struggle was long and severe.

A Prince of Croy fell here in the early part of the action. In the *vizier's* encampment was found the Polish envoy Proski, who, from the period of his sovereign's junction with Austria, had been kept in fetters, under constant menace of the sabre or the bowstring, and now owed his life and liberation to the confusion of the moment. Kunitz also, an agent in Caprara's suite, who had been detained in the Turkish camp, and had found means to send occasional intelligence to Stahremberg, escaped in a Turkish disguise during the action. A Polish writer, Rubinkoski, gives a rough list of the artillery and its appurtenances abandoned in the lines: 60 guns of 48 lbs., 60 of 24 lbs., 150 of various lesser calibre, 40 mortars, 9000 ammunition waggons, 100,000 oxen, 25,000 tents, 1,000,000 lbs. of powder. To this may be added 10,000 camels, 5000 oxen, mules, sheep, &c., and immense stores of other provision.

Among those accidental results of events which the political economist and the philosopher loves to notice, is the fact that the popular use of coffee in Germany is to be dated from this period, and is due to the plunder of the Turkish camp. Stahremberg's brave and faithful messenger, Kolschitzki, was rewarded by permission to set up the first coffee-house in Vienna. The head of the corporation of coffee providers is bound to this day to have in his house a portrait of this patriarch of his profession.

★★★★★★

The first coffee-house in Europe was established in Constantinople in 1551. A century later, in 1652, a Greek established one in London. The first in France was at Marseilles in 1671, in Paris the following year. In Germany that of Kolschitzki was the first, the second was opened at Leipzic in 1694. In 1700 Vienna counted four, in 1737 eleven. In the city and suburbs there are now one hundred.

★★★★★★

Another inventory of the siege-stores actually brought into the arsenal of Vienna shows a considerable amount, as well as variety of articles, but can give but an imperfect notion of the vast provision accumulated, as the army authorities could but glean after the plunderers of the three first days. The king writes to his wife that the quantity of ammunition saved was at most a third of the whole, and says that the continual explosions in the camp were like the last judgment. His letters give some very amusing details of that portion of the spoils of the *vizier's* tent which he contrived to rescue for his own share from the fangs of his officers. They illustrate also the character of the man whose penetralia were thus rudely exposed to investigation, and show that Kara Mustapha had superadded every description of refinement to the simpler sensuality of the East.

Tissues and carpets and furs are natural appendages of Oriental rank and wealth, and jewelled arms and quivers, studded with rubies and pearls, were equally consistent with his functions as commander of the armies of the faithful. Baths, fountains, a rabbit warren, and a menagerie, were found within the encampment. A parrot took wing and foiled the pursuit of the soldiers. An ostrich had been beheaded by the *vizier's* own hand, as if it had been a woman of the harem, to prevent its falling into Christian hands. This rarity had been taken from the Imperial Menagerie at the Favorita, where the king mentions having found a famished lioness and a small body of *Janissaries*, who had been left behind at that post, and still held out some days after the action.

The *Janissaries* surrendered to the personal summons of the king. Their lives were spared, and the lioness fed by order of the good-natured conqueror. "The *vizier*," writes the king," is a *galant homme*, and has made us fine presents: everything in particular which came near his person is of the most *mignon* and refined description. Father Louis will have reason to rejoice, for I have in my possession the medicine chest of the *vizier*. Among its contents are oils, and gums, and balms, which Pecovini, (king's Italian physician), is never tired of admiring. Among other things we have found some rare fishes called Eperlans de mer. *Informezvous-en, mon coeur, chez le Père Louis; ce doit être une chose précieuse pour rechauffer les entrailles."* Among the treasures of the *vizier*, diamonds were found in great profusion; many, set in girdles and otherwise, fell into the hands of the king, and many more carried off by the officers and soldiers. The king remarks that they were not used for ornament by the Turks of his day, and conjectures that they were destined to adorn the ladies of Vienna when transferred to the *harems* of the *vizier* and his *pachas*.

Among other trophies of interest, Roman Catholic historians have particularized an oaken cross six ells in height, remarkable from the fact that in the camp of the *infidel* it was set up for the daily celebration of mass by one of their Christian allies, Servanus Kantacuzenos, Prince of Wallachia. A chapel was built for it in the so-called Gatterholz, near Schönbrunn, on the spot where it had thus braved the scoffs of the Moslem. It was stolen thence in 1785.

As far as a considerable lapse of intervening years, permits us to decide, this great action appears to have been planned with surpassing judgment, and conducted with that steady valour and perseverance on the part both of officers and men, to give scope and effect to which all rules of war were invented, and without which these rules are useless.

History presents few instances in which an extensive operation has been conducted with such cordial concert between bodies of different nations commanded in several cases by their respective sovereigns, and in which jealousies of precedence and professional rivalries appear to have been so completely laid aside during the action. The only instance of any apparent deficiency in this respect is that of a refusal of the Prince of Waldeck to support an attack directed by the Duke of Lorraine; but even in this case there is every reason to suppose that he considered it to involve a departure from the earnest injunctions of the chief in command, the king, who had directed him to keep his troops in hand for the support of the right wing.

When the discomfiture of the Polish cavalry had compromised the safety of that wing, and with it the fate of the battle, we find the German troops, probably the Bavarians, prompt and efficient to the rescue; and on the left, Saxons, intermingled with Austrians, fought together, as if under one common banner. The stout elector himself was in the thickest of the fray. He is said to have been splashed with Turkish blood so as scarcely to be recognised. With the exception of the first somewhat rash attack of the Poles, there is no appearance of any indulgence of that untempered enthusiasm which the occasion might have excused. Order and steadiness seem to have pervaded the whole area of the Christian operations. Attacks were everywhere duly supported, failures retrieved, and obstacles of ground successively overcome, in a manner which showed a grave consciousness of the magnitude of the stake at issue.

Chapter 16

September 13

At sunrise of the 13th the Viennese rushed forth in crowds to taste the first sweets of their liberation from a two months' imprisonment. The only gate yet open, the Stuben, was soon clogged with the multitude, and the greater number clambered over the rubbish of the breaches, eager to gratify in the Turkish camp their curiosity, or their rapacity, or both. With respect to the more transportable articles of value, the Pole had been before them; but in the article of provisions there was yet much for hungry men to glean. Prices rapidly fell, and superfluity succeeded to starvation.

Among those who sought the camp with other purposes than plunder or curiosity, was the good Bishop Kollonitsch. His inexhaustible benevolence found employment there in collecting and saving some 500 infants, whose mothers, many of them, as is supposed, Turkish women, had perished by the swords of their ruthless masters. The king mentions one instance of a beautiful child whom he saw lying with its skull cloven; but in general even Turkish inhumanity had shrunk from the task of child-murder. These, with many half-murdered mothers and some Christian adult survivors of the massacre, the bishop transported to the city in carriages, at his own cost, and took measures for the future support and education of the infants thus rescued.

Popes may spare themselves the trouble of the forms, the ceremonies, and the intrigues necessary for adding such names as that of Kollonitsch to the list of saints in the Romish calendar: the recital of these actions puts the Devil's advocate out of court, and the simple record, though traced by a Protestant pen, is their best canonization. Another worthy member of the church, the Father Aviano, had recently performed a service for which the Duke of Lorraine and the army had doubtless reason to thank him. As confessor to the emperor he had used his influence to prevent the latter from embarrassing the army with his presence at Crems, and distracting men and officers from their duty by the etiquettes and ceremonies which that presence would have inflicted, and the intrigues which it would have fostered.

On the news, however, of the victory, the emperor had dropped down the river as far as Durrenstein, and thither the Duke of Lorraine despatched the Count Auersperg with the details of the late occurrences. At ten a.m. of the 13th, the Commandant Stahremberg issued forth from the walls he had so stoutly defended to visit the camp and exchange congratulations with the leaders of the liberating army. On this morning, too, the Duke of Lorraine and the Elector of Saxony met with the King of Poland for the first time since the mass of the Kahlenberg. The meeting between all these worthies had every appearance, in the first instance, of cordiality. They perambulated the camp and the approaches together amid the acclamations of the troops; but when they entered the town, the king had the shrewdness soon to perceive that, though the gratitude of the people was as warm as the cordial and kindly nature of the Viennese could make it, its full expression was checked by authority.

In two churches which he entered the people pressed to kiss his hand; but when a few voices uttered the *vivat*, which had evidently been forbidden by the police, he recognised at once in the clouded mien of the Austrian authorities that jealousy and ingratitude which proved afterwards the only guerdon of his vast services. At an angle of the wall between the Burg and Scottish gates, the king, wearied by the heat of the day, rested for a while; a stone, with his name inscribed, marked the spot till the year 1809, when the French engineers blew up the rampart. In one of the above-mentioned churches, that of the Augustines, a grand *Te Deum* was sung. The Abbé Coyer remarks that the magistracy were absent from this ceremony, which perhaps explains a passage in a letter of the king, in which he says:—

> I perceive that Stahremberg is not on a good understanding with the magistrates of the city.

The sermon was preached from the famous text—"*There was a man sent from God, and his name was John*" a happy plagiarism from the quotation of Scripture by Pope Pius V. on the occasion of the victory of Lepanto. The service concluded, 300 cannon shots from the ramparts spread wide the intelligence of the relief of the city—no superfluous announcement; for in Wiener Neustadt and other places the trembling inhabitants had drawn a contrary conclusion from the sudden cessation of the firing, and thought the city lost. The king, after dining with the *commandant*, only delayed his departure to hold a long discourse with a man of much accomplishment, the court interpreter, Meninski, whose conversation had probably more charms for him than that of the dull notabilities by whom he was surrounded. He was himself a good linguist, and a proficient in the Turkish language. This over, he hastened to quit the scene of cold civilities for the camp. He was escorted to the gates by the populace.

It may be mentioned that during the dinner an alarm was raised that the Turks had rallied, and were advancing. The king desired his officers present to leave the feast and mount, and was doubtless preparing to follow, when they returned with assurance of the falsehood of the report. This circumstance is mentioned in a very simple and detailed diary of the siege by the Doctor of Laws, Nicholas Hocke, one of the most curious of the many contemporary publications.

The electors of Saxony and Bavaria appear to have been exempt from any share of the feeling of jealousy manifested by Austria. Both in the first hour of enthusiasm offered to accompany the king to the end of the world. The former indeed soon found his appetite for a Hungarian campaign subside, and shortly withdrew with his army to his electoral dominions. The younger Bavarian thought fit to pass a longer apprenticeship under so great a master in the art of war. The Duke of Lorraine had little exercise of his own discretion; he knew too well by what tenure the command of the army of Austria was held to do otherwise than reflect the livid colour of the spirit in which the hereditary sovereign of the House of Hapsburg contemplated the elective King of Poland.

The king's letters are full of complaints of the unworthy treatment which he daily received from the duke and his subordinates; but we may charitably ascribe such mean conduct on the part of so great a commander to influence from above. In an early letter the king describes him by report as speaking little, and timidly, from the constant dread of infringing on the instructions of the court. Some jealous feeling was doubtless excited, and might be excused by the fact that the chances of battle had given the Polish sovereign and his army prior and exclusive possession of the spoils.

The king, immediately on his return to his quarters, directed a removal of them in advance. Some of his cavalry indeed were already on the track of the enemy, killing and taking prisoners in great numbers.

There were cogent reasons, both political as well as military, for his removing himself as soon as possible from the immediate neighbourhood of Vienna. The heat of the autumnal season had made the camp and its environs one vast charnel, swarming with flies and vermin. This circumstance had caused the Duke of Lorraine to transfer his quarters from Ebersdorf to Mansdorf, and would alone have induced the king to follow such example. He was however also aware that his presence at Vienna was an obstacle to the expected entrance of the emperor, who shrunk from any public acknowledgment of the services which had saved his crown from danger and his capital from destruction, at the expense of the most trifling infringement of etiquette, or the momentary concession of a point of which he was peculiarly tenacious.

The practice, as regarded the reception of crowned heads in general, offered no difficulty. It was not derogatory to the Imperial dignity in French phraseology to give them the right; but the claim of an elective monarch to this distinction had always been disputed by Austria. The king writes;—

Je suis fort aise d'éviter toutes ces cérémonies.

He moved to the neighbourhood of Schwechat in the first instance. He writes on the 17th from Schonau, some fifteen miles from Vienna, on the road to Presburg, describing the interview which, after the removal of difficulties, did take place with the emperor. The latter, having ascertained the departure of the king, landed at Nussdorf on the 19th, where he was received by the princes and other commanders of the German troops. After inspecting the camp and defences, he attended a solemn thanksgiving in the cathedral, at which the bishop Kollonitsch presided, and reviewed and thanked the *burgher* guard and free companies, &c. who lined the streets.

On the 15th he reviewed the Bavarian forces near St. Marx, and afterwards took heart of grace and accomplished the dreaded interview with the king at Schwechat. That it ever took place at all was due, however, to the straightforward proceeding of the king, who, finding himself put off with excuses of the clumsiest manufacture, asked the courtier Schafgotsch the plain question whether the ceremonial of the right hand was or was not the cause of the delay. He extorted for once the plain answer, Yes, and gravely proposed an expedient for obviating the difficulty, which was, that the two sovereigns should meet face to face on horseback, and remain in that position, at the head the one of his army, the other of his suite; the one attended by his son, the other, as the head of the Empire, by the Electors. This happy expedient was accepted, and the interview took place.

The king's own account of this singular interview is doubtless more to be depended upon than the numerous Austrian relations, which extol the condescension and cordiality of the emperor.

Of the Electors, the emperor was only accompanied by the Bavarian. Saxony had already quitted him. He had in his suite some fifty horsemen, *employés*, and ministers of his court. He was preceded by trumpets, and followed by body guards and ten foot attendants. I will not draw you a portrait of the emperor, for he is well known. He was mounted on a Spanish bay horse. He wore an embroidered *juste au corps*, a French hat, with an agrafe and red and white plumes; a belt mounted with sapphires and diamonds; a sword the same. I made him my compliments in Latin, and in few words.

★★★★★★

Note:—The king was practised in this language, which he always used in his addresses to the Polish diets. When the young Charles XII. of Sweden opposed the usual resistance of boyhood to his Latin preceptor, he was informed of this fact; and the example of the great soldier proved an efficient substitute for flogging. Sobieski learned Spanish at the age of fifty.

★★★★★★

He answered in prepared phrases in the same language. Being thus facing each other, I presented to him my son, who advanced and saluted him. The emperor did not even put his hand to his hat. I remained like one terrified. He used the same behaviour towards the senators and Hetmans, and even towards his connexion the prince palatine of Belz. (Constantine Wisnowiecki, allied to the Imperial family by the marriage of the king Michael with the Archduchess Eleanor). To avoid scandal and public remarks, I addressed a few more words to the Emperor, after which I turned my horse round; we saluted, and I retook the route for my camp.

The Palatine of Russia, (the appellation of Russia at this period applied to the province of Gallicia, the territories of the *Tzar*, which have since assumed it, came under the general designation of Muscovy), showed my army to the emperor, at his desire; but our people have been much provoked, and complain loudly that the emperor did not deign to thank them, even with his hat, for all their pains and privations. Since this separation, everything has suddenly changed; it is as if they knew us no longer. They give us neither forage nor provisions. The Pope had sent money for these to the Abbé Buonvisi, but he is stopped at Lintz.

The king does not mention the words of his reply to the emperor's harangue, "I am glad, Sire, to have rendered you this small service." The emperor is said two days afterwards to have sent, with a present of a sword for Prince James, a clumsy apology for the silence and coldness of his demeanour.

We cannot certainly judge of passages like these by the standard of our present modes of European thought and action. There may be circumstances under which these apparent air-bubbles become ponderable realities. In dealing, for instance, with the Emperor of China, the slightest abandonment of a point of etiquette might involve the most serious consequences, and the concession of a diplomatist could perhaps only be retrieved by the guns of an admiral. At the worst we might smile at the pedantic tenacity of the courts of Vienna or Versailles of the seventeenth century on points of ceremonial and precedence, but no such considerations can temper the indignation which the perusal of Sobieski's letters excites, at the practical and substantial ingratitude and neglect he experienced at the hands of Austria from the moment that his services ceased to be indispensable.

That some quarrels and jealousies should arise from the juxtaposition of the Sclavonic and Teutonic elements was perhaps inevitable. To be cheated, starved, and neglected, is usually the lot of armies serving in the territory of an ally whom they cannot openly coerce and pillage; but the Polish sovereign had to endure more than this. His sick were denied boats to remove them down the river from the pestilential atmosphere of the camp; his dead, even the officers, were denied burial in the public cemeteries. The starving soldier who approached the town in search of provisions was threatened to be fired upon. The baggage, including that of the king, was pillaged—the horses of stragglers on their road to rejoin the army carried off by force men on guard over the guns they had taken, robbed of their effects; and every complaint treated with cold neglect and every requisition dismissed almost without an answer.

The royal tent, which before the battle, though, as the king observes, spacious enough, could not contain the throng of distinguished visitors, were now deserted, and the demeanour of the Duke of Lorraine himself and every other Austrian authority, showed that this treatment was deliberate and systematic. It may have been some satisfaction to Sobieski, it almost becomes one to his admirers now, to find that the Austrian government was impartial in its ingratitude, and exercised on others, besides the Poles, its singular talent for disgusting and offending those who had done it service. The Elector of Saxony, as we have seen, lost no time in withdrawing his person and his troops. The father Aviano departed for Italy, disgusted with the intrigues of the court and the licence of the camp.

The Duke of Saxe Lauenburg retired, offended by the only instance in which the emperor appears to have shown a creditable sense of his obligations. The hero of the defence, Count Stahremberg, was justly rewarded with 100,000 crowns, the golden fleece, and the rank of field-marshal. The Duke of Saxe Lauenburg, who had held high command in the late action, considered himself ill-used by this promotion over his head of an officer inferior to himself, as also to Caprara and to Leslie, in length of service. Lastly, the Duke of Lorraine himself had as little reason as anyone to be satisfied. The king writes of him later, more in pity than in anger, "the poor devil has neither any of the spoils of war, nor any gratification from the emperor." We have indeed met with no instance but that of Stahremberg in which any signal mark of favour or munificence was bestowed on any party conspicuous in the late transactions. Gold medals and nominations to the dignity of state counsellor were indeed awarded to many of the city officials.

The young volunteer, Eugene, was attached to the service for which he had quitted that of France by his nomination to the Colonelcy of a regiment of dragoons which still bears his name; but this promotion only took place in December, and was rather a retaining fee to a young man of high rank and promise than a reward for positive service. Kollonitsch received a cardinal's hat from the Pope; and Daun, Sereni, and other distinguished officers, obtained from the liberality of the city rewards in plate and money, more commensurate with the exhausted state of the municipal exchequer than with the value of their services; the sums varying from 400 *rix*-dollars to 100 florins.

The state of affairs above described affords some reason for surprise, that the king should have persevered any further in his co-operation with the Imperial troops. He was as free to depart as the Emperor of Saxony. The Abbé Coyer supposes that he still entertained hopes of procuring a bride for his son in the person of an Austrian archduchess, and, as a consequence of such a connexion, the establishment of his descendants on an hereditary throne in Poland. The treatment, however, which he experienced at the hands of Austria could have left him little reliance on such expectations, and his letters to the queen indicate a higher motive for his perseverance, in a sense of the obligation of the oath by which he had bound himself to the assistance of the emperor. This, and his appetite for military success, are sufficient to account for his endurance.

The emperor, on the other hand, if we may trust the *abbé*, would have heard of his departure for Warsaw with pleasure, being advised of some Hungarian intrigues for raising up a rival to Tekeli in the person of the young Prince James, and placing him on the throne of Hungary. There is no evidence to show that Sobieski was influenced by any ambition but that of serving the common cause of Christianity, and adding to the military laurels which, in his case, almost hid the crown. One satisfaction Sobieski allowed himself in writing an autograph letter to the King of France, to whom, as the writer well knew, the tidings it contained would be gall and wormwood. The king also made over to the Elector of Bavaria some choice articles of the Turkish plunder, in the hope that, through him, they might find their way to the *Dauphiness* of France, and to the Tuileries. The following Pasquinade of the time is neat and bitter enough to deserve insertion here:—

TRIA MIRANDA!
Omnes Christian! arma summit contra Turcam,
Praeter Christianissimum.
Omnes filii Ecclesiac bellum contra Turcam parant,
Prateer Primogenitum.
Omnia animalia laudant Deum ob partam de Turcis victoriam,
Praeter Gallum.

The endeavours which Louis XIV. had made to detach, at all risks to Christendom, the King of Poland from the Austrian alliance, and the satisfaction with which he had viewed the critical position of the Austrian capital, were no secret. It is true that, to preserve appearances, he had raised the siege of Luxemburg and forborne an invasion of the Spanish Netherlands on pretence of setting free the King of Spain to assist his Austrian relations. These devices, however, deceived no one, and it was generally believed that it was his intention, after the humiliation of Austria should have been accomplished, to come forward at the head of the large force he was collecting on the Rhine as the saviour of Christendom.

A sovereign more deeply concerned in the issue than Louis, the *Sultan*, was perhaps the better prepared of the two for the reception of the unwelcome tidings of the relief of Vienna. The report of the confidential emissary despatched by him to the camp had been so unfavourable as to dissipate at once the expectation of success which no one down to that period had dared to represent as doubtful. Every preparation indeed had been made at Constantinople for a general illumination, and effigies of the Pope and of the principal Christian sovereigns had been prepared as materials for a bonfire. The report in question raised the Sultan to such a pitch of fury, that it required the influence of the *Mufti* to restrain him from directing a general massacre of all the Christians in his dominions. It had, however, the further effect of preparing him for the news of failure, and before it reached Constantinople, his rage had subsided into a deep melancholy. No sudden order for the destitution or death of Kara Mustapha betrayed his indignation, and the *vizier* continued for a while to exercise and to abuse the powers with which he had been intrusted.

CHAPTER 17

From the End of September to the End of December, 1683

The emperor's stay in his rescued capital was brief. He quitted it for Lintz on the 16th, leaving to the local authorities a heavy task to be performed of repair, and reconstruction, and purification. The Christian prisoners had been compelled to labour in the Turkish trenches, and in like manner Turkish captives were now compelled to repair the damage they had contributed to effect. The events of the siege had shown the danger occasioned by the near vicinity of suburban buildings in possession of an enemy, and an order was now issued for preventing the establishment either of buildings or gardens within a distance of 600 paces from the city rampart, to which edict the present glacis owes its origin. In this, the metropolitan seat of wealth and power, the work of restoration proceeded with speed and regularity; the affairs of mankind soon fell into their accustomed order, and material objects resumed their former aspect.

It was far different in the country, where, through whole districts, human hands were wanting to build upon the sites of ruined villages, to replant the vineyard and orchard, and to restore to cultivation the fields which the Tartar had converted into a wilderness. It was necessary in many instances for the government to colonize before it could cultivate, and it required years of peace and security to repair the ravages of a few hours of Turkish occupation.

The failure of so vast a scheme of invasion produced in the minds of the Viennese a reasonable sense of security against any reappearance of the horse-tails before their walls. It might be long, indeed, before the aggressive power of the Porte should be restrained within the limits of a well-defined frontier, and awed into quiescence by experience of its inability to cope with Christian Europe. The Turk was still in possession of fortresses, such as Neuhausel, within a few hours' march of the capital, but another investment of Vienna was an event not within the scope of reasonable calculation. It was therefore now determined to remove from public gaze a conspicuous and not very creditable memorial of the former liability of the city to the insult which it had twice experienced: namely, the crescent, which, since the siege of 1529, had surmounted the spire of the Christian Temple of St. Stephen.

It was generally held to have been placed there on an understanding with Soliman, that, like the black flag, which in modern warfare frequently protects an hospital, it should exempt the building beneath from the fire of an attack. Some writers, jealous of their country's honour, have indeed disputed this version of its origin. Be this as it may, the talisman had lost its virtue, for the malignity of Kara Mustapha had selected the cathedral as a principal object for his batteries, though the Turkish gunners had only succeeded in two or three instances in disturbing the celebration of its services, and the return of killed and wounded in its congregations exhibited only one old woman whose leg had been carried off by a shell.

At the suggestion, according to some authors, of Sobieski, but more probably of Kollonitsch, the crescent was now removed to the arsenal, where it is still preserved, and replaced in the first instance by an iron cross, which being fixed was shortly carried away by a storm. In 1587, a rotatory double eagle of brass was placed on the pinnacle, which it still adorns.

CHAPTER 18

Aftermath

Though the main interest of the drama ceases with the liberation of the city, the fate of a principal actor, Kara Mustapha, remains to be noticed; and some further events of the campaign will be found neither deficient in historical importance nor destitute of instruction to the soldier.

The situation of the Polish Army, and the general prospect of affairs some days after the battle, can hardly be better indicated than by the following extract from Sobieski's letter to the Queen of the 17th September. After giving a long list of the grievances and sufferings of his people, whose condition on the banks of the Danube he compares to that of the Israelites by the waters of Babylon, he proceeds:—

> You will extract from this letter a gazette article, with the understanding, however, that all my topics of grievance are to be kept out of sight. We must not forget the old adage of Kochanouski, 'the man who knows not how to conceal his disgust makes his enemy to laugh.' Say only that the commissaries of the Emperor have deceived our army with respect to the provisions and forage which they promised us, and for which the Pope has destined considerable sums; that the bridge is not finished; that the army suffers much; that the Imperial troops are still under the walls of Vienna; that the Saxons have retired; that the king is in advance; that his light cavalry is pressing the enemy; that if it were not for the horrible devastation of the country not a Turk would have escaped; that the king is constantly sending to the emperor to press him to enter the enemy's territory and to invest at the least two fortresses; that Tekeli has sent emissaries to me submitting everything to my decision; and so on.

Of the Hungarian fortresses at this time in the hands of the Turks, Neuhausel and Gran were the two which the Imperial commanders were most desirous to reduce, Neuhausel derived importance from its proximity to Presburg and Vienna, and from its situation in face of that vast Schütt island of the Danube of which the fortress of Komorn fortunately gave the Imperialists the command. Gran, often mentioned by authors by its Latin name Strigonium, was situated lower down the river on the right bank of the Danube. Its bridge, protected on the northern shore by the fortress of Barkan, gave the Turks the power of operating on both sides of the river; and a strong body of Turkish cavalry had thrown itself into the *tête-du-pont*, under the command of Kara Mehemet, a young *pacha*, worthy, by his courage, of the charge of a post of so much military importance.

Some difference of opinion seems to have arisen in the first instance between the king and the Imperial generals, the former inclining to postpone operations against Neuhausel and to move at once upon Gran, with the view of ulterior operations against the still more important city of Pesth, to which the *vizier* had transferred his headquarters. The king, however, acquiesced in the views of the Imperialists, which were influenced by the proximity of Neuhausel to the capital; but the decision of both was overruled by events. In any case it became necessary to throw a bridge over the river in the neighbourhood of Komorn, and the king complains in his letters of the delay in this operation. He was anxious to cross the river, both for the purpose of further encounter with the enemy and from the exhausted state of the country on the left bank. The passage of the river was effected on the 4th or 5th October.

The troops, during their occupation of the rich island of the Schütt, had been better supplied with forage and provisions, but had suffered dreadfully from the various forms of contagious and deadly disease for which the autumnal climate of Hungary is notorious. Sobieski remarks that the Germans, generally more delicate than the Poles, suffered less by the prevalent fever which decimated officers and men in his own army. He describes his own people as dissatisfied with the rich wines of Hungary, and pining for their beer and smoky cottages. Drunkenness, it would appear, was a preservative against the prevalent fever, and possibly the Poles were less addicted than the Germans to this prophylactic. Many Polish officers of distinction were swept off.

The Turks, meanwhile, were little in condition to take advantage of Austrian delays, or Polish sickness, for the purpose of stemming the tide of victory and pursuit. Detractors from the reputation of Sobieski have not been wanting to censure the laxity of the pursuit, and to ascribe it to the attractions of the *vizier's* tents. That he was fond of money his admirers have not denied. His apologists have alleged in his defence, on this head, the temptation to which the holder of a life interest in a crown is exposed to accumulate wealth for those descendants who on his decease may sink into a private station. Perhaps a law of celibacy would be no unreasonable condition of elective sovereignty.

No female reader of his letters will, however, blame the complacency with which he describes the treasures destined for the boudoir of the wife whom he styles "his incomparable," but who appears, by her taste for dress and intrigue, to have been very comparable indeed to many of her countrywomen. It is unnecessary to detail the many circumstances which must have made an active and immediate pursuit of the flying foe a military impossibility. It is sufficient to point to the forest denies through which the allied force had toiled for three weary days from the Danube to the heights of the Kahlenberg, during which time the horses had fed on nothing but the leaves of the trees which impeded their progress.

The *vizier's* first halt was under the walls of Raab; his first reassertion of his authority, which, in the confusion of defeat and flight, had been in abeyance, was to select a man he hated as an expiatory victim. The veteran Pacha of Pesth, whose original counsels, if followed, would have probably led to less fatal results, was ready to his hand. This old and distinguished man, with two other *pachas* and the *aga* of the *Janissaries*, were beheaded on a charge of cowardice, and some fifty other officers of less note strangled. After a halt of three days, employed in such proceedings as these, and in rallying and collecting the troops, he pursued his march towards Pesth, not unmolested by the garrison of Raab, but throwing reinforcements into Neuhausel and Gran as he passed.

The Polish Army had, as has been stated, crossed the Danube near Komorn on the 4th and 5th, and the Imperial cavalry had followed; but the mass of the infantry was still behind. The king took the advance with a small body of his own cavalry, in the hopes of an easy conquest of the Turks, whom he knew to have hastily occupied the *tête-du-pont* of Barware. Forgetting, in his contempt for a beaten enemy, and in his anxiety to seize the Turkish bridge of boats hear Barkan, the first rules of military science, and pressing forward without support or reserve, and without due security for co-operation from the more cautious Lorraine, he sacrificed some of his best troops, and narrowly escaped, in his own person and that of his son, the last penalty a soldier can pay for imprudence. The affair began with the advanced guard, which, according to the king's rather exculpatory but graphic report to his wife, committed itself prematurely, and contrary to his orders, in a skirmish with the Turks near Barkan.

Some accounts state that the latter were crafty enough to lure them on, by causing a herd of oxen to retire slowly before them. The Palatine of Russia, proceeding to the front, found it necessary to send in all haste for assistance, and the king in person brought up to the rescue his whole disposable force, making his numbers in the field some 5000 men, without infantry or artillery. He would have done more wisely to have left his advanced guard to their fate. He found it routed and disorganised, and himself with his small force, not yet deployed, within some hundred paces of an enemy flushed with success, and immensely superior in numbers. The Palatine of Russia, who saw the danger, implored him to leave the field. He replied to this invitation by charging at the head of his best available squadron. The charge succeeded, but at the same moment the centre and left wing, though not yet engaged with the enemy, gave way, and the conflict degenerated into a race for life and death.

The young prince, who in this affair, as in the Battle of Vienna, had followed his father like his shadow, received from him a positive command to fly. The king himself lingered till every effort he could make to rally his people had utterly failed, and he was left with six companions. To two of these, Czerkass, a Lithuanian gentleman, and a nameless soldier of heavy cavalry, he himself mainly attributed his salvation. The latter, who shot down with his carbine one of two horsemen who had come up with the king, and wounded the other, perished; the former lived to enjoy a pension of 500 crowns paid to him by the queen on every anniversary of this disastrous skirmish.

For some two miles and more the furious race continued: The Palatine of Pomerelia fell, horse and man, and was cut to pieces. The ground was heavy, and intersected with deep furrows: The king, though not so inactive as the French ambassador had described him, was both tall and corpulent; and when at length he pulled up and rallied his people on the cavalry and guns of the German troops, which at the instance of the Austrian General Dunnewald, attached in this affair to the staff of the king, were coming up to his support, breathless, and covered with bruises from rough contact with the companions of his flight, he lay for a while exhausted on a heap of straw.

The Abbé Coyer has a story of the king's witnessing the escape of his son, as he left his cloak in the hand of a Turkish horseman. The king expressly states that Fanfan, as he always calls his son, was *bien en avant* with the grand *écuyer* Mateinski, to whom the abbe and others also have attributed the preservation of the king. Most of the king's personal attendants, pages, &c., perished; he mentions a negro boy, a young Hungarian, master of several languages, but dwells with most interest on the fate of a little Calmuck, a famous rider in the king's hare-coursing pastimes.

★★★★★★

In the intervals of war and business the king had always been devoted to the chase. One of his objects of pursuit was the aurochs, now confined to a single forest of Lithuania, where alone it continues its species under imperial protection. One of the most eminent of living geologists, Sir R. I. Murchison, has broached a theory, founded at least on a profound investigation of the features of the district, that the species is a sole survivor of one of those great geological changes which have obliterated other forms of animal life. Sobieski's Queen wore a girdle of the skin of this animal. Down to a recent period it was an object of royal chase in Poland. Sir C. Hanbury Williams, in a letter from Brodi, describes a royal *battue* in which many of them were surrounded and driven over a steep bank into the river.

★★★★★★

In spite of his horsemanship he was captured, but by some strange accident spared by the Turks. After their subsequent defeat he was found in their camp and recognised by the Poles, but an unlucky German cut him down. There are many instances in which the greatest commanders have had to ride for their lives. In our own times the list would comprise names no less than, those of Napoleon, Murat, and Blücher; but the Cossack *hourra* of Brenne, and the skirmish near Leipzick, were accidents of warfare which no prudence could avert, and the gallant charge of Ligny few would be found to censure. The race of Barkan is historically valuable for the lesson it conveys of caution in the hour of success. An adherence to the simplest rules of military science would have saved two thousand lives.

Sobieski's character shines out conspicuously in the manner in which he took this severe check. Like the old Prussian of 1815, though bruised and stiffened, and scarcely able to sit his horse, he was up and ready on the following day, pressing the Duke of Lorraine to move against the Turks. In his religious convictions he was earnest, perhaps to the verge of bigotry, and in his letters to his wife in tracing the disaster to the judgment of Providence on the licence and crimes of the army, he passes over rather lightly the share which his own incaution had in producing it.

It required all the magic of Sobieski's influence to repair the moral consequences of this discomfiture in his own ranks, in which at first an ominous inclination displayed itself to concede the post of honour, the right of the line, to the German troops. We can hardly believe, on the sole authority of Rycaut, that the king himself was disposed to yield to this suggestion. His letter, written on the field, breathes nothing but an impatience for the arrival of the imperial infantry. Lorraine, on his part, seems to have needed no pressing, and it was determined to attack the enemy on the 9th. The young *pacha*, who had struck so serious a blow at the veteran conqueror of Choczim and Vienna, now himself fell into the error of abiding the chances of unequal battle; for though he had been strongly reinforced from Gran, he had but 25,000 men to oppose to some 50,000. Tekeli, too wise to believe the *vizier's* message announcing the total destruction of the Christian Army, and engaged in tortuous negotiations with Sobieski, was hovering almost within sight, but kept aloof from action.

The *pacha* fell into the still graver error of meeting the enemy with a chain of hills on his right, the river of Gran in his rear, and no retreat but by the bridge over the Danube. The consequence of this arrangement was a defeat, rendered bloody and complete by the failure of the bridge, which gave way under the fugitives. Barkan itself was carried by storm. Kara Mohammed himself escaped, but the Pacha of Karamania was killed, and the Pacha of Silistria taken. The amount of the Turkish loss is variously stated. The Poles, eager for vengeance, and excited by the sight of the heads of their countrymen stuck on the palisades of the fort, gave little quarter, and artillery was brought to bear upon the crowds who attempted to swim the river.

This success was purchased at the loss of 400 Poles and 70 of the imperial troops. Sobieski, in the moment of victory, writes of it as a victory greater than that of Vienna—an exaggeration only to be excused by the excitement of the moment. Its importance, however, was manifested by the speedy fall of Gran, the seat of the Hungarian primacy, containing the tomb of Stephen, the first Christian King of

Hungary, but which from the year 1605 had been desecrated by Turkish occupation. The Turkish bridge having been demolished during the battle, the Imperialists brought down their own bridge of boats from Komorn, which was ready for the passage of the troops a league above the city on the 13th. The town was carried by storm. The garrison, some 4000 strong, which had retired into the citadel, surrendered on the 27th, on condition of their safe conveyance to Buda, with their women and children, and retaining their small arms. The *vizier*, on receiving at Buda intelligence of the fall of Gran, departed in haste for Belgrade, but left with Kara Mehemet an order for the execution of the officers who had signed the surrender. His own bloody rule was meanwhile drawing to a close. His first reports and excuses for his failure before Vienna had been received at the court of Adrianople with simulated favour, and his messenger had returned with the usual tokens of royal approbation, a sword and a pelisse.

Influence, however, both male and female, was busy for his destruction; the friends of the murdered Pacha of Pesth, and all those who had originally opposed the expedition, were powerful and zealous. Tekeli, and the dying *Sultana* mother, Valide, threw their influence into the scale. At length the vacillation of the *Sultan* was overcome, and a chamberlain of the court rode out from Adrianople with the simple order to return as soon as might be with the head of Kara Mustapha. The officer, on approaching Belgrade, communicated his mission to the *aga* of the *Janissaries*, who gave his prompt acquiescence and ready assistance to the objects of the mission. The transaction was conducted, on the part of the servants of the crown, with that decent privacy and convenient expedition which usually attend the execution of Turkish justice, and submitted to by the patient with the quiet dignity with which the predestinarian doctrine of Islam arms its votaries against all accidents.

The insignia of authority were, politely demanded and quietly resigned. The carpet was spread, the short prayer uttered, the bowstring adjusted. In a few moments the late dispenser of life and death, the uncontrolled commander of 200,000 men, was a corpse, and his head on the road to Adrianople. It met with some subsequent adventures; for, having been returned to Belgrade by the *Sultan*, and deposited in a mosque, it was discovered after the surrender of that city to the Christians, and forwarded by them to the Bishop Kollonitsch. The prelate made over the grisly memorial of the man, who had threatened to send his own head on a lance's point to the *Sultan*, to the arsenal of

Vienna, where it still keeps its place among the other trophies of a long struggle of race and religion.

With the catastrophe of so leading a personage this work may properly reach the termination which its limits now demand. For the winter march by which Sobieski withdrew his forces to his own frontier, and the fortresses which he picked up by the way, his negotiations with Tekeli, and his passing successes over the Turks, the reader who wishes to pursue the subject will do well to consult his correspondence so often quoted, and the ample work of M. de Salvandy. From the above pages, concerned as they have been with a principal passage in the public career of one of the greatest characters in modern history, some faint idea may be derived of his qualities as a soldier. As a king, a statesman, an orator, and a man of letters, he must be estimated from other and fuller sources. After learning what he was in all these respects, we shall be prone to conjecture what he might have been.

As a husband and a father, if he had not married a bad and mischievous woman, *daturam progeniem vitiosiorem*—as a commander, if, instead of leading ill-disciplined levies to transient victories by the example and personal exposure of a partisan, he had brandished the staff of a Marlborough or a Eugene at the head of a permanent and organised force as a king and a statesman, if his better fortune had placed him at the head, not of a horde of turbulent, intriguing, and ungovernable slave-owners, but of a civilized, free, and united people it is scarcely too much to suppose that he might have realised the greater projects which it is known entered into his large conception, that the Turk would have been rolled back upon Asia, and that Greece might have dated her emancipation from the seventeenth century.

Appendix

No. 1.

The number of pieces of artillery furnished from the imperial arsenal of Vienna for the defence in 1683 was 262. The thirty years' war had led to many improvements in the construction and use of artillery. Gustavus Adolphus and Wallenstein had both effected important alterations, and in 1650 a Jesuit of Warsaw had invented the elevating screw as a substitute for the quoin. Whatever improvement, however, had taken place in the system as applied to field movements, it would appear that for purposes of stationary defence it was still one of much complexity and confusion.

The 262 pieces used at Vienna were of no less than 26 denominations and calibres, the capacity of the latter ranging from 1lb. to 48, and in the case of some large pieces called böller or pöller, used as mortars for vertical fire and discharging stone shot, from 60 to 200 lbs. There were of these four of 200, two of 150, five of 100, and ten of 60. Fifty other pieces furnished from the city arsenal were planted, not on the defences, but at various points in the city, and worked by 100 men of the burgher force. Of these hundred volunteer artillerists 16 were killed and 5 of the pieces ruined: 72 pieces in all had been rendered unserviceable at the close of the siege.

Thirty-seven officers were killed, which, considering the frequency of assaults and sallies, operations which require great personal exposure on the part of the leaders, would appear rather a small proportion to that of 5000 rank and file among the regular troops. The loss in action among the citizens is scarcely possible to arrive at. The only two officers of much distinction who fell were the Col. Count Dupigny and the engineer, Rimpler.

The Turkish loss is stated at 48,544. It appears to have fallen heaviest on the miners, of whom 16,000 perished, and 6000 of their artillerists. The formidable corps of the *Janissaries* was reduced by a loss of 10,000: 544 officers, including 3 *pachas*, were also killed. As this list is taken from a return found in the tent of the *vizier*, it does not include the loss of the Turks in the battle. These statements are naturally liable to much allowance for inaccuracy from many causes. A comparison of the various sources of information leads to a rough conclusion that the *vizier* sat down before the place with about 220,000 men. Of these it is supposed not more than 50,000 regained the Turkish frontier.

No. 2.—Order of battle of the Christian army before Vienna on the 13th September.

The left wing was commanded by the Duke of Lorraine; the centre by the Elector of Saxony and the Prince Christian Louis von Waldeck (it is idle to adjoin to these the Bavarian Elector, who was present, but had the good sense to consign the direction of his troops to Waldeck); the right wing by the Polish Field-Marshal Jablonowski; the whole by the King of Poland. The army was drawn up in three lines.

FIRST LINE.

Right wing.—19 divisions and 4 battalions of Poles; 8560 cavalry, 3120 infantry.

Centre.—9 divisions, Austrians; 7 divisions, Bavarians: 4 divisions, troops of the Circles; 5 battalions, Bavarians; 3 battalions, Circles; 5 battalions, Saxons; 5768 cavalry, 8600 infantry: commanders, the Elector of Saxony and the Prince of Waldeck.

Left wing.—10 divisions, Austrians; 5 divisions, Saxons; 6 battalions, Austrians; 5660 cavalry, 4242 infantry; commanded by the Duke of Baden.

Total of first line, 19,788 cavalry, 15,962 infantry.

SECOND LINE.

Right wing.—6 divisions, Poles; 8 divisions, Austrians; 4 battalions, Poles; 5568 cavalry, 3120 infantry: commanders, Generals Siniousky and Rabatta.

Centre.—5 divisions, Bavarians; 3 divisions, Circles; 4 battalions, Bavarians; 5 battalions, Circles; 3 battalions, Saxons; 6 battalions, Austrians; 1725 cavalry, 11,442 infantry: commanders, Field-Marshal Golz and Field-Marshal the Prince of Baireuth.

Left wing.—4 divisions, Saxons; 8 divisions, Austrians; 4528 cavalry: commanders, Field-Marshal Leslie and Prince Lubomirski.

Total of second line, 11,819 cavalry, 12,562 infantry.

THIRD LINE OR RESERVE.

Right wing.—9 divisions, Poles; 6 divisions, Austrians; 3 divisions. Bavarians; 3 battalions, Poles; 1 battalion, Bavarians; 6855 cavalry, 2940 infantry: commanders, great standard-bearer Lesno Lescynski and Field-Marshal Dunnewald.

Centre.—3 battalions, Bavarians; 2 battalions, Saxons; 2 battalions, Austrians; 4014 infantry: commander, Field-Marshal Leika.

Left wing.—3 divisions, Saxons; 7 divisions, Austrians; 3762 cavalry: commander, Field-Marshal Margrave Louis of Baden.

Total of third line, 10,617 cavalry, 6954 infantry.

Total force in the battle

Cavalry	42,224
Infantry	35,478
	77,702

Total of the army, including detachments

Cavalry, 127 divisions	46,100
Infantry, 57 battalions	38,700
	84,800

Artillery, 168 pieces, of all calibres, of which the Austrians counted 70, the Saxons 30, the Bavarians 26, the Franconians 12, and the Poles, 30. It is impossible, considering the difficulties of the march from Tuln, that all these pieces should have been brought into action: they were distributed along all parts of the line of battle.

To the above may be added Croats and other irregulars, and volunteers about 10,000. This detail of the force is extracted from the Military Conversations Lexicon, art. Wien.'

No. 3.—ANECDOTES OF THE SIEGE, FROM A TRACT BY THE ADVOCATE CHRISTIAN W. HUHN, AN EYE-WITNESS.

In the night of August 2nd some troopers of Dupigny's regiment, with divers foot soldiers of the garrison, made a sally by the covered way at the Scottish gate, and returned with forty-seven head of oxen and a captured Turk. The cattle were allotted partly to the wounded and sick soldiers, and partly to the captors, who made their gain from them, inasmuch as meat, which when the siege began had fetched one grosch the lb., rose afterwards to nine and more, and a fresh egg did not wait for a customer at half a dollar. Whosoever also fancied Italian cookery might purchase of one of the women who sat in the high market a roof hare (cat), roast and larded, for one florin, to be washed down with a cup of muscat wine at the Italian vintners; and truth to say, this animal, when the sweetness of the flesh was tempered with the salted lard, was an unusual, indeed, but not an unacceptable morsel.

The 9th August was a fine clear day, on which a young and spirited Turk chose to disport himself for bravado on a caparisoned horse, performing strange antics with a lance in his right hand. While he was caracoling at a distance of full 300 paces from the counterscarp, Henry Count von Kielmansegge, who happened to be with his foresters on the Kärnthner bastion, took such good aim at him with a fowling-piece that he jumped up with a spring from the saddle and fell dead amid shouts and laughter from the besieged.

A lucky shot of the same kind was executed by a student of the university, who sent a bullet through the head of a Turk near the counterscarp palisade, and dragged the body to him with a halberd. Having learned from experience of others that the Turks, *either to strengthen the stomach*, or when mortally wounded, to rob the Christians of their booty, were accustomed to roll up their *ducats* together and swallow them, without further ceremony he ripped up the corpse and found six *ducats* so rolled up within it. The head he cut off and bore it round the city upon a lance-point as a spectacle of his ovation.

In the assault of the 17th August a common soldier, having mastered and beheaded a Turk, and finding 100 *ducats* upon him sewed up in a dirty cloth, as one who had never seen so much money together before, went about the city like one distracted, clapping his hands and showing his booty to all he met, encouraging them by his example to win the like, as though it rained money from Heaven. On the 13th September, the day following the relief of the city, the Poles being masters of the Turkish camp, many soldiers, citizens, and inhabitants, while as yet no gate was opened, clambered down over the breaches and by the secret sally-ports to pick up what they might of provisions, ammunition, or other articles of small value.

The King of Poland and his people having fallen on the military chest and the *vizier's* tent, had carried off many millions in money, and the *vizier's* war-horse, his quivers, bows, and arrows, all of countless value, together with the great standard of their Prophet, inscribed with Turkish characters, and two horsetail standards. I, with many others who had been enrolled in a volunteer body during the siege, thought to pick up our share of the spoil. I, therefore, gained the counterscarp by the Stuben gate, passing between the ruined palisades on horseback to the Turkish camp.

I did not, however, dare to dismount, by reason of the innumerable quantity of flies and vermin, which, although at so advanced a time of the month of September, swarmed up from the bodies of more than 20,000 dead horses and mules, so as to darken the air, and so covering my horse, that not the space of a needle point remained free from them, the which was so insufferable to him, that he began to plunge and kick in front and rear, so that I was fain to get me clear of the press and make my way back to the city, but not till I had persuaded a passer-by to reach to me the bow and arrows of one who lay there, and also the cap of a *janissary*, and some books which lay about, and which had been plundered in the country, and secured them in my saddle-bags. After the which I re-entered the city, not as one *ovans* on foot, but *triumphans* on horseback with my *spolia*. I had no want of predecessors before or followers behind, for everyone who had legs to carry him had betaken himself to the camp to plunder it. Although I had gained the counterscarp and the inner defences, I passed a good hour making my way through the pass, and my unruly horse was compelled to move step by step for such time before I could extricate him and regain my quarters.

No. 4.—SPECIFICATION OF THE CHRISTIANS CARRIED OFF INTO TURKISH SLAVERY OUT OF HUNGARY, AUSTRIA, AND THE ADJACENT DISTRICTS IN 1683. FROM A CONTEMPORARY MS.

Old men	6,000
Women	11,215
Unmarried women, 26 years of age at the oldest, of whom 204 were noble. . . .	14,922
Children, boys and girls, the oldest between 4 and 5 years of age .	26,093
Total . .	57,220
Villages and hamlets burnt in the Viennese territory	4,092
In that of Presburg .	871
	4,936

The Great Siege of Vienna, 1683

Contents

Synopsis of Events

1663. Ahmed Kiuprili Grand Vizier.

1664. Montecuculi defeats the Turks at St. Gotthard.

Twenty years' truce with Austria, by which the Turks retain most of Hungary. 1669. The Turks take Candia from the Venetians.

1671. Conspiracy in Hungary against the emperor crushed.

1672. French attack upon Holland provokes a general war. Treaty of Buksacs between the Turks and Poles. Poland cedes most of Podolia and the Ukraine, and pays tribute to Turkey.

1673. The Polish nobles break the treaty. Great victory of Sobieski over the Turks at Choczim.

1675. Sobieski crowned King of Poland.

1676. Treaty of Zurawna between Turks and Poles; the former retain most of their conquests.

1677. Death of Ahmed Kiuprili. Kara Mustapha Grand Vizier.

1678. Tekeli heads an insurrection in Hungary against the Emperor. The French intrigue with him.

1678-79. Treaties of Nimuegen between the French and the allies.

1681. Louis XIV. seizes Strassburg and makes other aggressions upon the Empire. Treaty between Holland and Sweden against France.

1682. Treaty of Laxenberg between the emperor and the Upper German Circles against France, followed by similar treaties between the other Circles, the Emperor and Sweden. The Turks openly aid the Hungarians.

1683. League of the Empire, Poland and the Pope, supported by other anti-French powers, against the Turks. Turkish invasion of Austria. Siege of Vienna. Defeat of the Turks by John Sobieski and the Duke of Lorraine, September 12. The French attack the Spanish Netherlands in the autumn.

1684. Truce of Ratisbon between France and the Empire. 1686. Buda recovered from the Turks. League of Augsburg between the emperor and the Circles of Western Germany, joined ultimately by Spain, Holland, the Pope, Savoy and other Princes of the Empire, against the French. 1688. The English Revolution secures England for the side of the League, which she joins next year. General war with France follows.

1696. Death of Sobieski.

1697. Treaty of Ryswick between France and the allies.

Eugene defeats the Turks at Zenta, in Hungary.

1699. Peace of Carlowitz. The Turks cede nearly all Hungary, Transylvania, Podolia, the Ukraine, the Morea and Azof. The first great diminution of Turkish territory in Europe.

CHAPTER 1

The Threat from the East

At the present moment, in 1883, the power of Austria is driven as a wedge into the midst of the former dominions of the *Sultan*. That this is so, perhaps that Austria even exists as a great power, and can hope to be a greater in south-eastern Europe, is owing in no small degree to the Polish aid which in 1683 defeated the Turkish armies before the gates, and saved Vienna. The victor, John Sobieski, King of Poland, then deserved and enjoyed the gratitude of Christendom. But the unequal fate of a man great in character and in abilities, but born out of due time, in an incongruous age and in a state unworthy of him, has seldom been more conspicuously illustrated than in his career.

The great men of the last quarter of the seventeenth century whom we most readily remember are men of western Europe. Louis XIV., with the resources of France behind him, William III., wielding the power of England, of Holland, and of Protestant Germany, are the kings who fill the stage. The half-crazy hero, Charles XII. of Sweden, is a more familiar character than the great Polish king, the deliverer first of Poland, secondly of Germany, perhaps of Europe. The causes are not far to seek. The country which he ruled has disappeared from the roll of European nations. The enemy whom he defeated has become, in his last decrepitude, the object merely of scorn, or of not disinterested care.

It seems now so incredible that the Turks should have been a menace to Europe, that it is no great claim to remembrance to have defeated them. Sobieski, too, in his greatness and in his weakness, was a mediaeval hero. He was out of place in the age of Louis XIV. He was a great soldier rather than a great general, a national hero rather than a great king. His faith had the robust sincerity of that of a thirteenth-century knight, his character was marred by the violent passions of a mediaeval baron. His head was full of crusading projects—of the expulsion of the Turks, of the revival of a Catholic Greek state, not without principalities for his own house. His plans would have commanded support in the days of St. Louis, but were impracticable in a Europe whose rulers schemed for a balance of power. Poland herself perished, partly through clinging to a mediaeval constitution in the midst of modem states. Her medievally-minded king and his exploits are eclipsed by other memories, even upon the scene of his greatest achievement.

For the traveller who from the Tower of St. Stephen's, in the centre of the old-town of Vienna, looks down upon the places made remarkable by great historic actions in the valley of the Danube, has his eye turned first northward and eastward upon the Marchfeld. There, he is told, are Aspern and Essling, where the Archduke Charles beat Napoleon in 1809. There is the island of Lobau, where Napoleon repaired his forces, and whence he issued to fight yonder the great and terrible conflict of Wagram. The scene, not of a greater slaughter, not of a more obstinately contested fight, than Wagram, but the scene of a battle more momentous in its consequences, lies upon the other side.

Among the vineyards, villages, and *châteaux* which cover the lower slopes of the Wiener Wald, among the suburbs of Nussdorf and of Hernals, Charles of Lorraine and John Sobieski smote the Turkish armies in 1683. There at one blow they frustrated the last great Mohammedan aggression against Christendom, and set free the minds and arms of the Germans to combine against French ambition upon their western frontier. The victory was one of those decisive events which complete long pending revolutions, and inaugurate new political conditions in Europe.

The treaties of Nimuegen in 1678-79 had marked a pause in a general European contest. France and the Empire, Holland, Spain, Sweden, Brandenberg, all retired from their active conflicts, to plot and strive in secret, till an advantageous opening for war should again present itself. Poland and the Porte had a little earlier concluded their strife by the peace of Zurawna. But in the general breathing-time the eyes of all were turned with anxiety upon Eastern Europe. So much of Hungary as was not in the hands of the *Sultan* was in insurrection against the Emperor. The insolence of the Turks, and their support to the insurgents, were continually becoming greater. The whole East resounded with warlike preparations, and it was without doubt evident that a great enterprise was being prepared which might make the reign of Mahomet IV. as illustrious for Islam, as calamitous for Christendom, as that of Mahomet II. had been. Rome, Venice, Vienna, were the three capitals in more immediate danger, but the whole continent was interested, and all other designs were necessarily suspended till it became clearer where this storm would fall, and what resistance could be made to it.

For, two hundred years ago, the Ottoman Empire still stood high among the greatest of European powers. Spain ruled over wider territories; but the dominions of Spain were scattered over the Old and New Worlds, and her European lands, in the Netherlands and in Italy, were divided from her by the sea, or isolated by the interposition of the frontiers of powerful and often hostile neighbours.

A compact yet widely spread collection of kingdoms and of provinces obeyed the head of the Mohammedan world. Northern Africa, Western Asia, Eastern Europe were ruled from the Bosphorus. All the chief centres of ancient civilization, Rome alone excepted, Thebes, Nineveh and Babylon, Carthage, Athens and Constantinople, bowed beneath the Crescent. The southern frontiers of the *Sultan's* territories reached beyond the Tropic of Cancer, the northern touched nearly the latitude of Paris.

The modern kingdoms of Greece, Servia, Roumania were wholly his; the kingdom of Hungary, the dominions of Austria and of Russia were in part his also. The Black Sea was entirely encircled with Turkish or tributary territory; no other power possessed the same extent of coast line on the Mediterranean. Not only the Euphrates, the Tigris, the Nile, but the Danube, the Boug, the Dneister, the Dneiper and the Don flowed for a great part of their course between banks subject or tributary to the Porte, and reached the sea by mouths wholly under Turkish control.

The armies of the *Sultan* were unapproachable in numbers, unsurpassable in valour, by those of the Christian powers. Their discipline and warlike science were no longer what they once had been, the first in Europe; but their inequality in these respects to their enemies was not yet so marked as at present. Military and administrative skill were y et to be found in their empire. From the first appearance of the Turks in Europe Mohammedan rule had been, on the whole, extending. The Christian reconquest of Spain was balanced by the inroads of this new enemy upon the Eastern Empire. The Spanish reconquest of Grenada, in the fifteenth century, was more than counterbalanced by the Turkish conquest of Hungary in the sixteenth.

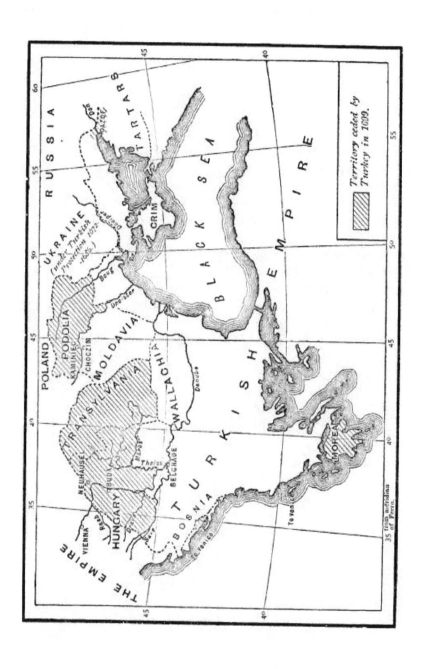

The Turks upon the middle Danube were a menace at once to Poland, Germany, and to northern Italy. Nor was this a mere temporary inroad of theirs. Two-thirds of Hungary were then more firmly held in their grasp than Macedonia is at present, and their frontiers were not going back. In the seventeenth century the Ottoman power still more than held its own in Eastern Europe. Though the Spaniards and Venetians had destroyed their fleet at Lepanto in 1571, though Montecuculi at the head of the Imperial troops had routed their armies at St. Gotthard in 1664, though Sobieski and the Poles made the great slaughter of Choczim in 1673, yet the frontiers of the Turks were advanced by every war. After Lepanto, the peace confirmed them in the possession of the newly acquired Cyprus; after St. Gotthard, they retained the strong city of Neuhausel, which they had just won, in Hungary, and conquered Candia; after Choczim, they were confirmed in their possession of the province of Podolia, and their supremacy over the Ukraine, the Marchland of Poland.

Of their soldiers the most formidable were the *Janissaries*. The policy of the earlier *Sultans* had demanded a tribute of boys from their Christian subjects. These children, early converts to Islam, were brought up with no home but the camp, no occupation but war; and, under the title of *Janissaries*, or the New Troops, were alternately the servants and the masters of the Ottoman *Sultans*. The strength of the Christians was drained, the strength of the Ottoman armies multiplied, and the fields of Paradise replenished at once, in the judgment of pious Mussulmans, by this policy. At this time the ranks of the *Janissaries* were not solely filled by this levy, but it has been computed that 500,000 Christian boys may have become instruments for the subjugation of Christendom, from the first institution of the tax in the fourteenth century down to the final levy made in 1675. Our commiseration for the Christian parents may be mitigated by the consideration that to sell their children into slavery, uncompelled, was a not unknown practice among the subjects of the Eastern Emperors, before the Mohammedan conquest.

These *Janissaries* formed a disciplined body of regular infantry. In the seventeenth century the Turks clung to the sabre, the musket, and even bows and arrows, as their arms, neglecting the pike, "the queen of infantry weapons," as Montecuculi calls it, just as afterwards they neglected the bayonet. But in the use of their arms every man of the Janissaries was a trained expert. The Turkish horsemen were famed for their rapidity of action, being generally more lightly armed and better mounted than the Germans or Poles. The *Spahis*, or royal horse-guards, were the flower of the cavalry. The feudal levy from lands held by military tenure, swelled the numbers of their armies, and every province wrested from the Christians provided more fiefs to support fresh families of soldiers. Thus the children and lands of the conquered furnished the means for new conquests.

Light troops, who were expected to live by plunder, spread far and wide before an advancing Ottoman host, eating up the country, destroying the inhabitants, and diverting the attention of the enemy. The Ottoman artillery was numerous, and the siege pieces of great calibre. Auxiliaries, such as the Tartars of the Crimea, the troops of Moldavian, Wallachian, Transylvanian, and even Hungarian princes, made a formidable addition to their forces. These armies lay, a terror to the inhabitants, a constant anxiety to the rulers, upon the frontiers of Germany and of Poland;—a black storm of war, ever ready to break in destructive energy upon them. Whatever schism divided Turks and Persians, towards Europe at least, from the Caspian to Morocco, Islam presented an unbroken front, contrasting powerfully with the bitter divisions of Christendom.

United Islam, which had preceded her western rival Spain in greatness, seemed also destined to long outlive that power's decay.

When Spain, in the sixteenth century, had been at the zenith of her power under Charles V., the Turks, under their great Emperor Solyman, had been not unworthy rivals to her. Even then Solyman had penetrated to the walls of Vienna, in 1529, and probably the lateness of the season, October, and the absence of his heavy artillery, stuck deep in the soil of Hungarian roads, saved the capital of the Austrian dominions more effectually than the valour of the garrison or the relieving forces of Charles could have done. Then the tide of Turkish power touched its farthest limit, but the fear of its return was not destroyed till after the lapse of one hundred and fifty years. Till after the siege of 1683, it is said that a crescent disgraced the spire of St. Stephen's, the cathedral of Vienna—a sign to avert the fire of Turkish gunners.

In the seventeenth century, when the great empire of Spain was fast approaching dissolution, when France was the great power of Western Europe, the Turks were still the great power of the East, with territories even more widely extended than in the previous age. It is true that, after the death of Solyman, a series of incapable rulers and the natural decay of an eastern despotism had paralyzed the great powers of Turkey; but the stern reforming vigour of Amurath IV. (1623-40), and, still more, the wise administration of the first two *grand viziers* of the house of Kiuprili, had done much to restore good government, vigour and efficiency to the Ottomans.

★★★★★★

Ahmed Kiuprili, the second *vizier* of his race, was one of the greatest ministers of his day. He was described by the Turkish historians as "the light and splendour of the nation, the preserver and administrator of good laws, the vicar of the shadow of God, the thrice learned and all accomplished *Grand Vizier*." He seems to have really deserved some of the praise.

★★★★★★

Their empire, the speedy downfall of which had been predicted by the English Ambassador, Sir Thomas Koe, at the beginning of the seventeenth century, had since fully recovered its former reputation. A clever Frenchman, M. de la Guillatière, who visited the camp of Kiuprili in Candia in 1669, formed the highest estimate of the military genius of the Turks, and of their political insight into the power and designs of the Christians. He judged of the greatness of the *Sultan* by considering the number and quality of the persons who feared his displeasure.

When he makes any great preparation, Malta trembles, Spain is fearful for his kingdoms of Naples and Sicily, the Venetian anxious for what he holds in Greece—Dalmatia and Friuli, the Germans apprehensive for what remains to them in Hungary, Poland is alarmed, and the consternation passes on as far as Muscovy, and, not resting there, expands itself to the Christian princes in Gourgistan and Mingrelia; Persia, Arabia, the Abyssinians are all in confusion, whilst neither man nor woman nor beast in all this vast tract but looks out for refuge till they be certain whither his great force is intended.—De la Gaillatière, *Account of a Late Voyage, etc., and State of the Turkish Empire.* Trans. 1676.

It is a striking estimate of Turkish power, but not beyond what experience confirmed. It was not till the second siege of Vienna, and her relief by Sobieski in 1683, that the real instability of the power of the *Sultan* was disclosed, that his armies were routed, his frontiers curtailed, his power rolled back within the Save and the Carpathians.

Not for the first time, in the summer of that year, Europe trembled at the progress of the Crescent. Since then, the tide of victory has run almost uninterruptedly in favour of the Cross, and Turkey has sunk from being the terror to the position of *protégée*, tool, victim, or tolerated scandal of Europe.

The decline of her forces, the reversal of the former position of Turk and Christian in the East, date from this great catastrophe of Islam. For Eastern Europe at least the battle before Vienna was a decisive battle. We must remember, indeed, what is meant by a decisive battle, or by any other so-called decisive event. They are rather the occasions than the causes of the transference of power. The causes lie deep which can produce such great and such lasting results. The operation of many influences, throughout a length of time, brings about ultimately the striking revolutions in the history of mankind. No chance bullet which strikes down, or avoids, a commander; no brilliant display of military genius in the person of one man; no incapacity of a single officer, can do more than alter the minor circumstances of great events. The great man is not successfully great, unless his genius can seize upon the opportunities offered by a rising tide of popular opinion, or profit by the accumulated energy of a nation.

The incapable leader can seldom make shipwreck of a power unless it be built upon unsafe lines. The presence of a thoroughly incapable commander argues something rotten in his cause. The revolution, the reformation, the reaction, the transference of empire will come; if not in one way, in another; if not in one year, in the next, or in following years. The foundations of success and of failure, are laid deep in the moral, religions and political habits and institutions of nations. The invincible determination and high political and military training of the Roman aristocracy bore them safely through the catastrophes of a Second Punic War and the revolt of their allies.

The ordered liberty, and the generations of successful adventure, which were the heritage of the English nation, had won Trafalgar before a shot had been fired from the *Victory*. The Persian host went forth predestined to choke the Gulf of Salamis with corpses. No Kosciusko's valour could redeem the long anarchy and blindness of Poland. Napoleon, marching from victory to victory, but approached the nearer to that fall, which must await one man against a continent in arms. So the Turkish myriads, victorious at Vienna, would have fallen upon some less noble field before the skill of some other Sobieski. But the genius and courage of individuals may well determine the fate of armies for a day. One day's victory may call for years of warfare to accomplish its undoing. A few years of delay may work great changes in the fortunes of men.

It is no mistaken estimate of the relative value of causes, it is no unintelligent interest which makes us prone to linger over the one dramatic moment—that moment when the courses of the tendencies of ages are declared within the compass of a day. By no hard effort of imagination, we identify our interest with that of the actors in the scene. To them, however confident, the result is never clear; to them the delay of a few years in the overthrow of some inevitably falling wrong may make that difference for which no ultimate success can compensate.

It was cold comfort to the inhabitants of Vienna, or to the King of Poland, to know that even if St. Stephen's had shared the fate of St. Sophia and become a mosque of *Allah*, and if the Polish standards had been borne in triumph to the Bosphorus, yet that, nevertheless, the undisciplined Ottomans would infallibly have been scattered by French, German and Swedish armies on the fields of Bavaria or of Saxony. Vienna would have been sacked; Poland would have been a prey to internal anarchy and to Tartar invasion. The ultimate triumph of their cause would have consoled few for their individual destruction.

Prompted by feelings such as these we dwell upon the decisive hours, when the long assured superiority asserts itself, for good and ail. We can hail Marathon, Salamis, Tours, or Vienna as the occasion, if not the cause, of the triumph of civilization over barbarism, of Europe over Asia. We must remember, too, that, if the day for a permanent advance of Turkish power was over, yet that a temporary Turkish victory, and a protracted war in Germany, could not have been confined in their influence to the seat of war alone. So cool and experienced a diplomatist as Sir William Temple did indeed believe, at the time, that the fall of Vienna would have been followed by a great and permanent increase of Turkish power.

★★★★★★

If the Turks had possessed this bulwark of Christendom (Vienna), I do not conceive what could have hindered them from being masters immediately of Austria, and all its depending provinces; nor, in another year, of all Italy, or of the southern provinces of Germany, as they should have chosen to carry on their invasion, or of both in two or three years' time; and how fatal this might have been to the rest of Christendom, or how it might have enlarged the Turkish dominions, is easy to conjec-

189

ture.—Sir W. Temple, Works, iii. 393, edit. 1814.

******

Putting this aside however, there were other results likely to spring from Turkish success. The Turks constantly made a powerful diversion in favour of France and her ambitions designs. Turkish victories upon the one side of Germany meant successful French aggressions upon the other, and Turkish schemes were promoted with that object by the French. The author of the memoirs of Prince Eugene writes bitterly, but truly enough, of this crisis:

> *Le roi très-chrétien avant d'être dévot, secourait les chrétiens contre les infidèles* (at St. Gotthard and at Candia), *devenu pourtant un grand homme de bien, il les agaçait contre l'empereur, et soutenait les rebelles de Hongrie, Sans lui ils ne seraient jamais venus, les uns et les autres, aux portes de Vienne.*

"If France would but stand neutral, the controversy between Turks and Christians might soon be decided," says the Duke of Lorraine. But France would not stand neutral.

CHAPTER 2

The State of Europe

The emperor was exposed on either side to these two implacable enemies. At Versailles, as at the Porte, had the destruction of the house of Austria been sworn.

But France was the power which, in the latter half of the seventeenth century, menaced most seriously the independence of her neighbours. Turkey was, perhaps, from her internal weakness and faulty constitution, in no condition to effect a lasting conquest, however great her mere destructive energies might be. An ingenious nation and an ambitions king, able ministers and skilful generals, revenues, ships, colonies, commercial enterprise, a central situation among divided foes, combined to render France the dominant power of the age.

The great Turkish *vizier*, the restorer of order and prosperity, Ahmed Kiuprili, had had a greater counterpart in the French minister, Cardinal Richelieu. The *Sultan*, Mahomet IV., was wanting in all those qualities which made Louis XIV. for long the successful administrator of a despotic power. The armies of France, under the leadership of a Conde, a Turenne, a Luxembourg, were the finest of the world, the envy of neighbouring princes, the pattern for all soldiers. The Duke of Marlborough and John Sobieski both learnt their first lessons in military affairs under French command. Prince Eugene vainly sought employment in the French troops; their opposition to himself taught William III. The art of war,

Nor was the French ascendency won by arms alone. The order and splendour of her government, the genius of her authors, the attractions of her Society, the diplomatic skill of her ambassadors, made a French party in every court in Europe.

Portugal may be said to have owed her independent existence to France; Holland till 1672 ranked as a French ally; Sweden, too far

191

removed to be a rival, was an almost constant friend, till Louis' aggressions alienated her also in 1681. France had a party in Poland; the petty princes and republics of Italy vacillated between her and the Empire; in England she had had Cromwell as an ally, and she held both Charles II. and his opponents in her pay. She maintained an understanding with Turkey. Discontented Romanists in England and Ireland, unruly Protestants in Hungary, were alike taught to look to her for advice and for assistance. Her frontiers were steadily advancing at the expense of Spain and of the German princes. Neither force nor treaties seemed to avail aught against her superior strength and cunning. The Lotharingian bishoprics and their dependencies; Elsass, Breisach and Bar, Roussillon, Franche Comté, parts of Flanders, of Artois, of Hainault and Luxemburg, the free imperial city of Strassburg, the territory of Orange, were steadily absorbed by her, and thoroughly incorporated with the French kingdom.

Her opponents saw no possibility of resistance, save in a great confederacy against her. Her power was not finally checked, nor her ambition confined within bounds, till such a confederacy was made. But it is hardly too much to say that such a confederacy would have been scarcely possible had the Turks been completely victorious at Vienna in 1683.

Three years later than that deliverance, in 1686, the League of Augsburg was formed. It was ultimately the union of the Emperor, the German princes, Sweden, Spain, Holland and the Pope, against an ambition that menaced ail. This League was the basis of that Grand Alliance which finally defeated France under Marlborough and Eugene. But the true foundations of a similar alliance had been laid before, in 1682, principally by the endeavours of the Prince of Waldeck, in the treaty of Laxenberg between the Circles of Upper Germany and the emperor.

This incipient League against France had been practically suspended by the Turkish invasion. A Turkish success must have dissolved it. The Pope had been zealous in forming the "Holy League" against the Turks and in promoting union against France. Had Vienna fallen, fear of the *Sultan* would have driven him into the arms of Louis, and he would have drawn the Catholic powers at least along with him. Probably all the States united in the "Holy League" must have demanded French support for their own salvation. With Austria and Poland beaten, France, and France alone, could have assumed the leadership of Europe against the East. The German Protestant princes would have been ranged under the command of Luxembourg and of Vendome; Louis would have triumphed upon the Danube; the house of Austria would have existed only by the sufferance of her ancient enemy; and French influence would have been riveted, as a chain, by the force of admiration and of gratitude, upon the neck of Europe. Such an event Louis expected, and the Emperor feared. As the Turks drew near, the French armies lay ready upon the frontier, ready to take advantage of the approaching catastrophe—ready to avenge, but not to save the Empire.

We in England, safe as we were from Turkish invasion, were by no means unaffected by the struggle. Nothing which tended to increase or diminish the power of France or of the German princes could be indifferent to us, and at that particular time our fortunes were closely bound up with those of the powers opposing France.

The motive which induced the Dutch Government and the other allies of Augsburg to sanction the descent of William III. upon our shores, and to withdraw, at a critical moment, the flower of their forces upon such a doubtful enterprise, was the necessity of including England in their league. Though James II. would no doubt have awakened resistance in some form or other anyhow, the plot which actually overthrew him was hatched abroad among the allies, and executed by the help of foreign troops and foreign money. English men, ships, and money were needed to beat the French. No method was open for obtaining them except by the superseding of King James, entirely or practically, by William, as king or regent. No personal aims nor admiration of Whig principles would have justified the risks William ran.

In truth, neither the allies nor the Dutch Government would have allowed him to run such risk at all, save for the common good of the League and of Europe. But a Turkish victory at Vienna would have meant the probable non-existence of the League, by the rallying of half its members to the side of France. It would certainly have meant such a change of circumstances upon the continent, as would have rendered it highly improbable that an army, principally furnished from Germany, could be spared to go to England. James and the Whig nobility would have fought their quarrel alone, with the High-Church Tory majority of the country as arbiters of the strife. Therefore, had the Battle of Vienna been fought differently, the Boyne, La Hogue and Blenheim might never have been fought at all. Forces supplied by England, or paid by England, commanded by Marlborough at Blenheim and at Ramilies, broke French power. The power of making the alliance which fought at Blenheim and at Ramilies was won at Vienna.

To turn to Sir William Temple's views again, so convinced was he that a Turkish invasion of Austria would tend to the great advantage of France, that he believed that the Turks themselves would see it, and for that very reason refrain from the enterprise; it being against their interest to make any one Christian power so strong as France would then become.

★★★★★★

If the *Grand Vizier* (Kiuprili) be so great a man as he is reputed in politics as well as in arms, he will never consent, by an invasion of Hungary, to make way for the advance of French progress into the Empire, which a conquest of the Low Countries would make easy and obvious; and so great accessions (with others that would lie fair and open in the Spanish provinces upon the Mediterranean) would make France a formidable power to the Turk himself, and greater than I suppose he desires to see any in Christendom.—Sir W, Temple, Works, ii.. 212, edit. 1814.

★★★★★★

It is certain that Louis XIV. fully appreciated the value of that diversion of their attention from himself, which an attack from Hungary upon the rear of the German powers would cause. It is equally certain that lie, the eldest son of the Church, the most Christian King, the persecutor of the Huguenots, had some understanding with Mohammedans and with Hungarian Protestant malcontents. And this, too, at a time when religions passions still ran high; when the forces of Europe were everywhere divided, owing to religious intolerance; when France herself was about to be fatally injured by the Revocation of the Edict of Nantes. Louis, however, intrigued as readily with Hungarian Protestants as with Irish Romanists, and the intolerance of the emperor gave every opportunity for interference.

Indeed, the attacks of the Emperor Leopold upon the religion of some of his Hungarian subjects well-nigh proved fatal to Austria. The Protestants preferred Mohammedan rule, which, if contemptuous, may be just, and is not avowedly persecuting, to the oppressions of a court dominated by the Jesuit fathers. Attempts to Germanize their nation and to override their laws united Hungarians of all religions in a common hostility to Vienna. A dangerous conspiracy, fomented by France, was discovered, and crushed in 1671 by the execution of the principal leaders. But Emerich Count Tekeli, the son of one of the chiefs involved, escaping into Transylvania, threw himself upon the protection of the Turks, and with their assistance commenced a guerilla warfare in Hungary. Numbers of the inhabitants, irrespective of their religion, joined his standard. A levy, under French officers, was made even in Poland for the assistance of the insurgents. With the almost open aid of the Pasha of Buda, their operations assumed the character of regular warfare, and they fully held their own against the Imperial generals.

It was fortunate for Austria that, just as the obligations of a peace and internal confusion h ad prevented the Turks from attacking Hungary during the Thirty Years' War, so this rising was not taken advantage of by the Porte, in spite of French solicitations, till after the peace of Nimuegen in 1679. During the contest with France, from 1673 to 1679, the Polish war had occupied the attention of the Turks, and the Austrian government had been untroubled. They had not at the same time to wage open war with the East and West. Yet even now, though peace nominally continued in Western Europe, France was glad to avail herself of those difficulties of the Court of Vienna, to which she herself was contributing. Louis seized Strassburg, and quietly annexed other places by the pretended legal decisions of packed tribunals.

He attacked the Spanish Netherlands, and conceived himself to be acting generously in that he refrained from taking Luxemburg. It was enough that Austria should be spared the task of fighting, at the same time, on behalf of Spain against the French, and on her own behalf against the *Infidels*. That the house of Bourbon should strive to embarrass the house of Hapsburg, by intrigues in Turkey, in Hungary and in Poland, was but in accord with a traditional policy, which no danger to their common Christendom could be expected to overrule.

But 1683 was a year of disaster for Louis. In that year he lost two of his natural sons, his Queen, and his greatest minister, Colbert. Above all, in that year his designs against the emperor were destined to be foiled by the interference of Sobieski, the *Deus ex machina* for Christendom and for the Empire.

CHAPTER 3

The Turks March Out

To return, therefore, to the troubles in Hungary, which gave occasion for French intrigue and for the interference of the Porte. The Turks, reinvigorated by the policy of the late Vizier Kiuprili, but directed no longer by his cool experience and judgment, were now not slow to take advantage of the difficulties of Austria. After their defeat at the hands of Montecuculi at St. Gotthard in 1664, they had consented to a twenty years' truce, by which they were still left in possession of the greater part of Hungary, and of that part where the pure Magyar population most prevailed. This truce had not expired when the oppressions exercised in the part of their country remaining to the emperor drove the Hungarians to arms, and Count Tekeli to seek aid from the *Sultan*.

Ordinarily scrupulous in the observance of their treaty obligations, the Turks were on this occasion overcome by the temptations held out to them of an easy extension of their frontier and of their influence. With the active aid of the Hungarians, and with the tacit consent of France, they deemed it possible to deal a mortal blow at the house of Austria. The *Sultan*, Mahomet IV., was perhaps not over ambitions, but he was spurred on by the zeal of a servant. The *grand vizier*, Kara Mustapha, though a nephew of the great minister Kiuprili, owed his advancement more to the beauty of his person and to the favour of the Sultana Valide, or Queen Mother, who ruled the ruler of Islam, than to other connexions or to ability. His ambition, however, was believed to aim at no less than a dependent kingdom for himself in Hungary or at Vienna. Here, at all events, and not against the Poles or Russians, did Kara Mustapha determine to gather his laurels and his booty. He had, indeed, already essayed a Russian campaign with little profit. A more striking success and greater glories, more abundant plunder with

196

fewer toils, seemed to be promised by a campaign in the valley of the Danube, than by one among the marshes and forests of Poland, or of the Ukraine.

Too late, in 1681, the court of Vienna attempted a conciliatory policy in Hungary. The spirit of rebellion had been aroused, and the offers of redress and justice made by the emperor were distrusted as a veil for treachery, or despised as the confession of weakness. Tekeli defied the emperor, and assumed the offensive even beyond the borders of Hungary. Neither was the Porte to be propitiated. In vain an Imperial Embassy to Constantinople sought a prolongation of the truce, which was on the point of expiring at the end of the stipulated twenty years. The demands of the Turks rose with the progress of their preparations.

A principality for their ally, Count Tekeli, in Hungary; extension of territory, with the strongest border fortresses for themselves; a great war indemnity—such were the terms which implied a determination not to negotiate. The ambassador, Count Caprara, was compelled as a prisoner himself to witness the departure of the Turkish hosts for the frontier. At the end of the year 1682 the main body were drawn together at Adrianople. Mahomet IV. encouraged his troops by his countenance in the camp, and beguiled the tedium of winter quarters by his favourite pastime of hunting. The sport was carried on upon a gigantic scale with thirty thousand beaters, many of whom perished by exhaustion. "No doubt they have spoken ill of me, and God hath dealt them their reward," was the reasonable conjecture of the *Sultan* upon their fate.

This mighty hunter, however, relieved his army of his presence when the spring of 1683 saw it finally set in motion for the Danube. Kara Mustapha was invested with complete command. Accounts vary as to the precise point where Mahomet left his army. The ambition of his *vizier* perhaps was interested in removing so soon as possible from the field the *Sultan*, to whom the glory of success would have been necessarily ascribed. Similar motives had, according to M. de la Guillatière, caused others before this to keep the easily persuaded prince back from the camp, whither his first impulse would have led him.

Oriental exaggeration is prone to magnify the hosts which Asiatic despots can command for their service. The muster-roll, found in the tent of the *grand vizier* after his defeat, affords a better basis for calculation. We find there, in round numbers, 275,000 fighting men enumerated, as the original strength of the Turkish Army. Judging by the analogy of our Indian armies, the attendants and camp followers of all descriptions must have doubled these numbers. In Hungary, the *vizier* effected a junction with Count Tekeli, who was at the head of nearly 60,000 men—Hungarians, Transylvanians, Turks and Tartars.

Even French officers and engineers were to be found in Tekeli's ranks; and the character of his cause was vindicated by coins which he caused to be struck with the inscription, *Pro Deo et Patria*. Half a million of men probably, of all creeds and races that lie between the Carpathian Mountains and the Arabian deserts, were arrayed under the standard of the Prophet in the Valley of the Danube. Again, according to the Turkish returns, of these 50,000 men perished in the operations before the decisive battle that relieved Vienna. Of the whole vast multitude not more than 50,000 it was computed, ultimately regained the Turkish frontier.

But even if drawn up with the best intentions, the accuracy of such returns and estimates can never be more than an approximation to the truth. It is sufficient that hundreds of thousands were marshalled beneath the Crescent to burst in a storm of desolating war upon the Christian lands.

For the struggle between Turk and Christian was not of the character of those operations to which the term of civilized warfare is convention ally applied. Prisoners were seldom made. The Christian slaughtered; the Turk, if he spared, sold into slavery his captives; prisoners we cannot call them to whom future release was denied. Far and wide before the Turkish armies, the Tartars and the irregular horsemen, whose sole pay was plunder, whose diversion and whose business at once was rapine, spread in a desolating cloud over the country. The whole of the unconquered Hungary, the Austrian duchy, the plains of Moravia and the mountains of Styria were swept or threatened by the scourge.

Poland they had long held to be their licensed field of plunder, and now Bavaria, and Bohemia even, trembled at the terror of their approach. The painful curiosity of their friends has attempted an estimate of the numbers of Turkish captives taken in this invasion. 32,000 grown persons, the great majority women, 204 of whom were maiden daughters of the nobility; 26,000 little children were, they tell us, carried off into slavery. This return seems to make no mention of lads, nor of elder girls, who would perhaps form the majority of those spared for the slave-market. How many of these perished under their hardships, or by the Turkish disasters; how many others tasted death, but before slavery; how many others may have lost home, wealth and honour, must remain beyond enumeration or even conjecture. It is said that in lower Austria and on the frontiers of Hungary alone, 4936 villages and hamlets were given to the flames in 1683.

To meet this torrent of devastation, the Emperor Leopold could muster but scanty forces. A full half of the territory now united under the Austro-Hungarian monarchy was in the hands of the Turks, or of the Hungarian rebels; or then formed part of the territories of Poland. The finances of Vienna have never been a source of strength. "Business men laugh at our finance, for my pain I weep over it," said Eugene to the emperor not long afterwards, lamenting the want of the sinews of war. The Imperial influence of Leopold in Germany was small. The German princes were distant, jealous, slow to move. Brandenberg was irritated over the Silesian claims, that fruitful source of future war. France was all but openly hostile. Spain was powerless. Venice, a shadow of her former self. Poland alone, under her heroic monarch, John Sobieski, might give present and substantial assistance. Yet all knew that to lean upon the support of Poland was to risk leaning upon a bruised reed indeed.

Poland was, indeed, to all appearance, still a great country. The Prussian province of Poland, Lithuania, Gallicia, Posen, part of Prussia proper, were Polish. Roughly speaking, her frontiers stretched from the Dneiper to near the Oder, from the Baltic to the Carpathians. But a great territory does not make a great nation. The approaching fall of Poland was foreshadowed by her fortunes, even in the seventeenth century.

The extraordinary calamities of that country should not blind us to the means by which she brought some of her misfortunes upon her own head. Her constitution seemed skilfully contrived to unite the vices of aristocratic and democratic governments with the virtues of neither. Her people were turbulent without freedom, proud without steadiness of purpose. She lacked the equality and the popular support proper to a republic, as she lacked the fixed succession to the highest office and the consistent policy which are supposed to be the advantages of monarchy. A mob of tens of thousands of armed citizens pretended to form a deliberative diet. Their convention was always a signal for confusion; their dissolution was often the prelude to civil war.

In the huge concourse a single *veto* could stay proceedings, unless indeed the malcontent paid for his opposition with his life. An attempt to introduce representative assemblies was always resented, and the experiment restricted, by the jealousy of the citizens. Delegates, not representatives, came to the meetings. They were vigilantly observed, and strictly cross-examined on their return, by self-constituted judges, as to the performance of their mandate. Real debate and deliberation, free judgment and rational decision, were as impossible in one kind of assembly as in the other. Below these citizen-nobles, the people were slaves. The two halves of the state, Poland and Lithuania, were set against each other continually. The monarchy became purely elective in the sixteenth century.

The king was the nominee of some foreign country or of some domestic party, or family. Factions nourished from abroad were thus kept alive. Once elected, the king found his power curtailed on every side; and as generally as solicitous for the advancement, and future succession perhaps, of his family, as for the good of the state. He might be a stranger, or he might owe his position to the support of a foreign power. He seldom or never could be more than the nominee of some faction, the king of a party to the end of his days.

John Sobieski, the Polish king, and himself once a Polish noble-man, was not a candidate put forward by France for the Polish crown, but was generally supposed to lean towards a French connexion. His wife was French; he had passed some of his earlier years in France, and had served in Louis' musketeers of the Guard. His most formidable rival for the crown had been Charles Leopold of Lorraine, (see note following), the Austrian candidate, who was now commanding the Imperial armies. An ill omen for any unity of action in the future, between the two, against the Turks.

✶✶✶✶✶✶

The Duke of Lorraine had married the emperor's sister, the widow of the late Polish king, Michael. The French had driven him from his hereditary states, and he found employment at the head of his brother-in-law's armies, against them and the Turks.

✶✶✶✶✶✶

Sobieski had fought his way to royalty. He had contended against the enemies, from Sweden to Turkey, with whom Poland was contin-ually embroiled. His medals bore the proud device of a sword piercing three laurel crowns, with on its point a royal diadem, and the truthful motto below, *Per has ad istam*. Poland had been afflicted by Cossack insurrection, Tartar devastation and Turkish conquest. The king, Mi-chael, had signed the disgraceful peace of Buksacs, by which the Poles became Turkish tributaries. Sobieski and the other nobles repudiated

200

the treaty; and at Choczim, in 1673, Sobieski overthrew the Turks with such slaughter that "the turbans were floating thick as autumnal leaves upon the Dneister." The crown of Poland rewarded his victory; but the turbulence and inconstancy of his subjects prevented his reaping the fruits of success.

At the most critical moments lie was left destitute of men and of money, in the face of a host of Turks and Tartars. At Lemberg before his coronation, and at Zurawna after it, he was glad to have successfully defended the remainder of his country. The peace named from the latter town, left part of the Ukraine and nearly all Podolia with the fortress of Kaminiec, in Turkish hands.

The Turks scrupulously observing their part of the agreement, believed that they thereby secured the neutrality of Poland. Sobieski had suffered injuries and affronts at the hands of Austria. The punctilious pride of the Emperor was likely to add to the difficulty of forgetting these. At the last moment only would Leopold consent to address the man who was to save his empire by the title of Majesty. The Poles either were loath to begin a new Turkish war at all, or represented the advantage which might be gained by holding aloof, till both combatants were exhausted. If they fought, Podolia, not Hungary, the recovery of Kaminiec in the former, not the relief of Vienna, should be their object.

The Lithuanians were specially jealous of Sobieski, and slow to move. The Cossacks were not to be depended upon. The country was exhausted of men and money by former campaigns. The French ambassador, Forbin, Cardinal de Janson, was instructed to work upon the king by promises of the future support of Louis, of visionary crowns in Hungary, and of lands in Silesia as the price of his inactivity. No means were to be spared to detach Poland from Austria. The cardinal worked cautiously, being an old friend and in expectation of future favours from Sobieski; but a special agent who was with him, the Marquis de Vitry, spared no pains to foment jealousies and to excite fears, and distributed money among the partisans of a peace policy.

An abortive scheme was entertained for supplanting the king himself by another, more amenable to French influence. But the conspiracy was discovered, and the effect was disastrous to the French faction. The Poles rallied round the victor of Choczim and of Lemberg, and the authors of the intrigue against him were thrown into prison, or left the country. The French agent, Vitry, himself retired from Poland. Fortunately, also for Christendom, and for the house of Austria, the wife of Sobieski, Marie Casimire de la Grange d'Arquien, a French-woman, had determined to thwart the diplomacy of her native land. The failure of an intrigue, by which her father, a needy *marquis*, was to have been converted into a wealthy duke; a refusal of the French court to receive her, a French subject by birth, as an equal should she revisit France;—these causes made her an Austrian partisan.

Sobieski, at the age of fifty-three, still burned with youthful ardour for his wife of forty-one, though scandal would have it that this King Arthur had his Lancelot in the Field-Marshal Jablonowski, one of the foremost of his officers, "His incomparable Maria," as the king addressed his queen in his frequent letters, was at all events vain and intriguing, and seldom influenced for good the husband whom she also adored. Yet on this occasion her persuasions seconded the arguments which would undoubtedly have swayed Sobieski apart from her. His true atmosphere was that of the battlefield. His most glorious victories were won over the *infidels*. The danger which menaced Austria was a common menace to Christendom. Warsaw itself would not be safe if Vienna fell. The foremost champion of the Cross would not be wanting in such a crisis. In his enthusiasm he deemed it possible to unite the jarring elements of European society in a grand crusade.

Visions floated before him of a great League, including the Christian powers and the Persians, by which the Turkish Empire should be overthrown, Constantinople recovered, Moldavia and "Wallachia united to the Polish crown, and a republic of Athens and the Morea established. A scheme too great for accomplishment in the face of the selfishness of France and Austria and the inherent weakness of Poland.

But a general subscription was needed to put any army into the field at all. Rome and Italy were foremost in contributions; even ecclesiastical property was allowed to be mortgaged in the cause. The Pope, an economical reformer in Rome, as befitted the member of a banking family, the Odescalchi, was able to provide two million *scudi*, Christina, ex-Queen of Sweden, bestirred herself to increase the fund. The Regent of Portugal sent money, and sanctified the gift by a simultaneous holocaust of Jews. 1,200,000 florins were to be advanced by the emperor to pay the Polish troops. The Pope undertook to guarantee the repayment, and contributions were expected from the King of Spain.

Both these latter alike were swayed by the double motive—fear of the Turks, and the desire to set free the Empire to act against France again. Leopold, as his contribution to the harmony of the allies, had condescended to yield the title of "Majesty" to the King of Poland, and had held out hopes of a marriage between the son of Sobieski and an Austrian Archduchess, which might ensure the succession of the former to his father's throne. A dispensation from the Pope released the Poles from the duty of keeping their oaths to the Turks. The emperor and the king exchanged oaths not to resort to such a dispensation from their engagements to each other. The treaty of alliance was signed; but before the Polish troops could be mustered in any numbers, the Turkish Armies had united with those of Tekeli, and were pouring across the frontier.

CHAPTER 4

Battle is Joined

Charles of Lorraine, the Imperial commander, had under his orders less than 40,000. The levy *en masse* of Hungary produced 3000 soldiers only for the emperor's service, so wide was the sway of the Turks, or so universal the sympathy for Tekeli. Six thousand Hungarians, supposed to be raised for the emperor, went over to the enemy as soon as they advanced. Yet, contrary to his own opinion, Lorraine began with offensive operations against the Turkish fortress of Neuhausel. A partial success was followed by a disastrous repulse, and the army withdrew south of the Danube, as the main Turkish force approached upon that same side of the river. Lorraine had some idea of making a stand near the Raab to cover the Austrian frontier, but the number of the enemy and the temper of his own soldiers rendered such an attempt too hazardous.

He determined to retreat, and await the reinforcements already promised by the Princes of the Empire. Garrisons were hastily flung into Raab, Komorn, and Leopoldstadt. (over against Neuhausel, not the island suburb of Vienna), the infantry then recrossed the Danube and fell back towards Vienna along the Schütt island, under Count Leslie's orders. The cavalry marched upon the southern side of the river, but the superior rapidity of their retreat did not save them from molestation. On July 7 at Petronel, some twenty miles below Vienna, 15,000 *Spahis* and Tartars burst upon their march. For a time Count Taaffe, with the rear-guard of 400 men, was in extreme danger. The exertions of Lorraine and of Louis of Baden rallied the cavalry and speedily repulsed their disorderly assailants, but in the confusion several of the officers fell, including Prince Aremberg and Julius Louis of Savoy, an elder brother of Prince Eugene, and much of the baggage became the prey of the Tartars. Altenburg and Haimburg, posts upon the Danube, bad been already stormed, after a brief resistance, by the Turkish infantry.

Those stragglers who first leave the field are always apt to cover their own flight by the report of a universal overthrow. So fugitives came galloping to Vienna with a tale of disaster. They spread the rumour that the Duke of Lorraine was killed and the army totally defeated, while their alarm seemed amply confirmed by the glow of burning villages that brightened upon the twilight of the eastern horizon. The Imperial court, which had delayed its flight so far, in the hope that the enemy might linger about the fortresses of Raab or of Komorn, tarried now no longer. "Leopold could never bear to bear plain truths but when he was afraid," says Eugene. He had refused to recognise the imminence of the peril until now; and by his confidence had involved in his destruction others, who had not the same means of escape at the last moment which he himself possessed.

Yet means of escape were barely open to him, when at length he understood that he must defend or abandon his capital. The roads to Upper Austria and to Bavaria, along the southern shore of the Danube, were rightly distrusted. The emperor, his empress, and the empress mother, with all their train of courtiers, of ladies, and of servants, shorn of pomp and bereft of dignity in their flight, poured over the Leopoldstadt island and the Tabor bridge in all the misery of panic fear. The prompt destruction of the bridge of Crems, above Vienna, is said alone to have saved their route from interception by the Tartars. A part of their baggage actually became the prey of the marauders. The whole court, including even the empress herself, who was far advanced in pregnancy, were driven to seek rest in farms and cottages. Once they passed the night under a temporary shelter of boughs.

In the universal panic, small room was left for hopes of a return to the capital and to the palaces that they had quitted. Milan, Innspruck, Prague were thought of as their future refuge. On to Lintz, and from Lintz to the frontier they fled, till their confidence at last returned behind the fortifications of the Bavarian city of Passau. But they were not the only fugitives from Vienna. The bold march of the Vizier upon the city, leaving Raab, Komorn, and Presburg in his rear, to fall an easy prey when once the great prize was captured; this had taken the citizens by surprise. The retreat of Lorraine, and the skirmish at Petronel, had filled them with abject terror.

People from the surrounding country who had taken shelter in Vienna no longer relied upon her as a stronghold, but turned their thoughts to an escape to Bavaria, or to Styria, or even to the distant Tirol. From nine o'clock in the evening till two o'clock in the morning, on the 7th and 8th of July, a never-ending stream of carriages and of fugitives were following in the track of the Imperial *cortège*. East and south, upon the horizon, the glare of burning villages told that the Turkish horsemen were there. High on the summit of the Kahlenberg, the flames of the Camalduline Convent dreadfully illuminated the track of the fugitives.

Sixty thousand persons, it was believed, left the city in the course of a few days. Of those who, crossing the Danube, took the roads into Upper Austria or into Moravia, some fell into the hands of the Hungarian and Tartar marauders. But few of those who attempted to escape into Styria succeeded in reaching a place of safety. They perished by thousands, enveloped by the flying squadrons of the invaders.

In Vienna herself, deserted by her leaders and by so many of her children, violent tumult raged against the government, and against the Jesuits, who were supposed to have instigated the persecution of the Protestants of Hungary. There was ample cause for terror. The fortifications were old and imperfect, the suburbs encroached upon the Works, the number of the defenders was small. Thirteen thousand infantry, supplied by the army of Lorraine, and seven thousand armed citizens formed the garrison; and, besides these, about sixty thousand souls were in the city.

The command was entrusted to Ernest Rudiger Count Starhemberg, an officer of tried skill and courage. He had served with Montecuculi against the Turks, and against both Condé and Turenne with the same commander and with the Prince of Orange. He entered the city as the fugitives forsook it. He set the people to work upon the fortifications, organised them for defence, and assured them that he would live and die with them. But while writing to the Emperor that he would joyfully spend the last drop of his blood in defence of his charge, he confesses that the place is in want of everything, and the inhabitants panic-stricken. Fortunately, he and others with him were the class of men to restore confidence in the rest. Under him served many noble volunteers, for the example of the emperor was not universally followed.

The Bishop of Neustadt, once himself a soldier and a knight of Malta, was conspicuous among many brave and devoted men for his liberal donations to the troops, and for his superintendence of the sanitary state of the city. In one respect alone the place was well furnished; three hundred and twenty-one pieces of artillery were supplied by the Imperial arsenal for the fortifications. (Together with forty-two guns and eight howitzers from the city arsenal. Among the emperor's pieces were eleven gigantic mortars, described as 100, 150, and 200-ponnders, but two hundred and fifty-three of the guns were smaller than 12-pounders).

The city was defended after the existing fashion, with ten bastions, the curtains covered by ravelines, with a ditch mostly dry. On the side of the Danube was merely a wall with towers and platforms, and all the works were more or less uncared for and decayed. The work of fixing palisades was postponed till the Turkish Army was in sight. It is possible that by a slightly more rapid march the *vizier* might have secured Vienna by a *coup de main*.

On July 13, the Turkish regular cavalry came in sight, preceding the infantry of the main army; and at the last possible moment fire was set to the suburbs, which impeded the defence. A high wind speedily caused them to be consumed. On the 14th, the Turkish army took up its position, encamping in a semicircle, round the whole of the circuit of the defences not washed by the Danube. A city, surpassing in size and population the beleaguered capital, sprang up about the walls of Vienna.

The tents of the *vizier* were pitched opposite the Burg bastion, in the suburb of St. Ulric. The camp was crowded not only by soldiers, but by the merchants of the East, who thronged thither as to a fair to deal in the plunder of the Christians. The Imperial troops still attempted to hold the Leopoldstadt island; but on July 16, the Turks threw bridges across the arm of the Danube, and shortly drove the Christians to the northern bank of the river. The houses of the Leopoldstadt were given up to fire by the Turks; and the bridge, leading to the northern shore, destroyed by the Imperialists. The investment of Vienna was now completed upon every side. Batteries from the Leopoldstadt, and from the south and west, crossed it with fire in all directions. Trenches were opened, and the elaborate approaches and frequent mines of the Turks, advancing with alarming rapidity, enveloped the western and south-western face of the works from the Scottish gate to the Burg bastion.

Upwards of three hundred pieces of artillery played upon the crumbling defences and the devastated city. The pavement of the streets was torn up, that the balls might bury themselves in the soft earth where they fell. The upper floors and roofs of the houses were barricaded

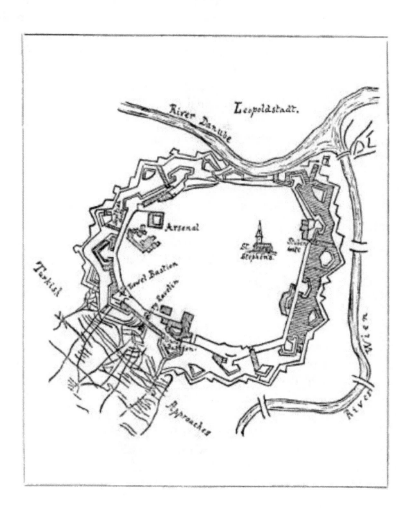

with heavy timber, or covered with sandbags, to guard against the fire of the dropping shells. The streets themselves were blocked behind the walls, chains drawn across them, and the houses loop-holed and prepared for defence to the last extremity. All the gates had been walled up but one, the Stuben gate, which, being partially covered by the stream of the Wien, was left open as a sally-port. Early in the siege, the assailed, frequently issuing forth, returned the attacks of the enemy, frustrated their operations, and even captured provisions in the hostile lines. But as time went on, the diminishing numbers of the garrison forbade the waste of life incurred even in successful sorties.

The progress of the Turks was rapid with sap and mine. They were famed for their skill with entrenching and engineering tools, and the Christians learnt much from them, though their approaches were unlike the ordinary European works.

Instead of parallel lines to the defences they drew curves, overlapping each other and continually approaching the place attacked. The trenches were deep, and fifteen or sixteen feet wide at the bottom where the ground allowed. The depth of the Turkish works effectually protected their soldiers, even when they had made a lodgement in the ditch; for the besieged could not depress their cannon sufficiently to hurt them. (Starhemberg to Duke of Lorraine, August 18).

They were protected skilfully by bomb-proof shelters of timber and of turf, beneath which thousands of men, hidden and shielded, crouched ready for attack, or for the repulse of sorties. Their mines penetrated in every direction to the counterscarp of the place, and ultimately to the walls themselves. At length the very cellars of the nearest houses were threatened by a subterranean enemy; and water and drums strewn with peas were placed in them, to tell, by the slightest vibration, of the work of the Turkish miner's pick below.

The Turkish miners were bolder than those of the garrison. The latter were hired labourers of the lowest class, of whom Starhemberg wrote to Lorraine that nothing would induce them to re-enter a mine after they had heard the sound of the enemy working near them. On the part of the enemy, men who had applied for a *Timar*, or military fief, often volunteered as miners to prove their courage and to win its reward.

At the very beginning of operations the city all but perished through a fire, which actually reached the windows of the Imperial arsenal stored with eighteen hundred barrels of powder. An explosion there would have opened a road for the Turkish Army into Vienna, at once deprived of the means of resistance and reduced to ruins. The exertions of Captain Count Guido Starhemberg, nephew of the *commandant*, who personally superintended the removal of the powder through the opposite windows, together with a lucky change of wind, saved the city. Rightly or wrongly, an incendiary was suspected. The fear of treachery was added to the legitimate terrors of the citizens. Desertions took place to the enemy, and spies were actually apprehended within the walls. Hungarians and other Christians were arrayed upon both sides, and this community of language and manners, between besiegers and besieged, rendered such a danger more real.

But from the open force of the attack the worst calamities were to be feared. On the 23rd, 25th, and 27th of July the opening assaults were delivered. all were repulsed, but with loss of lives ill-spared.

Closer and closer crept the Turkish sappers. Assault after assault upon the outer fortifications gradually wrested important positions from the besieged. The Burg and Löwel bastions, with the connecting curtain between them and the Burg ravelin, were reduced to an almost shapeless ruin by the Turkish mines and artillery. Every device was tried to retard the attack. The arts and ingenuity of a great city were at the service of the besieged. They made their own powder; and, when hand-grenades began to fail, the invention of an officer supplied their place with grenades of earthenware. Nevertheless, on August 7, the Turks made a lodgement upon the counterscarp, after twenty-three days of firing and terrible losses upon both sides.

The *Janissaries* now stood upon the very threshold of the city. Hand to hand fighting was carried on in the ditches. The citizens armed with Scythes upon the end of poles contended with advantage from above against the Turkish sabres. Boiling pitch and water stood continually ready to overwhelm the assailants as they struggled up the shattered slope of the ramparts. Besiegers and besieged were continually within pistol shot of each other, and showers of Turkish arrows descended on the town. As yet no footing was obtained by the Turks within the body of the place, though the streets and houses stood ready barricaded against such an event.

But the *vizier* commanded two hundred thousand men, Starhemberg but twenty thousand. Disease and the toils and losses of the defence told fearfully upon the latter. Starhemberg himself was disabled by dysentery early in the siege, and did all that man could do, carried in a chair from post to post, amidst the hottest of the fire. On the other side, Kara Mustapha made his rounds in a litter rendered shot-proof by plates of iron. The chief engineer of the garrison, Rimpler, fell. Colonel Bärner, commanding the artillery, and the Prince of Wurtemberg were disabled. Five thousand men, more than a third of the regular soldiers, perished. Food became scarce, vermin were eagerly sought for by the poor, and dysentery followed inevitably in the train of want. Fever sprang from the confinement, filth, and bad air inseparable from their condition.

Sixty persons a day were dying of dysentery alone towards the conclusion of the siege. But the humour of the Viennese asserted itself still among their calamities, and the spoils of nocturnal chase upon the tiles were sold as "Roof Hares" in the market. The courage of long endurance, that rarest of all courage, was tried to the uttermost. The Bishop of Neustadt, bravest of the brave defenders, laboured unremittingly among the sick, nor cared less for the safety of the whole, by undertaking the control of sanitary measures. The otherwise useless non-combatants were organized by him into bands of scavengers, hospital attendants, and carriers of the wounded.

A despatch from Starhemberg, dated August 18, came safely to the hands of Lorraine. The *commandant* wrote boldly, perhaps with an eye to the probability of his intelligence reaching the Turkish and not the Imperial general.

> I must in the first place, tell your Highness that we have up to this moment disputed the works with the enemy, foot by foot, and that they have not gained an inch of ground without paying for it dearly. Every time that, sword in hand, they have attempted a lodgement, they have been vigorously repulsed by our men, with such loss that they no longer dare to put their heads out of their holes.

Nevertheless, he was providing for the worst.

> I have caused a new work, well ditched, to be made in the middle of the Burg ravelin; the Löwel and Burg bastions are also defended by a second line; and I am even now beginning another work behind these same bastions. I write this that your Highness may know that we are forgetting nothing, that we are wide awake, and taking all imaginable precautions. As in duty bound I assure your Highness, that to show myself worthy of the confidence which your Highness, and more especially his Majesty my master, repose in my small services, I shall never yield the place but with the last drop of my blood.

This despatch was safely carried to Lorraine by Kolschitzki, a Pole. Many other letters had miscarried, for few messengers penetrated, at the risk of life, between the city and the slowly mustering forces of Lorraine. Some swam the arms of the Danube. The most skilful, however, was this Kolschitzki, who relied upon his knowledge of the Turkish tongue and manners, and in Turkish dress penetrated the besieging lines, much as a countryman of our own relied on similar knowledge in a scarcely less memorable siege.

The name of Kolschitzki of Vienna may be named side by side with that of "Lucknow" Kavanagh, though the Pole not only passed out through the besiegers, but succeeded in returning again in a like manner into the city with despatches, to sustain the courage of the defenders. From his stone chair, high up in the fretted spire of St. Stephen's, the watchman saw the rockets which rose as signals from the Christian outposts north of the Danube. But from the southern bank must the march be made for the deliverance of the city; and was it possible that Lorraine, or even Sobieski, could carry a force across the river in the face of such an army?

The garrison record, with painful exactness, the terrible annals of the siege; what ravelin is deluged with the blood of assailants and of defenders; where mines have blown the counterscarp into the ditch, or shattered the salient angle of a bastion; what new quarter of the city is devastated by the cannonade; what much-prized life is taken; when the bread begins to fail; what false hopes of relief, or what exaggerated tidings of calamity, circulate among the citizens. These details, of overwhelming interest to every man at the moment, and printed indelibly upon his mind, bring to the distant observer but one confused and appalling panorama of suffering and of endurance, of courage and of despair.

The growing anxiety of the city appears in a second despatch of Starhemberg's, dated August 27. He still tells of attacks repulsed, of sorties boldly executed, and of mines discovered and foiled, but he acknowledges the need of succour.

> We are losing many men and many officers, more from dysentery than from the enemy's fire, the deaths from that disease alone are sixty daily. We have no more grenades, which were our best defence; our guns are some of them destroyed by the enemy's fire, some of them burst before firing fifty rounds, from the bad material used by the founder; and the enemy, seeing

they can hold their lodgements in the ditch with a few men, are massing great numbers on the counterscarp, to have a large force ready there for some extraordinary effort. . . . We await, therefore, your Highness's arrival with extreme impatience; for my own part not so much from a wish to be relieved as that I may have the honour of respectfully assuring your Highness of my obedience, being, as I am, your Highness's most humble and obedient servant, Starhemberg.

The courtly bravado of the subscription is in strong contrast with the hurried postscript that follows:—

My miners tell me that they hear the enemy working beneath them under the Burg bastion; they must have run their gallery from the other side of the ditch, and there is no time to be lost.

When this despatch was written, both sides believed that the supreme crisis was at hand.

The 29th of August was looked for as the decisive day. On that anniversary Stuhlweissenberg and Belgrade had fallen before the Ottomans. (Not Pesth and Rhodes, which are sometimes added. Rhodes fell on Christmas day). Above all, on that day the strength of Hungary had been smitten, and her king, Louis, had died, before the hosts of the great Solyman, on the disastrous field of "The Destruction of Mohacs"—that battle which first opened Hungary and Austria to the invader.

But the 29th came and passed, with no general attack from the besiegers. A mine was sprung under the Burg ravelin, nearly completing the ruin of the work; and three or four hundred Turks attempted to establish themselves upon the remains, but were driven back again. Another mine was sprung by the Burg bastion, but no assault followed. From St. Stephen's considerable movement was noticed among the Turkish detachments on the left bank of the Danube, occasioned by the march of Lorraine's army.

In the camp murmurs and dissensions ran high. The Janissaries clamoured at their lengthy detention in the trenches. They openly accused the incapacity, or worse faults, of the *vizier*. There seems little doubt but that he had it in his power to have overwhelmed the defenders by a general and prolonged assault, towards the end of August.

Ottoman leaders had known well how to avail themselves of the obedience and fatalist courage of their soldiers. Amurath IV., when he won back Baghdad from the Persians, Mahomet II., at the taking of

Constantinople, had shown how cities could be won. Before the city of the *Khalifs* for three days, before the city of the Caesars from a May sunrise till well-nigh noon, had torrent after torrent of brave, devoted, undisciplined soldiers wearied the arms and exhausted the ammunition of the defenders, until the Janissaries arose, fresh and invincible for the decisive charge. Wave after wave of stormers, fed from inexhaustible multitudes, had rolled upon the besieged, and, like broken waves, had rolled back in ruin, until the last and greatest should burst in overwhelming force upon the breaches.

Such an assault would have been surely successful against Vienna. But the *vizier*, in vain security, pictured to himself the advantages of a surrender, which should preserve the city as a trophy of his conquest—the seat, perchance, of his sovereignty. The riches which he dreamed it to contain, he hoped to receive as his own spoil; not to yield as the booty of the army after a storm. So, while the decisive days passed, the signal for attack was delayed, except by small bodies upon single points, until the courage of his soldiers was dissipated and their confidence destroyed. On the contrary, the unexpected reprieve gave courage to the defenders. The *Janissaries*, on the other hand, impatiently invoked the appearance of the relieving army to end their sojourn in the trenches by the decisive event of a stricken field. Slowly, but at last, ere yet too late, that army was approaching.

CHAPTER 5

The Approach of the Relief Force

The duties which had been imposed upon Charles of Lorraine were of the most arduous kind. With a handful of troops, but slowly reinforced by the German levies, whose assistance was rendered less useful by the jealousies of the sovereign Princes in command, he was opposed both to the Turks and to Tekeli. He was expected to be ready to support the garrisons of Presburg and of Komorn, to hinder the incursions of the enemy into Upper Austria and into Moravia—above all, to prepare the bridges above Vienna, by which alone a relieving army could arrive. Though driven from the Leopoldstadt island, and from all immediate communication with the city, his presence yet animated the besieged with hope of succour. He fixed his headquarters finally at Krems, on the Danube, where the Saxon contingent presently arrived, followed by the troops of the Circles and the Bavarians.

Before their arrival, towards the end of August, he felt strong enough to advance and rescue Presburg from Tekeli. He followed up the operation by a defeat inflicted on the combined forces of the Turks and Hungarians upon the Marchfeld. A detachment of four thousand Polish horse, under Lubomirski, originally raised to assist Tekeli, were already present with the army of Lorraine. But decisive operations were of necessity postponed till after the coming of the King of Poland with the bulk of his forces, and of the rest of the German troops.

Lorraine, in these movements, undoubtedly proved his title to generalship; but nothing except the extraordinary apathy of the *vizier* rendered them possible. A skilful employment of the enormous force of Turkish cavalry must have forced the Imperial army to retire for want of supplies. The ravage, aimlessly and mercilessly inflicted upon Austria and the confines of Moravia, would, if directed against Poland, have probably prevented the march of Sobieski. An able commander,

215

with such forces at his command, might have prevented, or at least hindered, the junction of the Poles and Germans. Nor were any steps taken by the Vizier to stop the construction of the bridges at Krems and at Tuln, nor to guard the defiles of the Wiener Wald, over which the Christian army must advance to raise the siege.

So extraordinary indeed was the neglect of the enemy, that a secret understanding has been supposed between Tekeli and Sobieski, by which, in return for the future good offices of the latter, the former was not to molest Poland nor hinder the junction of the Christian forces. Be that as it may, the secret information of the Poles was as good as that of the Turks was bad, and the king knew thoroughly with what foes he had to deal, (Salvandy, vol. xi.).

Meanwhile, in spite of French intrigues, in spite of backwardness in Lithuania and of distrust in Poland, Sobieski had left Warsaw for Cracow on July 18. Up to the last moment the Turks disbelieved in his coming in person, and the emperor and the French king both doubted it. He was gouty, he was rheumatic, he was too fat to ride; such was the tenour of the information of the baffled French agent Vitry. Nevertheless, on the 22nd of August, he was on the Silesian frontier with the main part of his army. It consisted mostly of cavalry, of those Polish horsemen matchless in prowess, but the most unstable of forces. His infantry was less numerous and inferior, their shabby accoutrements contrasting sharply with the gaudy equipment of the cavaliers.

"They have sworn to dress themselves better in the spoils of the enemy," said the king of one regiment, deprecating the criticism of the Germans.

His march lay through Silesia and Moravia, through the borders of the lands devastated by the Tartars, where the trembling inhabitants thronged around him, hailing him already as their deliverer. Urged by message after message from Lorraine, he left his army to follow under the leadership of the Field-Marshal Jablonowski, and hurried on himself at the head of two thousand cavalry, his son Prince James by his side.

We can follow every movement of the campaign from the letters which, amid the hurry of the march, during short hours snatched from sleep, once at least during the thunder of a Turkish cannonade, he found time to despatch continually to his queen. *Seule joie de mon âme, charmante et bien-aimée Mariette,* as he calls her. Her letters in reply are his continual consolation amid the labours of the campaign, the ingratitude of the emperor, and the insubordination of his subjects.

I read all your letters, my dear and incomparable Maria, thrice over—once when I receive them, once when I retire to my tent and am alone with my love, once when I sit down to answer them.

Such is his answer to her expression of a fear that the distractions of his enterprise may leave no time for interest in aught besides. On August 29 be writes, from near Brunn in Moravia, sending the news of the retreat of Tekeli after his defeat by Lorraine, and adding that he hopes the next day, on nearing the Danube, to bear the cannon which tell that Vienna is still untaken. On the 31st he is near Tuln, above Vienna. He has passed the distant thunder of the cannonade upon his left hand, and has effected his junction with the army of Lorraine. Despairing of the arrival of the Lithuanians, he has distributed the arms intended for them among the imperfectly equipped Poles. Still more is he distressed at the non-appearance of the Cossacks, whom he expected, and whom he knew as invaluable for outpost duty. Menzynski, who should have conducted them, is lingering at Lemberg. "*C'est un grand misérable.*"

Most interesting of all is the passage in which he gives his wife his first impressions of his future colleague, the Duke of Lorraine. Lorraine had been a competitor with Sobieski for the crown of Poland, and it must have been a singular meeting when the rivals first came face to face co-operating together in a mighty enterprise. Sobieski the king, whose offspring were not to reign; Charles the duke, the destined ancestor of the Imperial line of Austria.

******

The grandson of the Duke of Lorraine married Maria Theresa, Queen of Hungary, and was himself Emperor. The granddaughter of Sobieski was the mother of Charles Edward, the hero of the Forty-Five.

******

The one in the semi-Oriental magnificence of his country, he went into action before Vienna in a sky-blue silk doublet; the other in the dress of a campaigner, best described in Sobieski's own words. The duke he finds modest and taciturn, stooping, plain, with a hooked nose, marked with small-pox; clad in an old grey coat, with "a fair wig ill-made," a hat without a band, "boots of yellow leather, or rather of what was yellow three months ago."

Avec tout ça, il n'a pas la mine d'un marchand, mais d'un homme comme il faut, et même d'un homme de distinction. C'est un homme avec qui je m'accorderais facilement.

The friendship of the former rivals was cemented by a banquet, and the duke's accustomed monitor being first overcome, Lorraine himself was induced to proceed from his native Moselle, which he drank usually mixed with water, to the strong Hungarian wines—to the improvement, as the king tells his wife, of his conversation. Besides Lorraine, Sobieski found a crowd of German princes awaiting his arrival: John George of Saxony, speaking no French nor Latin, and very little German; Waldeck, of the house of Waldeck-Wildungen, (of the family, not an ancestor, of the present Duchess of Albany), William the Third's right hand man in the Netherlands, here commanding the troops of the Circles, and winning high praise from the king for his activity and zeal; Maximilian of Bavaria, whose courage and ill-fortune were hereafter to be signalized at Blenheim and at Ramilies, now aged twenty-one, wins notice as "better dressed than the others."

There were two Wurtembergers and the Prince of Brunswick-Lüneburg, afterwards our George I.; the Prince of Saxe-Lauenberg; a Hohenzollern and a Hessian; three princes of Anhalt; Hermann and Louis of Baden, the latter was with Marlborough at Schellenberg; two sons of Montecuculi, the conqueror of St. Gotthard; last and youngest, though not least, Eugene of Savoy, the future conqueror of Zenta and of Belgrade, and the colleague of Marlborough in his greatest battles. There was Count Leslie, of that Scotch house which had given generals to half the armies of Europe; Count Taaffe, the Irishman, afterwards Sir Francis Taaffe and Earl of Carlingford, whose elder brother fell fighting for King James at the Boyne, but whose services to the allies secured the earldom from forfeiture. There were gathered veterans of the Thirty Years' War, men who might have seen Gustavus or Wallenstein, and men who were to reap their brightest laurels hereafter in the war of the Spanish Succession.

As was wittily said, the Empire would have been there had only the emperor been present. The Brandenberg troops also were wanting. The "Great Elector" was jealous of Poland—once his superior in the Prussian duchy—had formerly been injured by Sobieski acting with the Swedes in the interests of France, and moreover was not on the best terms with the emperor. Brandenberg, then as ever, was playing with skill and patience her own game. The fortunes of the future Prussian monarchy were not to be lightly risked for the sake of Austria. But the emperor himself must not be rashly charged with want of courage for his absence from the camp. He was not trained to war; the presence of his court would have been embarrassing to the operations, perhaps would have been inseparable from intrigues and jealousies that would seriously have crippled the army.

A certain stubborn manhood Leopold had shown in not yielding to the pressure put upon him to make terms with Louis XIV. in this extremity. The aid of France could have been purchased by the election of the Dauphin as King of the Romans, probably by smaller sacrifices. The Diet at Ratisbon had been not disinclined to yield, but the emperor had steadfastly refused to subject either his own house or the Empire to French dictation. That one crowned head was in the field was of the greatest importance, especially when that one was the King of Poland.

Everywhere the most cheerful deference was rendered to Sobieski by all who were present. The princes, jealous of each other before, now vied with each other in zealous obedience to the conqueror of Choczim. His experience of Turkish warfare was unique, his personal character commanding. He tells his wife how Lorraine, Waldeck, Saxony, Bavaria would send or even come personally for his commands. The ascendancy exercised by Sobieski is nowhere more decisively illustrated than in the conduct of five hundred Janissaries, a trophy of his victories, who now formed his body guard. He offered them leave of absence from the battle, or even a free passage to the Turkish camp, but they besought leave to live and die with him, (Salvandy).

The king himself was fully prepared to accept the advice of generals like Lorraine and Waldeck. He had left his royal dignity behind at Warsaw, as he told Lorraine, and at once agreed with the latter upon a plan for crossing the Danube at Krems and at Tuln, concentrating at Tuln and marching over the Kahlenberg to Vienna. He only complained of the backward condition of the bridges and of the slow assemblage of the troops, whereas the emperor had by letter assured him that all was ready before he had left Poland. When finally assembled, the united armies numbered eighty-five thousand men. The Poles were more than twenty-six thousand strong. But allowing for detachments, not more than seventy-seven thousand men were available upon the battle-field. The artillery numbered one hundred and sixty-eight pieces, of which few came into action.

On September 4, the king still writes from near Tuln. If an excess of glory is often the share of a successful commander, yet an excessive toil is his always. Sobieski tells his wife that he has a continual cold and headache, and is night and day in the saddle. The French stories were so far true that he could not mount without assistance, yet in the midst of such operations no rest is possible. The Turks are, he says, either really ignorant of his presence, or refuse to believe it. The *vizier* was incredibly ill-supplied with information.

He really was uncertain whether Sobieski was in the field; and whether the Polish Army, or partisan corps only, like that of Lubomirski, had joined Lorraine. The smallest resistance would seriously have retarded the passage of the Danube, performed by the Germans at Krems, by the Poles at Tuln. As it was, the difficulties were terrible. The pontoons sank under the weight of the artillery and waggons. The latter had to find fords over the smaller branches of the river, while the bridges upon the main stream were strengthened to sustain them. Even then much baggage was left north of the Danube; much more upon the southern side, entrenched and defended.

On September 8, when the concentration of the army upon the southern bank was being completed, Marco Aviano, the Emperor's Confessor, celebrated a solemn mass, and gave a formal benediction to the Christian army. Sobieski then steppe d forward, and after addressing some words of encouragement to the assembled officers, bestowed the honour of knighthood upon his son James.

★★★★★★

Schimmer, *Sieges of Vienna*; Count Thûrheim, *Life of Starhemberg*; and Salvandy, *Hist. de Pologne*, vol. ii. misplace this solemn benediction of the army and the knighting of Prince James on the morning of the 12th. Sobieski's own testimony, in his letters to his queen, is decisive for the 8th, Nor on the 12th was there time for the ceremony.

★★★★★★

An enthusiastic votary of his religion, he desired to impress upon his army that their cause was the cause of God, against the enemies of the Faith. Even the Lutheran Saxons and North Germans could, with more justice than the Hungarian renegades, claim to be fighting *Pro Deo et Patria*. Upon the coming struggle depended the question whether the frightful devastation, which had desolated Hungary and Austria, was or was not to be repeated in all the south German lands.

The flat ground upon the southern side of the Danube, from near Krems to Tuln, the Tullner Feld, offered a convenient space for the mustering of the army after passing the river. Vienna was not further

220

than about sixteen miles as the crow flies, but the intervening country was of a difficult nature, even should the Turks attempt no interruption to the movements of the relieving forces. The Wiener Wald, rising to more than nine hundred feet above the level of the Danube, runs into a north-easterly direction between Tuln and Vienna, and advances up to the very current of the river, which flows north-eastward and then south-eastward round the mountain barrier. The roads were few and difficult, and trees covered the slopes of the hills. Sobieski had decided to advance with his left wing covered by the Danube, and to throw succour into Vienna upon that side; while with the right he threatened the rear of the Turkish camp on the side of Dornbach and Hernals. With this object the march was directed upon the Leopoldsberg and the Kahlenberg, the last heights or ridges of the mountains above the Danube, to the north-west of Vienna.

And at length, on the 10th of September, the forward movement upon the Kahlenberg began. Already as early as the morning of the 6th, a reconnaissance had been pushed to the summit, and as evening fell had cheered Vienna with a flight of signal rockets, in answer to the fiery messengers of distress which nightly rose from the spire of St. Stephen's. But to carry an army up the Kahlenberg was a harder task. Sobieski wrote that the country was horribly wasted. There was neither food for man nor forage for horses, beyond what the army could carry with them. Indeed, the leaves of the trees upon the Kahlenberg had to eke out the supplies of the latter. There was all need for despatch. The last despairing message had come from Starhemberg, borne by a swimmer on the Danube to Lorraine, in language as brief as significant, "*No time to be lost; no time indeed to be lost.*"

CHAPTER 6

The Critical Moment

There was no time to be lost indeed. The fortifications of Vienna were a mere heap of ruins. The Imperial Palace was battered to pieces. Nearly one whole quarter of the city was in ashes. On the 3rd of September, the long contested Burg ravelin was yielded to the Turks. On the 4th, the salient angle of the Burg bastion was blown into the air, and an attack was with difficulty repelled. On the 6th, a similar mine and assault following cumbered the Löwel bastion with ruin and with corpses. For a moment, the horse tails were planted upon the ramparts. Driven back thence with difficulty, the Turks still clung to the Burg ravelin, and four pieces of cannon planted there, at frightfully close quarters, completed the ruin of the works.

But no new attack came. Informed of the advance of Lorraine, though still incredulous of the presence of Sobieski, the Vizier began to draw his troops towards the foot of the Kahlenberg. He still clung to the batteries and trenches; still kept the pick of his *Janissaries* grappling with the prize which but for him they might have already won. He rejected the advice of the Pasha of Pesth, to withdraw across the Wien and fortify a camp on the Wienersberg, secure that if the Christians attacked and failed Vienna would fall. He withdrew his troops indeed from the Leopoldstadt, and threw up some slight Works towards the Kahlenberg, but remained otherwise irresolute, halting between his expected booty and her deliverer.

Sobieski had already taken the measure of his opponent. In reply to desponding views of Lorraine at Tuln, he had said:

Be of good cheer; which of us at the head of two hundred thousand men would have allowed this bridge to have been thrown within five leagues of his camp?

To his wife he wrote:

> A commander who has thought neither of entrenching his
> camp, nor of concentrating his forces, but who lies encamped
> there as if we were one hundred miles off, is predestined to be
> beaten.

Viewing the Turkish force from the Kahlenberg, he said to his
soldiers:

> This man is badly encamped; he knows nothing of war; we shall
> beat him.

It was well for the Christians and for Vienna that none of the great
warriors who had served the Porte was now in command. No man
like Kiuprili, or even like Ibrahim "the Devil," the last Turkish commander against whom Sobieski had contended, was there, to use the
fidelity of the *Janissaries* and the valour of the *Spahis* to advantage. The
march up the defiles of the Kahlenberg presented, even without inter-
ruptions, extraordinary difficulties. The king himself pushed forward
to superintend the exploration of the way. He was so long parted from
his Polish troops that they became anxious for his safety. He rejoined
them at mid-day on the 11th, and encouraged them as they marched,
or, as he says, rather *climbed* to the summit. Some Saxon troops, first
arriving, with three guns, opened fire upon a Turkish detachment
marching too late to secure the important position.

The Turks retired, and the distant sound of the firing announced to
Vienna the first tidings of deliverance. It was not till the evening of the
11th, however, that the main body of the army had reached the ridge.
Even then many had lagged behind; the paths were nearly impracti-
cable for artillery, and the Germans abandoned many of their guns
in despair between Tuln and the Kahlenberg. But few pieces indeed
were fired after the first beginning of the battle on the following day,
Polish guns, for the most part, brought up by the vigour of the Grand
Marshal of the Artillery, Kouski, the same officer who had directed the
Polish field-pieces against the Turkish camp at Choczim.

September 11, as Sobieski and the generals stood at length upon
the crest of the hill:

> An hour before sunset, they saw outspread before them one
> of the most magnificent yet terrible displays of human power
> which man has seen. There lay the valley and the islands of the
> Danube, covered with an encampment, the sumptuousness of

which seemed better suited for an excursion of pleasure than for the hardships of war. Within it stood an innumerable multitude of animals—horses, camels, and oxen. Two hundred thousand fighting men moved in order here and there, while along the foot of the hills below swarms of Tartars roamed at will. A frightful cannonade was raging vigorously from the one side, in feeble reply from the other. Beneath the canopy of smoke lay a great city, visible only by her spires and her pinnacles, which pierced the overwhelming cloud and flame.—Coyer, *Memoires de Sobieski.*

Sobieski estimated the force before him at one hundred thousand tents and three hundred thousand men. Including the non-combatants, he was, perhaps, not far wrong; but the fighting men in the Turkish army by this time would be by many fewer than that number. One hundred and sixty-eight thousand men is the most which may be allowed from the muster-rolls found in the *vizier's* tent, and that certainly exceeds the truth.

★★★★★★

The roll includes the forces of Tekeli, who was not in the Turkish camp at all, and takes no count of the last losses which the Turkish detachments had suffered, nor of the loss from desertion the night before the battle, when many of the irregulars went off with their booty. The Turks had lost, according to this roll, 45,500 men before the battle.—See Thürheim's *Starhemberg.*

★★★★★★

All around, except where in the encampment the magnificence of the invader was proudly flaunted in the face of the ruin that he had made, the prospect was desolated by war. Whatever might be the fortune of the coming day, a generation at least must elapse before those suburbs are rebuilt, those villages restored and repeopled, those fields fully cultivated again. The army felt that it lay with them, under God, to provide against that further extension of the ravage which would follow, should the bulwark of the *Oesterreich*, the Eastern March of the Empire, be forced by Hun and Tartar.

Not distinguishable from the distance at which they stood, thousands of Christian captives lay in the encampment below. The morrow might deliver up the people of Vienna to a like fate with theirs. The city, as the king declared on entering it after the relief, could not have held out five days. As the wind now lifted the cloud of smoke, where should have been the fortifications, the eye could discern nothing but a circle of shapeless ruin, reaching from the Scottish gate to what had been the Burg bastion. Up to and on to it climbed the curving lines of the Turkish approaches.

Sobieski had only hoped gradually to fight his way into a position whence he could communicate with the besieged, and he had arranged his plan of battle at Tuln with that idea. But the inequalities of the country between the Kahlenberg and Vienna, broken with vines, villages, small hills and hollow ways, together with the unexpectedly rapid development of the attack when once it began, seem to have interfered with his original disposition.

His army occupied a front of half a Polish mile, or about an English mile and three quarters. It was drawn up in three supporting lines that faced south-eastward.

The first line of the right wing was composed of nineteen Polish (cavalry) divisions and four battalions; the second, of six Polish and eight Austrian divisions, and four Polish battalions; the third, of nine Polish, six Austrian, three German divisions, three Polish and one German battalion.

The centre was composed in the first line of nine Austrian and eleven German divisions, and thirteen German battalions; in the second, of six German divisions, ten German and six Austrian battalions; in the third, of five German and two Austrian battalions.

The left wing shewed in the first line, ten Austrian and five German divisions, and six Austrian battalions; in the second line, four German and eight Austrian divisions; in the third line, three German and seven Austrian battalions.

Lubomirski with his irregular Poles was on the left; the Polish Field-Marshal, Jablonowski, commanded on the right; the Prince of Waldeck, with the Electors of Bavaria and Saxony, the centre; the Duke of Lorraine and Louis of Baden, with Counts Leslie and Caprara, were on the left. The king was upon the right or right centre throughout the day. The total force, including detachments not actually engaged, was 46,700 cavalry and dragoons, 38,700 infantry; in all 85,400 men, with some irregulars, and 168 guns, many of them not in action at all. The dragoons fought on foot in the battle.

★★★★★★

The dragoons were mounted infantry, using horses to reach the scene of action only. They carried the infantry weapons, sword

225

and musket, but not pikes. The bayonet was just coming into use, but was still fixed in the muzzle of the gun, and had to be removed before firing.

★★★★★★

The army was, roughly, one-third Poles, one-third Austrians, one-third Bavarians, Saxons, and other Germans. (Count Thürheim, *Starhemberg*; and Sobieski to his wife, September 13). The fatigues of the march from Tuln would naturally diminish the number of effective soldiers on the day of battle; and the troops were not all in position when the evening of Saturday, September 11, fell. As the night however wore away, the rear guard gained the summit of the hills, and snatched a brief repose before the labours of the morrow.

But for the king there was no rest. The man whom the French ambassador had described as unable to ride, who was tormented certainly by wearing pains, after three days of incessant toil, passed a sleepless night preparatory to fourteen hours in the saddle upon the battlefield. The season of repose was dedicated to the duties of a general and the affection of a husband. At three a.m. on Sunday, the 12th, the king is again writing to his *bien-aimée Mariette*. He has been toiling all day in bringing his troops up the ravines.

We are so thin; we might run down the stags on the mountains.

As to the pomp or even comfort of a king, that is not to be thought of.

All my luggage which we have got up here is in the two lightest carts.

He has some more upon mules, but has not seen them for forty-eight hours. He had no thought of sleep; indeed, the thunder of the Turkish cannon made it impossible; and a gale of wind, which he describes as "sufficient to blow the men off their horses," bore the noise of their discharge with redoubled clamour to the relieving army. Moreover, the king writes, he must be in the saddle before daybreak, riding down from the right to the extreme left, to consult with Lorraine, opposite whom the enemy lies in force; not entrenched, he hopes, as on that side he means to break through to the city. A two days' affair, at least, he thinks. Then, "my eighth letter to your sixth," he adds, with other familiar and gentle conversation, with tidings of her son and of other friends, but with no word of fear or of apprehension. He had made his will before setting out from Warsaw, but he entertained no thought of failure. Then closing his wife's letter, the affectionate husband becomes again the heroic king and careful general.

He rides from right to left along the lines, in that boisterous autumnal morning, makes the last dispositions with Lorraine, with him and with a few others takes again the Holy Communion from the hands of Marco Aviano before the sun has risen, and then returns to his post upon the right wing, ready for the advance that was to save Vienna. His next letter to his wife was dated "September 13, night. The tents of the *vizier*."

CHAPTER 7

The Attack

The position of the Christian Army on the Kahlenberg was, from the left wing, the nearest point, about four miles from Vienna. The centre and right were further removed. The intervening country, far from being a plain, as Sobieski had been led to believe when he formed his first plan of battle, is broken up into hillocks and little valleys, intersected by streams, full of vineyards, and interspersed with the ruins of numerous villages burnt by the Turks. Beyond these lay the Turkish encampment and approaches, mingled with the vestiges of the suburbs destroyed by Starhemberg at the beginning of the siege.

The Turkish army was stretched over a front of about four miles from point to point, but slightly curving with the convex side towards the attacking force. Their right rested upon the Danube, and held the Nussberg before the villages of Nussdorf and Heiligenstadt; their left reached towards Breitensee near the Wien, and the Tartars swarmed still further on the broken ground beyond. Their camp straggled in an irregular half-moon from the river above Vienna to beyond the Wien, and their troops were, at the beginning of the action, drawn up before it.

Some hasty entrenchments had been thrown up by them here and there, of which the most considerable was a battery between Währing, Gerstorf and Weinhaus, (*Turkenschanze*, traces of which lately remained), but the bulk of their artillery remained in their lines, pointed against the city, and the clamour of the ensuing battle was swelled by the continuous roar of their bombardment, kept up as on previous days. In the trenches lay a great body of *Janissaries*; and the Turkish Army was further weakened by the dispersal of Tartars and irregulars on the night before the fight, doubtful of the event, and anxious at any rate to secure their plunder.

As the king had said, the Turks were badly posted, their camp was long and straggling, too valuable to be abandoned and not easy to defend. In case of a reverse, their right wing would run the risk of being driven into the Danube, or else have to fall back upon their centre and left, to the confusion of the whole army. Fighting with a river and a fortified city upon their flank and rear, repulse for them would mean certain disaster. But the incapacity of the *vizier* could not be fully fathomed till the attack began.

We have the assurance of Sobieski himself that he hoped upon the first day merely to bring his army within striking distance of the enemy, and to establish his left well forward near the bank of the Danube, ready to deal a decisive blow, or to throw succour into Vienna on the morrow or following day. He closed his letter to his wife in the grey of the windy morning of the 12th of September, ignorant that the decisive moment, bringing a victory greater than that of Choczim, was at hand.

The Turks had pushed their outposts forward up the banks of the river, and soon after daybreak Lorraine upon the left was engaged, and the fight thickened as his attack towards Nussdorf and Heiligenstadt was developed. Eugene of Savoy began his distinguished career in arms by carrying tidings from Lorraine to the king that the battle had commenced in earnest. Eugene, barely twenty, had left Paris that year, slighted by Louis, and had entered the service of the emperor. His memoirs dismiss briefly this his first essay in war:

> The confusion of that day can be but confusedly described. The Poles, who had clambered up to the Leopoldsberg—I know not why—went down again like madmen and fought like lions. The Turks, encamped where I threw up lines in 1703, did not know which way to front, neglected the eminences, and behaved like idiots.

★★★★★★

Note:—In 1717 Eugene, in like case with the *vizier* now, was besieging Belgrade, and was himself surrounded by a large Turkish Army. However, he defeated the relieving army and took the city.

★★★★★★

The young *aide-de-camp*, carrying orders through the hottest of the fire, could not yet penetrate the System which underlay the apparent confusion of the march and battle. Advancing in columns with a comparatively narrow front down the difficult slope of the hills, the infantry gradually deployed right and left upon the lower ground, while the cavalry of the second line advanced to fill the gaps thus left in the foremost. The Turks resisted gallantly, but they were principally dismounted *Spahis*, not a match for Lorraine's favourite troops, the German foot, though regaining their horses they would retreat with great rapidity, to again dismount, and again resist, as each favourable position offered itself.

The fighting was obstinate, and the losses heavy upon both sides, but the tide of fight rolled steadily towards Vienna. The Germans carried the height of the Nussberg, above Nussdorf, and their guns planted there disordered the whole of the Turkish right with their plunging fire. Osman Ogoli, Pasha of Kutaya, the Turkish general of division, pushed forward three columns in a counter-attack, boldly and skilfully directed. The Imperial infantry were shaken, but five Saxon battalions, inclining to their left from the Christian centre, checked in turn the onset of the Ottomans, and restored the current of the battle. But had the whole force of the enemy been commanded as their right wing, the allies would scarcely that night have been greeted in Vienna.

No false move in the advance escaped the skill of Osman. As the Turkish attack recoiled, the Prince of Croy had dashed forward with two battalions to carry with a rush the village of Nussdorf. Checked and overwhelmed, he fell back again, himself wounded, his brother slain. Louis of Baden, with his dismounted dragoons, came up to the rescue, and checked the pursuing enemy. As they recoiled slowly the fight grew fiercer, and then more stationary about Nussdorf and about Döbling. Houses, gardens, and vineyards formed a series of entrenchments, sharply attacked and obstinately defended. A third time the fiery valour of the Turks, charging home with their sabres among the pikes and muskets, disordered the allies, and all but regained the summit of the Nussberg.

Again the superior cohesion of the Christians prevailed, and the Turkish column outflanked fell back, still stubbornly contesting every foot of ground. From the long extended centre and left of their line no support came to them, as the *vizier* in anxious irresolution expected the advance of the centre of the allies and of the Poles upon their right. His infatuation, moreover, had kept in the batteries the bulk of his artillery, and in the trenches the best of his Janissaries. In dire want of the guns, which roared idly upon the already shattered defences of the city, Osman was driven through Nussdorf and through Heiligenstadt, upon the fortified defiles of Döbling, where at last a battery of ten guns and a force of Janissaries opposed a steadier resistance to the advancing Germans.

It was now noon. Lorraine had already won the position which had been marked out for his achievement for the day, and slackened his attack while he reformed his victorious battalions. The centre and right of the Christian Army, separated by a longer distance from their foes, bad been slowly gaining the field of action, and had scarce fired a shot nor struck a blow, except for the support accorded to the left by the centre. The whole of the infantry and cavalry had at mid-day gained the positions assigned to them, and, in the absence of most of his artillery, Sobieski would have hesitated to continue his advance had not his lines, upon the left especially, become so deeply involved that it was difficult to suspend the conflict for long.

Yet a momentary lull succeeded to the sharp sounds of close combat. A sultry autumn day had followed the boisterous night and morning, and the heat was oppressive. (There is a proverb, "*Vienna aut venenosa aut ventosa.*" She was giving to her deliverers successive displays of her character). The Poles upon the right halted and snatched a hasty meal from the provisions they had brought with them. But as the rattle of the small arms and the clash of weapons died away, the roar of the battering guns and the answering fire of the city rose in overwhelming distinctness.

Behind the smoky veil, Starhemberg and his gallant garrison could perchance barely guess, by sounds of conflict, the progress of their deliverers. Tidings from the watch-chair on St. Stephen's would spread alternate hope and despair among the citizens. The fate of Vienna trembled in the balance. The garrison stood ready in the breaches, the rest of the inhabitants cowered upon the housetops to watch, or knelt in the churches to pray; but to the *vizier* came swiftly tidings of the foe with whom he had to deal, the foe whose presence he had obstinately refused to credit.

Reforming after their brief delay, the Polish cavalry in gorgeous arms came flashing from the woods and defiles near Dornbach on his left. Those who had before fought against him, knew the plume raised upon a spear point, the shield borne before him, the *banderolles* on the lances of his body guard, which declared the presence of the terrible Sobieski.

"By *Allah*, but the king is really among them," cried Gieray, Khan of the Crimea. And all doubt was at an end as the shout of "*Vivat So-*

bieski" rolled along the Christian lines, in dread and significant answer to the discordant clamour of the *Infidels*.

Profiting, however, by the interruption in the battle, the *vizier* had reformed his line, brought up infantry from the trenches, and now directed his attack upon the Poles and the most formidable of his opponents, hoping by their overthrow to change the fortune of the day, while the Imperialists and Saxons still halted before his entrenchments at Döbling. The Turks advanced with courage. For a moment a regiment of Polish lancers were thrown into confusion, and the officers, members of the nobility of Poland, who strove to rally their lines, fell; but Waldeck, moving up his Bavarians from the centre, restored the fight. The attack was defeated, and advancing in turn the headlong valour of the Poles drove the Turks back from point to point, over the Alserbach and its branches upon the confines of their camp. To relieve the pressure upon the right and centre. Lorraine had renewed his attack with the left of the allies. Horses and men had recovered breath and order, and their artillery had moved up in support.

The defiles of Döbling were cleared by the Saxons; and at about four or five o'clock the Turkish redoubt before Währing was carried by Louis of Baden with his dismounted dragoons. Falling back in confusion upon their approaches and batteries, the Turks desperately endeavoured, too late, to turn the siege guns upon the enemy, whose advance now threatened them upon all sides. The caution of Sobieski had, up to the last moment, inclined him to respect the superior numbers and the desperation of his foes, and to rest content with the advantage won; but now, in the growing confusion, he saw that the decisive hour had arrived. The Elector of Bavaria and the Prince of Waldeck hastening from the centre already saluted him as conqueror.

The desperate efforts of the *vizier* to gain room by moving troops towards his left from the centre, and so extending his lines beyond the Polish right, served but to increase the confusion. The Field-Marshal Jablonowski covered that wing, and the Queen of Poland's brother, the Count de Maligni, pushing forward with infantry, seized a mound, whence his musketry fire dominated the spot where the *vizier* stood. The last shots were fired from the two or three cannon which had kept pace with the advance. A French officer rammed home the last charge with his gloves, his wig, and a packet of French papers. Already the roads to Hungary were thronged with fugitives, whose course was marked by dust in columns, when the king decided to seize the victory all but in his grasp already. *Non nobis, non nobis, Domine exercituum, sed Nomini Tuo des gloriam*, he cried in answer to the congratulations of his friends, as he began the decisive movement.

Concentrating as rapidly as possible the bulk of the cavalry of the whole army, German and Polish, upon the right wing, (Sobieski's letter of September 13), he led them to the charge, directly upon the spot where the *vizier* with blows, tears, and curses, was endeavouring to rally the soldiers, whom his own ill-conduct had deprived of their wonted valour. The Turkish infantry without pikes, their cavalry without heavy armour, were incapable of withstanding the shock of the heavy German *cuirassiers*, or of arresting the rush of the Polish nobles, whose spears, as they boasted to their kings, would uphold the heavens should they fall. Their king at their head, they came down like a whirlwind to the shout of "God preserve Poland."

The spears of the first line were splintered against the few who awaited them, but their onset was irresistible. *Spahis* and *Janissaries*, Tartars and Christian allies alike went down before the Polish lances, or turned and fled in headlong confusion. The old Pasha of Pesth, the greatest of the Turkish warriors in reputation, had fled already. The Pashas of Aleppo and of Silistria perished in the *mêlée*.

"Can you not help me?" cried the *vizier*, turning to the Khan of the Crimea.

"No," was the reply; "I know the King of Poland well, it is impossible to resist him; think only of flight." (Sobieski's letter of September 13. He must have heard of the conversation from the *vizier's* attendants taken in his encampment).

Away through the wasted borders of Austria, away to the Hungarian frontier, to their army that lay before Raab, poured the fugitives. There seldom has been a deliverance more complete and more decisive. The terror which had so long weighed upon Eastern Christendom was dissolved in that headlong rout. It was more than the scattering of an army; the strength of an empire was dissipated on that day. Resources which had been accumulating for years were destroyed; and such an expedition, so numerous and so well furnished, never was sent forth by the Ottoman again. The victory lacked nothing to render it more striking, either in suddenness, in completeness, or in situation.

The whole action had been comprised in the hours between sunrise and sunset, before the gates of one of the greatest capitals in Europe. We may borrow indeed the words of Eugene, used in his despatch describing the last victory of the war at Zenta, to picture the last hours of that evening before Vienna. For upon the summits of the

Weiner-Wald, whence the allies had descended that morning to a yet doubtful field, "the sun seemed to linger, loath to leave the day, until his rays had illumined to the end the triumph of the glorious arms" of Poland and "of the Empire." There was no want of individual courage among the Turks.

"They made the best retreat you can conceive," wrote the king, for hard pressed they would turn sword in hand upon their pursuers. But the head which should have directed that courage was wanting; and for that want they were a gallant mob, but no longer an army. Grateful for the result though we may be, there is something pathetic in the magnificent valour of a race of soldiers being frustrated by such incapacity. The Christians, exhausted by the toils of the last few days, could not pursue to any distance. The Imperial General Dûnewald indeed with a few squadrons of Austrians and Poles, the stoutest steeds or the keenest riders, despising both plunder and fatigue, pushed straight on through the twilight to Enzersdorf, where the road crossed the stream of the Fischa, ten miles from Vienna, and there bursting on the line of flight made a slaughter of the fugitives, which showed how much they owed to the night and to the weariness of their conquerors.

But there was no general pursuit on the part of the allies. Their commanders were doubtful of the full extent of their victory, and feared lest from such a multitude some part might rally and destroy the too eager followers whom they still outnumbered. But without pursuit their work was done. At seven, Louis of Baden had opened a communication with the besieged, and the garrison sallying forth joined the relieving army in the slaughter of the Janissaries who had remained, neglected or forgotten, in the trenches. Even then one miner was found, doggedly toiling in his gallery beneath the ramparts, ignorant of the flight or death of his companions; perhaps from among so many the last staunch soldier of the Prophet.

I cannot conceive, wrote Sobieski, how they can carry on the war after such a loss of *matériel*. The whole of the artillery of the Turks, their munitions, and their baggage were the spoil of the victors. Three hundred and ten pieces of cannon, twenty thousand animals, nine thousand carriages, one hundred and twenty-five thousand tents, five million pounds of powder are enumerated. The holy standard of the Prophet had been saved, but the standard of the Vizier, mistaken for it, was sent to the Pope by the conqueror, while his gilded stirrups were despatched at once to Poland to the queen, as a token of victory. Never, perhaps, since Alexander stood a victor at Issus in the tents of

Darius, or the Greeks stormed the Persian camp at Plataea, had a European army entered upon such spoil.

Much money had been saved by the Turks in their flight; but precious stuffs and jewelled arms, belts thick with diamonds, intended to encircle the fair captives of Vienna, the varied plunder of many a castle of Hungary and of Lower Austria, were found piled in the encampment. In the *vizier's* quarters were gardens laid out with baths and fountains, a menagerie, even a rabbit warren. His encampment alone formed a labyrinth of tents, by itself of the circumference of a little town, and with its contents declared the character of its late owner. An ostrich, previously taken from an Imperial castle, was found beheaded to prevent recapture. A parrot, more fortunate, escaped upon the wing. The Polish envoy was discovered in the camp in chains, forgotten during the turmoil, and thus saved from the death promised him if his master should take the field.

The Imperial agent at the Porte, Kunitz, had escaped into the town during the battle; but the mass of Christian captives had not been so happy. Before the battle the *vizier* had ordered a general massacre of prisoners, and the camp was cumbered with the bodies of men, women, and children, but for the most part of women, foully slaughtered. The benevolent energy of the Bishop of Neustadt, above-mentioned, found employment in caring for five hundred children, who had, with their mothers in a few cases, escaped the sword. The night was passed in the camp by the victors, who were intent on securing their victory or their plunder.

Not till the following morning did the king meet Lorraine and exchange congratulations upon their success. Then, with the Commandant Starhemberg, they entered the city, passing over those well-contested breaches, which but for them might have been that day trodden by the *Janissaries*. They repaired to the churches for a solemn thanksgiving. Sobieski himself sang the *Te Deum* in one of them. Nothing could exceed the enthusiastic gratitude of the people, who barely allowed a passage to the horse of their deliverer.

The priest, after the *Te Deum* ended, by a happy inspiration or plagiarism, gave out the words, "*There was a man sent from God, whose name was John.*" (It was the exclamation of the Pope, Pius V., on hearing of the victory of Don John of Austria over the Turks at Lepanto, in 1571). A salute of three hundred guns proclaimed the victory far and wide, and the shouts of "*Vivat Sobieski,*" that filled the city outthundered the thunder of the cannon. Their walls were a chaos, their habitations a ruin, but the citizens rejoiced as those rejoice whom the Lord hath redeemed and delivered from the hand of the enemy. They were as men released not only from the sword, pestilence, and famine, but from prison besides. They poured forth to taste again the sweets of liberty, wondered at the trenches, or joined in the pillage of the camp, where the air was already sickening from the thousands of the slain and foul from the refuse of the barbaric encampment. But amid all the popular rejoicing, the king could not but observe the coldness of the magistracy.

The emperor could not endure that any but himself should triumph in Vienna, and his feelings were reflected in his servants. On hearing of the victory he had returned to the neighbourhood of the city. A council was held to settle the weighty point as to how the elective Emperor was to receive the elective king. "With open arms, since he has saved the Empire," said Lorraine; but Leopold would not descend to such an indecorum.

He strove to avoid a meeting with the deliverer of his capital, and when the meeting was arranged could barely speak a few cold words in Latin, well answered by Sobieski, who, saying, "I am happy, Sire, to have been able to render you this slight service," turned his horse, saluted, and rode away. A few complimentary presents to Prince James and to the Polish nobles did not efface the impression of ingratitude. The German writers minimise the coldness of the emperor, but Sobieski was at the moment undoubtedly aggrieved, and others were discontented.

CHAPTER 8

Victory

Neglected and distrusted by the sovereign whom he had delivered, Sobieski found consolation in detailing his victory, his spoil, and his wrongs alike to his wife. We find the great soldier again, in the full flush of his victory, writing indefatigably to his Mariette. It is on the night of the 13tb, in the *vizier's* late quarters, in the camp still cumbered with the slaughter of the combatants and of prisoners. The loss had been heavy in the fighting upon both sides, he tells us; and such an estimate, formed at such a moment by the victorious general, by far outweighs the accounts by which the French above all tried to minimise the slaughter made, and with it the greatness of the victory won.

★★★★★★

A moderate estimate of the Christian loss is five thousand men, or about one-fifteenth of those on the field; a loss in about the same proportion as that of both sides at Sadowa. The Poles alone confessed to the loss of one hundred officers killed, and they were neither so long nor so hotly engaged as the left wing. The loss of the centre was probably less. Thürheim and Schimmer give of the allies four thousand, and twenty-five thousand Turks; but the latter figures are quite uncertain, and the Christians made the least of their losses. As the fight was so much hand-to-hand, with little artillery fire, it would resemble ancient battles, where the loss of the vanquished was always disproportionately large. The memoirs of the Duke of Lorraine simply say, that "for about three hours the fighting was very bloody upon both sides." Fighting, however, had begun soon after daybreak, and the pursuit lasted till nightfall.

★★★★★★

He begins his letter:—

God be blessed for ever. He has given victory to our people; He has given them such a triumph that past ages have not seen the like.

All around, the explosions of the Turkish ammunition, fired by the plunderers from city and army, "make a din like the last judgment." He plunges into a description of the riches that the camp contains.

The *vizier* has made me his heir; he has done everything *en galant homme.*

You cannot say to me, 'You are no warrior,' as the Tartar women say to their husbands when they return emptyhanded.

For two nights and a day plunder has gone on at will; even the townsfolk have taken their share, and I am sure that there is enough left for eight days more. The plunder we got at Choczim was nothing to this.

There was a touch of the barbaric chieftain in the Polish king, and he keenly enjoyed not merely the victory, but the spoil which he had won. At the end of the seventeenth century, the character of this general of the school of Montecuculi, this admirer of Condé, recalls to us at once the ardour of a crusader, and the affectionate rapacity of a moss-trooper, reserving the richest plunder of a foray to deck his wife at home. He exults in the belts and in the watches studded with jewels, the stuffs and the embroideries which are to adorn his wife's *boudoir.* But he is still bent on action, he says:—

We must march tomorrow for Hungary, and start at the double, to escape the smell of the camp and its refuse, with the thousands of bodies of men and of animals lying unburied.

One letter, at least, he had despatched before writing to his wife. He knew well the feelings with which the King of France would regard the salvation of the Empire, and the setting free of the attention of Germany to be directed to his own designs. In Sobieski's own words to his wife, he thus reveals his triumph over the French king, whose intrigues had been ceaselessly directed to prevent his coming:—

I have written to the King of France; I have told him that it was to him especially, as to the Most Christian King, that I felt bound to convey the information of the battle that we have won, and of the safety of Christendom.

This letter remained unanswered. It is said that the proofs of Louis' dealings with the Turks had at that moment passed into the hands of the victors, amid the plunder of the *vizier's* quarters.

No sooner had Louis heard that the intrigues of his agents had failed, and that Sobieski was actually in the field, than his armies were let loose upon the Spanish Netherlands. Unable to anticipate the victory at Vienna, the French revenged it by seizing Courtrai and Dixmunde in the autumn, and bombarding Luxemburg before the end of the year. The French nobility had been forbidden to hasten to the defence of Christendom; and now were inclined to depreciate, at least in words, the victory they had not shared.

Amidst the general chorus of admiration and of thankfulness which rose from Europe, in France, and in France alone, were the deeds of Sobieski slighted. He had cut in pieces not only the Turks, but the prophecies which had filled Paris of the approaching downfall of the house of Austria. The allies of that house took a bolder tone; Spain talked of the declaration of that war against Louis which he had provoked for so long; the United Provinces listened to the warlike councils of the Prince of Orange; the Emperor spoke decidedly of succouring all his friends.

Far different was to be the progress of Louis' aggressions upon Germany, now that the overmastering fear of Turkish invasion was done away with, and the Turkish hold upon Hungary loosened. The alliance of Laxenberg and the other leagues were now to ripen into the great confederacy of Augsburg and the Grand Alliance.

Upon the Ottoman power the effect of the victory was decisive. Turkish rule in Hungary had received a blow from which it never recovered. It is true that Sobieski, advancing rashly with his cavalry alone, shortly involved himself in a disaster, near the bridge of the Danube, opposite Gran. The king himself had to ride for his life from the Turkish horsemen. The check, however, was avenged by the complete destruction of the force which had inflicted it; and the fortress of Gran, the most important place upon that side of Hungary, became the prize of the conqueror.

The views of Sobieski embraced the reduction of Buda, and, perhaps, of the whole of Hungary, in this campaign. But this was forbidden by the lateness of the season, still more by the jealousy of the Emperor. The king warred against the Turks, but not against the Hungarians. He sympathised with their efforts to regain their liberties, and strove to reconcile rather than to subdue Tekeli. Leopold was fearful of the establishment of a Polish interest in the country, and showed a studied neglect of his allies. But had other causes allowed, the insubordination of the Poles would have prevented further conquests. The Polish nobility, the political masters of their king, were foremost in clamouring for a return to their native country.

A prolonged career of conquest was impossible at the head of such a State and army. The hopes of a Hungarian alliance died away. Tekeli, after much hesitation, refused to enter into the negotiations which the king proposed; and reluctantly the deliverer of Christendom withdrew through Upper Hungary into Poland again, reducing some towns upon the road, but leaving his great work half done. His army melted in his hands. The tardy Lithuanians, too late for the fighting, arrived to add to his vexation in Moravia, where they disgraced their country by pillaging the people whom they had not helped to save.

But Sobieski was not alone in suffering from the emperor's ingratitude. Starhemberg, the defender of the city, was deservedly rewarded; but most of the others, from Lorraine downwards, who had participated in the battle, had little recompense for their services. Even the ardour of the Elector of Bavaria was for a time cooled by the coolness of the Emperor, though he returned again to the service of his future father-in-law. The Elector of Saxony, Waldeck, and others left the scene of the campaign to enjoy their triumph, or to plunge into other enterprises; but under Lorraine, and a series of generals, culminating in that Eugene of Savoy, who had seen his first service at Vienna, the Turks were driven foot by foot from Hungary. Kara Mustapha shortly paid for his defeat, as Ottoman commanders did pay—with his head, suffering not unjustly. But his successors, though less incompetent, were scarcely on the whole more fortunate than he.

In vain a new Kiuprili was found to head the Turkish armies and to reform the Turkish State.

A short gleam of success under his leadership was ended by his death in battle. In vain a *Sultan*, Mustapha II., again appeared himself at the head of his armies. The means of warfare of the Ottomans were to a great extent expended and lost beyond repair in the great disaster at Vienna. New enemies rose up against them in their weakness. Russia in the Ukraine, Venice in the Morea and in Dalmatia, began conquests at the expense of the Porte. The war indeed dragged on, delayed by the renewed contest between France and the Augsburg league; but the very weakness of Austria served merely to show more clearly the fallen fortunes of the Turks, who could make no lasting stand against her. Steadily upon the whole the fortunes of the Ottomans declined, though it was not till the great victory of Eugene at Zenta, in 1697, that they were driven reluctantly to treat. The peace signed at Carlowitz, in 1699, illustrates the altered relations of Europe since the beginning of the war, when the Turks h ad been a menace to Germany.

For the first time, a European conference considered the affairs of Turkey. England and Holland were mediators of the peace, that the Emperor might be more free to act with them in the coming war of the Spanish Succession. Sobieski had nearly three years earlier become a memory, with his victories, his schemes, and his disappointments, in the grave; and with him ended the ever unstable greatness of Poland. Another yet more notable northern sovereign, Peter the Czar, was a party to the negotiations. Everywhere was territory rent from Turkey. To Austria, she yielded nearly all of Hungary and Transylvania, with most of the Sclavonian lands between the Save and the Drave; to Poland, she gave up Podolia; to Russia, Azof; to Venice, the Morea and parts of Dalmatia.

One point she proudly refused to yield. The Hungarian Tekeli and his friends, who had sought her hospitality, were retained by her, safe from the vengeance of the emperor; as in 1849 other Hungarian exiles were shielded by the Turks, against the vengeance of Austria and of Russia combined. This was the first peace which had permanently reduced the frontiers of the Ottomans; it marked the termination of the last of the great Mohammedan aggressions upon Christendom; it saw the end of the secret understandings by which, since the days of Francis I., France had endeavoured to use Turkey for the subversion of Austria and for the ends of her own ambition.

The complete reversal of the former positions of the combatants, the disastrous termination of the war for Turkey the "rolling away of the stone of Tantalus that hung above *their* heads, the intolerable woe for the Germans, the far-reaching results of the struggle in the future history of Europe"—all are traceable to the day when the genius of Sobieski marked triumphantly, from the windy heights of the Kahlenberg, that fatal incapacity which should open for him the way, as victorious deliverer, to the foot of the ruined ramparts of Vienna.

But naturally, before concluding our consideration of the subject, we ask what gain did Poland, or the King of Poland, gather from the enterprise in which he had played so glorious a part? For a few months he was the centre of the admiring eyes of Christendom.

"L'empire du monde vous serait du si le ciel l'eût réservé à un seul po-

tentat," wrote Christina of Sweden from Rome, not without a glance at the pretensions of Louis XIV. To supremacy, and of Leopold to an imperial primacy in Europe. Never before had Poland filled so great a place in the eyes of the world. The cautions Venetians sought her special alliance. In the language of diplomacy, she was *Respublica Serenissima*; but untroubled she never was, and her greatness was of short duration.

It is true that the frontiers of the State were relieved of a constant fear. The Turks were for the time broken, the Tartars were crushed, the Cossacks of the Ukraine again reduced to submission. But Sobieski had fought and had conquered for others. His country was incapable of gathering the fruits of victory; incapable of prolonged effort, and therefore of lasting success. At the peace of Carlowitz, Podolia, with the fortress of Kaminiec, was recovered; but Moldavia had been in vain invaded by the Poles; and the Turks, it was soon seen, were beaten for the benefit of Austria; the Tartars for the benefit of Russia.

The King of Poland, alive to the shortcomings of his countrymen, was unable to correct them. A man who was at least the most eminent soldier, general we may not say, of Europe; a man who above all others living fulfilled the character of a hero; a king who had saved his country; a husband who was devoted to his wife, found himself thwarted by his subjects, and distracted by quarrels in his family. No doubt he laboured to render the crown hereditary in his house, a service to his country it would have been had he succeeded; but the jealousy of the Poles, still more that of the neighbouring sovereigns, and to some extent the misconduct of his wife, rendered this impossible. He found himself the object of an empty respect, but the wielder of no authority; he saw his country without order, without steadiness of purpose, unable to follow any settled policy in conjunction either with France or with the enemies of France.

The factions of the Diet left him without soldiers and without money. Not for the first, but nearly for the last time, the Poles were victorious in battle, but were destined to fail woefully in attaining the objects of war. The end was not far off. Sobieski was followed by a foreigner upon the throne, and within ten years of his death, Charles XII. of Sweden was disposing as a conqueror of the crown of Poland. The prey to the ambition of her neighbours his country has remained, now like her king a memory, to serve as a lesson of the consequences of the disregard of those restraints and of that self-control which alone can render freedom safe and liberty a blessing. For want of these her place has vanished from the map of Europe, sooner even than that of the foe whom she destroyed.

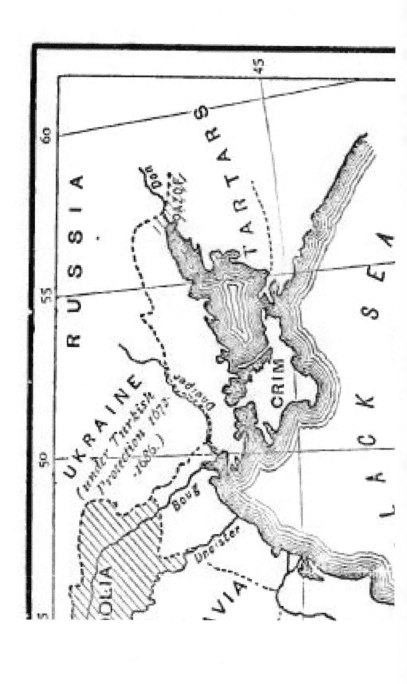

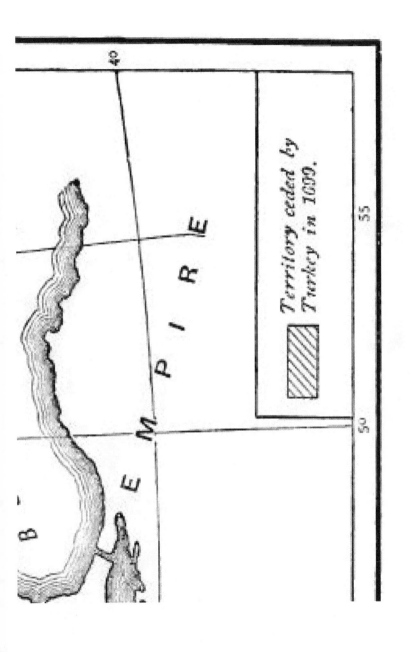

Territory ceded by
Turkey in 1000.

Sobieska at Vienna

(An extract from *The Life of King John Sobieski* by Count John Sobieski)

In the beginning of May, 1683, intelligence was received that the Ottoman forces were arriving out of Asia and Africa, in the vast and fertile plains of Adrianople, their usual place of rendezvous when they marched against the Christians. Mohammed came thither with his Court, in order to be nearer the scene of war and to give more life to the expedition. Lie might have attacked the empire of Germany, before the peace of Nimeguen, when Leopold was engaged with Louis XIV, and then the empire must have been destroyed. The Porte has been generally unfortunate in choosing its time to attack the Christians, who, by tearing one another to pieces so frequently, seem to, present themselves to its strokes. But, after all, if the danger was less now than before the peace of Nimeguen, it was still sufficiently great.

The general of the Ottoman forces was the Grand-Vizier Kara-Mustapha, the same who had already tried his fortunes against Sobieski at Trembowla and Leopol. He still continued in favour with the Sultana Valide; and, having also gained the high regard of Mohammed, had lately married his daughter. The *Sultan* does not give to every *vizier* his *catischerif*, that is to say, a full power; but the present had that honour conferred upon him, and perhaps never more unworthily so; a general who had hardly ever won a battle, who had done nothing to merit any such honour, he had received this distinguished token of regard from Mohammed from pure favouritism.

Never had ambition and pride, two passions that devoured him, a more extensive field in which to act. A hundred and forty thousand regular troops consisting of *janizaries*, *Spahis* and others; eighteen thousand Wallachians, Moldavians and Transylvanians, commanded by their respective princes; fifteen thousand Hungarians, led by Tekeli; fifty thousand Tartars, commanded by Selim-Gerai, their *cham*; and, if we include volunteers, officers of the baggage and provisions, work-men of all sorts and personal servants, the whole must have amounted to more than three hundred thousand men, thirty-one *bashaws*, five sovereign princes, with three hundred pieces of cannon; and the object of this mighty armament was equally great, the conquest of the western Empire.

The Imperial troops were commanded by Charles V, Duke of Lorraine, the same who was Sobieski's competitor for the crown of Poland in 1674. He was then young, but had already given proofs of having the soul of a hero. The duke's capacity, much more than his rank, procured him the command in chief which would have frightened any man but himself, for he had only thirty-seven thousand men to oppose that torrent of *Infidels* which came to overwhelm the Empire.

The *vizier* advanced on the right side of the Danube, passed the Save and the Drave, forced the duke before him and made a feint of attacking Raab while he detached fifty thousand Tartars on the road towards Vienna. The duke, perceiving the stratagem, made a stolen march in his turn; suffered a check at Patronel, and had scarce time to reach Vienna, where he threw in part of his infantry to re-enforce the garrison and took post in the island of Leopoldstadt, formed by the Danube on the north side of the city; while the Tartars arrived about the same time on the south.

Upon this occasion was seen one of those spectacles which ought to be a lesson to sovereigns and which move the compassion of their subjects, even when the sovereigns have ill-deserved their tenderness; Leopold, the most powerful emperor since Charles V, flying from his capital with the empress, his mother-in-law, the empress, his wife, the archduke, the archduchesses, and a great part of the inhabitants following the court in great disorder.

The whole country was filled with flying parties, equipages and wagons laden with goods—the last of which fell into the hands of the Tartars, at the very gates of Lintz. Even this city, which the Imperial family fled to in their first flight, did not seem a safe asylum, and they were forced to take refuge in Passaw. They lay the first night in a wood where the Empress, who was far advanced in her pregnancy, found that it was possible to sleep upon straw, surrounded on all sides by terror. Among the other horrors of this night, they had a view of the flames which already consumed Lower Hungary, and advanced towards Austria. The Turks were to be dreaded only as civilized warriors, who conquer by dint of valour; but the Tartars burned, murdered, and carried into slavery. They knew nothing of tenderness, of love, of mercy or of compassion. The deepest caves afforded an insecure retreat; the trembling victims were discovered by dogs trained to hunt men; and Tekeli, the chief of the Hungarians, upon this occasion, was a very Tartar.

The emperor, by only the first excesses that attended this eruption, paid dearly for his acts of violence in Hungary, and the blood of its nobles that he had spilt. He could not be persuaded that Kara-Mustapha would leave behind him such places as Raab and Comora and fall directly upon Vienna. The King of Poland, who knew better, as is always the case with those who make war in person, gave him warning of it but without effect.

Vienna had become, under ten successive emperors of the House of Austria, the capital of the Roman Empire in the West. Solyman, the Great, was the first Turkish emperor that marched against Vienna in 1529, after having been crowned King of Persia at Bagdad, making Europe and Asia tremble at the same time. He failed in his attempt not daring to contend against the fortune of Charles V, who marched to its relief with an army of eighty thousand men. Kara-Mustapha, who saw only a handful to oppose him, flattered himself that he should be more fortunate and began the siege on the seventh of July. The Germans are undoubtedly a brave people, but they have never appeared before the gates of Constantinople as the Turks have before those of Vienna.

The *vizier* pitched his camp in the plain on the southern side of the Danube and filled its whole extent, which is nine miles. This camp abounded with everything that was necessary for so vast a multitude, money, ammunition and provisions of every kind. The different quarters were commanded by *bashaws*, who displayed the magnificence of kings; but all this magnificence was eclipsed by the pomp of the *vizier*, who simply wallowed in luxury. A *grand vizier's* retinue usually consists of two thousand officers and servants, but the present had double that number.

His park, that is to say, the space enclosed by his tents, near the palace of the Favorite, was as extensive as the city he besieged. The lustre of the richest stuffs of gold and jewels seemed to contend with the highly polished glare of arms. It was furnished with baths, gardens, fountains and even curious animals for his amusement. He shut himself up with his young *icoglans* oftener than with his general officers. The *iman*, or minister of religion, who attended him in this expedition, threatened him with the divine indignation, but the *vizier* laughed at his menaces, and plunged himself deeper in debauchery.

In the meantime, the luxury of the general did not in the least diminish the valour of the *janizaries*, nor was the Turkish artillery at all less formidable.

Count Staremberg, a man of abilities and experience, who was now Governor of Vienna, and had formerly been so to his master, had set fire to the suburbs, and by a cruel necessity, burned the substance of the citizens, whom his object was to preserve. He had a garrison under him which was computed at sixteen thousand men, but in fact amounted only to eleven thousand at most.

The Duke of Lorraine, who had taken post on the island of Leopoldstadt and did his utmost to preserve a communication from thence with the city, thought himself obliged to retire from it, by the bridges which he had laid across the Danube and now ordered to bo broken down. Never was there a general in a more desperate situation. For, after he had thrown part of his infantry into Vienna, Raab and Comora, he had not thirty thousand men left to keep the field.

The Turks did not get possession of the counter-scrap till the seventh of August, after repeated engagements for twenty-three days together, with great loss of blood on both sides. Their mines, their continual attacks, the decrease of the garrison, the waste of provisions, all contributed to give the utmost uneasiness; and to so many real evils more imaginary ones were added.

The Duke of Lorraine wrote letter after letter to the King of Poland to hasten his march. Notwithstanding all the diligence he had used, his army could not be got together till towards the end of the month of August, 1683. He sent away the first bodies that arrived, and while the main body was getting ready, took up his residence at Cracow, where he did not throw away his time. His fondness for hunting, play and entertainments, never showed itself, but when the Republic was at peace. He examined into the details that he received of the siege; studied the situation of Vienna by a topographical map; considered the position of the Turks in every view; settled his order of battle and regulated his marches in order to fix the decisive day.

When he arrived at Tarnowitz, the first town of Siberia, he reviewed his army which amounted only to twenty-five thousand men and, consequently, far short of the number stipulated in the treaty. Before the review was over, he received a letter from the Emperor. A copy of it may serve to show the power of adversity upon haughty minds, and the return of their pride as soon as the danger was past.

The emperor says:

> We are convinced that, by reason of the vast distance of your
> army, it is absolutely impossible for it to come in time enough
> to contribute to the preservation of the place which is in the
> most imminent danger. It is not therefore your troops, Sire, that
> we expect, but your Majesty's own presence; being fully per-
> suaded that if your royal person will vouchsafe to appear at the
> head of our forces, though less numerous than those of the en-
> emy, your name alone, which is so justly dreaded by them, will
> make their defeat certain.

It must certainly have cost Leopold a great deal to make this condescension. As soon as he despaired of seeing the Polish army, nothing
hindered him from putting himself at the head of his own troops; but
the past and the present made him feel the necessity of another commander to whom he no longer scrupled to attribute the qualities of
a hero, or to accede the title of *Majesty*, which he had before refused
him. The emperor concluded his letter with a minute account of all
the troops that he was assembling, and which were to arrive forthwith
at the bridge where they were to pass the Danube, assuring the king
that the bridge was already finished. Time will show that the emperor
soon altered his language in regard to King John, and was mistaken in
his facts. His letter is preserved to this day in the archives of Poland.

★★★★★★

The critical situation of affairs, and the confidence which Leopold
reposed in the Polish ruler determined the king to take a step which
exposed his own person to danger.

Leaving his army to the care of the Grand-General Jablonowski,
he resolved to go forward himself, according to Leopold's request,
and even to give battle without it if the preservation of Vienna required it. In order to get thither, he had no route to take but across
Silesia, Moravia, and that part of Austria which lies to the north of the
Danube; three provinces that were infested by Hungarians, Turks and
Tartars whom the Duke of Lorraine, with all his splendid ability and
courage, despaired of keeping within bounds any longer.

The king, in his march, had only two thousand cavalrymen. Other
kings, even in the midst of an army, have a second army for their
guard. His equipage was no greater than that of the brave soldiers that
marched with him. Here was another instance of the democratic spirit
of the great king which endeared him so much to his soldiers; he did

not claim for himself more than he would concede to them. Nothing but a chaise attended him, which even Prince James, his own son, made no use of; they both travelled all the way on horseback. It is not every king that is formed to be a hero; indeed, very few of them, but whoever is animated with that glorious ambition must be able to endure fatiguing marches, suffer hardships and expose himself to dangers like a common soldier, whenever occasion requires it.

Napoleon the Great, of more modern days, was a fair example of this. John III was so far from discovering any fear that he himself recovered the whole country from its consternation. The peasants, who had sown only that they might not reap, and regretted the fate of their massacred friends, ran together from every hamlet to see their deliverer, and considered themselves as already delivered. His own troops that he had conducted through so many dangers, stood also in need of being encouraged, and he saw to it that no opportunity was left unimproved to strengthen and encourage them.

One morning, when he was a few miles from Olmutz, an eagle flew by him on the right, and, as the Poles had retained some faith in omens, he told them a story out of the Roman history, and the flight of an eagle was considered as a token of victory. Another day, upon the weather's clearing up, after a thick mist, an inverted rainbow (a phenomenon not common, but which sometimes happens) was seen upon the surface of a meadow. The reader will bear in mind that the symbol of the Turkish power was the crescent, and this rainbow formed a crescent, but was upside down. The soldiers fancied it to be miraculous, and the king did all he could to confirm them in this belief.

At length, the king reached the banks of the Danube which it was impossible to pass by the bridges of Vienna, in sight of the enemy. He therefore marched to Tuln, a small town on the right side of the river, fifteen miles from Vienna. Leopold had written to John that the bridge at Tuln was finished, whereas, they were now at work upon it. The same letter told him that he would find the German troops assembled in readiness; but he saw only the Duke of Lorraine's little army and two battalions that guarded the head of the bridge. At this sight he broke out in a passion:

Does the emperor take me for an adventurer? I have left my own army because he assured me that his was ready. Is it for myself, or him, that I come to fight?

The duke, whose prudence was equal to his valour, quieted his indignation.

The Polish Army was left at a great distance; and yet, to the amazement of everyone, it arrived before the Germans. The quickness of its march did great honour to the Grand-General Jablonowski who made his appearance on the fifth of September.

The German generals, leaving their troops behind, were come to attend the king and could not help expressing some disquiet at the great day that was approaching. The king says contemptuously:

> Consider the general you have to deal with, and not the multitude that he commands. Which of you at the head of two hundred thousand men would have suffered this bridge to be built within fifteen miles of his camp? This man has no ability to command. We shall conquer him easily.

The Polish Army was, by this time, passing the bridge. The cavalrymen were universally admired for their horses, their dress and fine appearance. This was probably one of the most remarkable bodies of cavalry that ever appeared upon a field of battle. Every man was a nobleman, that is, each possessed a title of nobility; every one of them was a knight and commanded by their king, the most knightly man of that age or any other age. The infantry, however, was not so well clothed, and did not make so good an appearance. One battalion among the rest being remarkably ill-clad, Prince Lubormirski advised the king, for the honour of the nation, to let it pass in the night. The king was of a different opinion, and when the battalion was crossing the bridge he exclaimed:

> Look at it well; it is an invincible body that has taken an oath never to wear any clothes but what it takes from the enemy. In the last war they were clad in the Turkish costumes.

If this encomium did not furnish them with clothes, it certainly armed them with courage.

The Poles, when they had crossed the bridge, extended themselves upon the right and were exposed for twenty-four hours together to be cut in pieces, if Kara-Mustapha had known how to make the most of his advantages. At length the bodies of German troops arrived, one after another, and the whole Christian Army was assembled by the 7th to the amount of seventy-four thousand men.

From the camp at Tuln, they heard the roar of the Turkish batteries. Vienna was reduced to the last extremity, and many officers of the first merit had lost their lives. The grave continued open, without ever closing its mouth. The dysentery, a disorder as destructive as the sword, carried off sixty persons a day. Staremberg himself was attacked by it. There were not more than three or four officers left to a battalion; most of these were wounded; and nearly all of their chief officers were gone. The soldiers, worn out with fatigue and bad rations, could scarcely walk to the bridge; and those who escaped the fire of the enemy died of weakness. The citizens, who at first partook in all the labours of the siege, had recourse to prayer as their only defence, and ran in crowds to the churches where the bombs and balls carried terror with them.

The Duke of Lorraine had just received a letter from Staremberg who, in the beginning of the siege, had the firmness and even confidence to write, "I will not surrender the place, but with the last drop of my blood." What a splendid contrast was the spirit of this noble commander compared with that of the cowardly, craven Emperor Leopold! At present he had scarce a gleam of hope remaining. His letter contained only these words:

No more time to lose, my Lord, no more time to lose.

The stupid inaction of Kara-Mustapha cannot be accounted for, except that it was a spirit of over-confidence. It is certain that if at this time he had made a general attack, Vienna must have fallen. But avarice extinguished the thunder that he held in his hand. He entertained a notion that the place of residence of the emperors of Germany must contain immense treasures; and he was afraid that he should lose this imaginary wealth by the city's being pillaged, as it inevitably would be, if taken by storm. He chose therefore to stay till the place surrendered; an event which, he continued to flatter himself, would occur at any hour. Nor did his presumption contribute less to blind him than his avarice. He jested at the weakness of the Christian Army, which he thought still weaker than it was, and could not suppose it would have the boldness to come and attack him. His intelligence was so bad that he was still ignorant of King John's coming in person. Of all the princes in the league, the *vizier* dreaded him the most, and we shall soon see that he had just cause.

The king, when he was just going to march, gave out the order of battle with his own hand; the following is a copy of it, as found among his manuscripts:

The centre is to consist of the Imperial troops to which we shall add the regiment of cavalry belonging to the Chevalier Lubormirski, Marshal of the Court, and four or five squadrons of our horse-guards; in the room of which we expect to have dragoons, or other German troops. This body is to be commanded by the Duke of Lorraine.

The Polish Army, commanded by the Grand-General, Jablonowski, and the other generals of that nation, is to make the right wing.

The troops belonging to the Electors of Bavaria and Saxony are to be placed on the left wing, to which we shall add also some squadrons of our horse guards, and other Polish cavalry, instead of which they are to give us dragoons on foot.

The cannon is to be divided, and, in case the Electors have not enough, the Duke of Lorraine is to furnish them with some of his. This wing is to consist entirely of the troops belonging to the Electors.

The troops of the circles of the Empire are to extend along the Danube with the left wing, inclining a little towards the right; and this, for two reasons: First, to keep the enemy in alarm, for fear of being charged in flank; and, secondly, to be in readiness to throw the enemy into the city, in case we should not make an impression upon the enemy so soon as we hope. This body is to be commanded by the Prince of Waldec.

The first line is to consist wholly of foot, with artillery, and to be followed closely by a line of horse. If these two lines were to be mixed, they would embarrass each other in passing the defiles, woods and mountains; but, as soon as we enter the plain, the cavalry is to take post in the intervals between the battalions, which shall be left for that purpose. This order is to be observed particularly by our own horse guards, which shall charge first.

If we draw up all our troops in three lines only, we shall take up more than a German league and a half, which would not be for our advantage; and, besides, we must, in this case, pass the little river of Vien, which ought to be left on our right. We must therefore make four lines; and the fourth will serve for a body of reserve.

For the greater security of the infantry against the first attack of the Turkish horse, which is always very warm, great use might be made of *spancheraistres* or *chevaux-de-frize*; but they must be very light in order to be carried conveniently and, as often as the battalions halt, be placed at their head.

I make it my earnest request to all the generals, that, as fast as the army comes down the last mountain to enter upon the plain, they will each take their posts according to the directions given in this present order.

They had only a march of fifteen miles to get at the Turks who were separated from them by nothing but a chain of mountains. Across these there lay two roads, one over the highest part of the ridge; the other in a place where the hills were lower and the passage more easy. The Council of War, being assembled, was for taking the latter; but the king determined upon the former which was much shorter; nor did any of the princes murmur, because he convinced them that the fate of Vienna depended upon a single moment, and that there are cases when expedition ought to be preferred to caution.

On the 9th of September the whole army was in motion. The Germans, after several attempts to draw up their cannon, despaired of success and left them in the plain. The Poles were more persevering, for Konski, Palatine of Kiovia, commander of the artillery, succeeded in getting over twenty-eight pieces and none but these were used on the day of battle.

This march, which was encumbered with all sorts of difficulties, continued for three days. Two of them passed without the king's being seen by his Polish Army, which began to demand where he was with the utmost anxiety. It appeared that the king had been among the troops of the Empire, endeavouring to encourage them to battle.

The army at length drew near to the last mountain, called Kalemberg. From the top of this hill, the Christians were presented, about an hour before night, with one of the finest and most dreadful prospects of the greatness of human power—an immense plain, and all the islands of the Danube, covered with pavilions whose magnificence seemed rather calculated for an encampment of pleasure than to endure hardships of war—an innumerable multitude of horses, camels, and buffaloes; two hundred thousand men, all in motion; swarms of Tartars dispersed along the foot of the mountain in their usual confusion; the fire of the besiegers incessant and terrible, and that of the besieged such as they could possibly make; in fine, a great city, distinguishable only by the tops of the steeples, and the fire and smoke that covered it.

The besieged were immediately apprised, by signals, of the approach of the army to their relief. To have an idea of the joy that the city felt, a person must have suffered all the extremities of a long siege, and be destined with his wife and children to the sword of a merciless conqueror, or to slavery in a foreign country. But this gleam of joy was soon succeeded by fear. Kara-Mustapha, with such an army, had still reasons to expect success though he did not deserve it. The King, who was examining the disposition of his forces, said to the German generals:

This man is badly encamped; he knows nothing of war; we shall certainly beat him.

It would seem that the quick, experienced eyes of Sobieski, with that wonderful intuition of a great commander, could quickly take in and notice all the faults of an antagonist. It is well known that Marshal Villars, then ingloriously employed in the Cevennes, foretold the defeat of Dillard from the bad disposition of his troops at the Battle of Hochstet, and every general who cannot prophesy in the same manner ought to give up his command.

The cannon on both sides was the prelude to the important scene of the following day, which was the 12th of September, a day that was to decide whether Vienna under Mohammed IV should have the fate of Constantinople under Mohammed II., and whether the Empire of the West should be reunited to the Empire of the East; perhaps also whether Europe should continue a Christian continent.

★★★★★★

A few hours before the break of day the king, the Duke of Lorraine and several of the Generals joined in an act of religion which was very much practiced in those days, not so much in ours. They asked the protection of the Son of God, while the Turks were invoking the one God of Abraham by repeated cries of *Allah! Allah!*

This cry redoubled about sunrising, when the Christian Army descended from the mountain with a slow and even pace, keeping its ranks together, preceded by its cannon, and halting every few steps, to fire and load again. The front grew wider and deeper in proportion as the space enlarged. The plain was a vast amphitheatre where the Turks, in the utmost agitation, beheld the motions of their enemies. It was at this time that the *cham* of the Tartars bade the *vizier* observe the lances adorned with streamers belonging to the Polish horse guards and said to him, "the king is at their head," words which filled him with dismay. However superior his own army was in point of numbers, he now knew that he must meet and must combat a leader who had never failed of victory.

The *vizier* ordered the Tartars to put all their prisoners, to the number of thirty thousand, to death. These prisoners had been gathered together, in the march to Vienna, from towns and villages *en route*. They were composed of all classes, rich and poor, bond and free, male and female, and of all ages. Instantly he then ordered his troops to march towards the mountain, and at the same time ordered a general assault to be made upon the place. This last order should have been given sooner, for the Christians had now recovered courage, while the *Janizaries*, provoked at their general, had lost it.

In the meantime, the Christians were coming down and the Turks ascended to meet them, so that the action was soon begun. The first line of the Christian Army, consisting wholly of foot, charged with such impetuosity that it made room for the line of cavalry which took post in the interval between the battalions. The king, the princes and the generals advancing to the front, fought sometimes with the horse and sometimes with the foot. The two other lines followed close upon the foremost. Konski, whose skill in military art was equal to his intrepidity in action, had the care of the artillery which was loaded with cartridge-shot, and fired at a very small distance.

The scene of this first engagement, in the ground between the plain and the mountain, was broken by vineyards, rising grounds, and little valleys. The enemy, having left their cannon at the entrance of the vineyards, suffered much from those of the Christians. The combatants, being dispersed about on the unequal ground, disputed it with great fury till towards noon when the Count de Maligni, brother to the Queen of Poland, got possession of a rising ground which took the Turks in flank, who, being driven from hill to hill, retired towards the plain and drew up along the border of their camp.

The Christian Army, the left wing in particular, transported at this success and crying out victory, must needs push their advantages without intermission. Their ardour was unquestionably noble but the king thought it dangerous. The German cavalry, being heavily mounted, would soon have been out of wind in the distance between them and the enemy. A still stronger reason was that all the different bodies having been engaged, sometimes upon rising grounds and sometimes in valleys, had inevitably fallen into some confusion and disturbed the order of battle.

Some time therefore was taken to repair the disorder, and the plain became the scene of a triumph which posterity will always have a difficulty to believe. Seventy thousand men marched to attack two hundred thousand, and the reader must keep in mind that the Turks and Tartars were well instructed and drilled in the art of war, and in accoutrements and in all preparations of a soldier they could not be excelled, and that they possessed qualities that made them regarded as being the best soldiers of the world. This will give the reader some sort of a conception of the daring of seventy thousand men in attacking this mighty host. In the Turkish Army, the Bashaw of Diarbekir commanded the right wing, the Bashaw of Buda the left, and the *vizier* was in the canter, having with him the *aga* of the *Janizaries* and the general of the *Spahis*.

The two armies continued motionless for some time, apparently like gladiators in the arena, each one waiting for the other to strike the first blow; the Christians in silence; the Turks and Tartars with their deafening cries accompanied by the sound of clarions. In this awful moment a red pavilion was erected in the midst of the *Infidels* and close to it the great standard of Mohammed, a sacred object to the professors of the Mussulman faith, like the *labanim* of the Roman emperors, or the *oriflamme* of the ancient Kings of France. But this imposture, which sometimes inspires them with as much courage as Truth can give the Christians, did not do its office on this great occasion, for the *vizier* had deprived it of all its virtue.

As soon as the king had given orders for the charge, the Polish cavalry, sabre in hand, pushed vigorously on to the *vizier*, whose post was made manifest by the standard. The first ranks were instantly forced and the Poles penetrated even to the numerous squadrons that surrounded the *vizier*. The *Spahis* disputed the victory, but all the rest, Walachians, Moldavians, Transylvanians, Tartars and even *Janizaries* themselves, showed no alacrity, a fatal effect of an army's hating and despising its general. It is doubtful whether in all the world's history we have a single instance where an army that has not the most complete and thorough confidence in its general has ever been victorious, and never where they distrusted or despised their leader.

The *vizier* attempted to recover their good opinion by showing courage and good behaviour, but he had lost his opportunity. He addressed himself next to the Bashaw of Buda and the other generals, who answered him only with a silence of despair.

259

"And thou," said he to the Tartar prince, "dost thou too refuse to help me?"

The *cham* saw no safety but in flight. The *Spahis* were now reduced to their last efforts. The Polish horse had broken and scattered them, and the great green standard of the Ottoman Empire disappeared, the *vizier* turned his back, and his flight made the consternation universal. It was soon communicated from the centre to the wings, which were hard pressed by all the divisions of the Christian Army at the same time; the left by Jablonowski, the right by the Electors, while the Duke of Lorraine fell upon the centre and the king animated the whole by his actions and his orders. That immense multitude which, under an able leader, ought to have surrounded and overwhelmed its enemies in so extensive a plain, was deprived by terror of all strength and presence of mind. Had night been farther off it would have been a total defeat; as things were it was only a precipitate retreat.

The king advanced next towards the *Janizaries*, who were left to continue the siege, but they had all disappeared and Vienna was completely delivered. The victorious troops would fain have entered the enemy's camp, allured by the immense riches that the Turks had left, but the temptation was a dangerous one at this juncture. The enemy, favoured by the darkness of the night, might return and cut in pieces an army which would be too much employed in pillage to make any defence. An order was therefore issued to continue all night under arms upon pain of death.

******

About six in the morning the enemy's camp was opened to the soldiers, whose desire for plunder was at first paralyzed, as it were, by a most shocking spectacle. In several parts of the camp mothers were butchered, some of whom had their children still hanging at their breasts. These women were of good repute, not like a certain class that sometimes follows the army and are always a pest to the army and the morals of the soldiers. They were virtuous wives whom their husbands chose rather to kill than to dispose to the lusts of the Christians. The children escaped this slaughter, and five or six hundred of them were preserved, whom the Bishop of Newstadt took care of and educated in the religion of the conquerors. It seems to have been a practice for the Mohammedans to take their families with them upon these campaigns. It seems so strange as we view it from our standpoint, that they should have in this way exposed their loved ones to all the horrors and the vicissitudes of war.

Never did an army get possession of more abundant spoil; for the Turks, who are economists in time of peace, display great magnificence in the field. The hero of the day had his share upon the present occasion. He wrote to the queen that the *grand vizier* had made him his heir, and that he had found in his tent the value of several millions of *ducats*. He added:

You will have no room to say of me what the women of Tartary say, when their husbands return empty-handed: 'You are no men because you come back without plunder.'

Among the many things which fell into the hands of the soldiers there were two which attracted the notice of all but excited the covetousness of none. One was a large standard which, in the hurry of joy, was taken for that of Mohammed. But this was certainly a mistake, for the singular precautions that the Turks used had always prevented this calamity. The standard is enclosed in an ark of gold with the *Alcoran* and the robe of the Prophet. This ark is carried by a camel which goes before the *Sultan* or *vizier*; and, when the standard is displayed in battle, an officer of the race of Mohammed, called the Naikbul-Eschret, was appointed to watch the event of the combat; and, when the victory inclines ever so little to the side of the enemy, the guard at once disappears with all haste from the field of battle with the sacred *deposinum*.

The *vizier*, upon the present occasion, accompanied this officer in his flight. But the Christians, who were fond of being mistaken in this fact, have persisted in declaring that they possess the famous standard; and the historians, one after another, not excepting the celebrated author of the *Annals of the Empire*, have adopted their mistake. The other sacred implement that made part of the booty was a picture of the Virgin found in the *vizier's* tent, with this inscription in Latin:

Per hanc imaginem victor eris, Johannes.
Per hanc imaginem victor ero Johannes.

The first line, "John, by this image thou shalt conquer," comes from the Virgin; to which John answers, "By this image, I, John, will conquer." It was evidently an imitation of the sign which Constantine claims to have seen in the air when he was marching to give battle to Maxentius.

The image gave occasion for much speculation. Some thought it very remarkable that the Vizier should have in his tent a presage of his approaching ruin which ought rather to have been in King John's possession. Others insisted that no miraculous facts should be admitted without an application of the test of severe criticism. The image, however, was placed in a magnificent chapel, built by the Queen of Poland and the supposed standard of Mohammed was sent to the Pope as an act of homage to the Lord of Hosts. All the cannon remained to the emperor and the Empire also. The Turks lost a great many colours and it is well known that colours are never surrendered but with great effusion of blood; and indeed, if we take only a transitory view of two armies disputing at first against each other, foot to foot, for six hours, a spot of ground full of eminences and vineyards, and afterwards coming to a general action, this will be sufficient to show that it could not be done without considerable loss; but this loss will, after all, be thought small and was so in effect for so great a victory.

The next day after the victory was a day of glory. Staremberg, the brave commander of the city, who had so resolutely and so gallantly and with so small a force of men, resisted the mighty hosts of the Turks for two whole months, had come to pay his respects to the deliverer of Vienna, for here King John thought he might show triumph without offending the emperor, and entered the city over its ruins amidst the acclamations of the people. His horse could scarce get through the multitudes that fell prostrate before him, coming to kiss his feet and calling him their father, their saviour, the noblest of all princes. Vienna in this moment of joy forgot that it had a jealous master; and that master was their cowardly craven Emperor.

Leopold, who expected to have a triumph in his capital, though he had not been present at the battle, advanced by the Danube, scarce venturing to cast his eye upon the smoking ruins of so many hamlets, villages, gardens and country-seats. As he drew near the city he heard the firing of cannon, not intended for him. He was wounded to the very heart with this thought, and turning to the Count de Sintzendors, said to him:

The weakness of the counsels that you have had a share in occasions me this disgrace.

These words, uttered with that imperious tone which always crushes a courtier, affected the minister so much, it is said, that he died the next day. A minister who should die of grief at having advised a measure productive of misery to the people, would deserve tears.

The emperor suspended his march, that he might not be a spectator of King John's triumph. A difficulty of ceremony contributed to stop him; the question was, whether an elective King had ever been present with an emperor, and in what manner he had been received? The Duke of Lorraine, who listened only to the voice of gratitude, answered, "With open arms, if he has preserved the Empire."

The emperor was attentive only to his Imperial dignity, and gave King John to understand that he would not give him his hand, which was the reception the King of Poland expected of a sovereign prince. After much negotiation, the matter was settled by arranging to have the two sovereigns meet on horse-back upon the open plain.

When the moment of the interview arrived, the King of Poland, in a Polish bonnet and plume of feathers terminated by a large pearl hanging loose, clad in the same armour that he wore on the day of the battle, with a Roman Buckler, on which were engraved, "Not the actions of his ancestors, but his own," and mounted upon a stately horse with magnificent equippings, approached the emperor with that heroic presence which nature had given him, and that air which his victory gave him a right to put on. The Emperor talked of nothing but the services done the Poles in all ages by the friendship and protection of the emperors.

At last, however, he let drop the word gratitude for the deliverance of Vienna. At this word the king, turning his horse, said to him: "Brother, I am glad that I have done you that small service." He was going to put an end to the discourse, which grew disagreeable, but he observed his son, Prince James, alight from his horse to pay his respects to the emperor: "This is a prince," said he, "whom I am educating for the service of Christendom."

The emperor, without saying a word, only nodded his head; and yet this was the young prince whom he had promised to make his son-in-law. Such a picture can only be truly outlined before our later and broader visions, as free dwellers in the free country of our adoption and the true outlines of such a scene serve to make the Polish king, regal democrat as he was, a kingly sight indeed.

The king's dissatisfaction with the emperor would naturally have induced him to return to his own dominions, after having saved the Empire. This was what the Republic intended, and the queen desired; and this is what he should have done. But he flattered himself that Leopold, notwithstanding his strange behaviour, would still perform his promises. The double hope of a match between an archduchess and his son, and of the crown of Poland's being made hereditary in his family, which hope he had, no doubt, deservedly nurtured, supported him against the Imperial pride.

Kara-Mustapha, after his defeat, retired to Buda where he expected his fate. His being the son-in-law of Mohammed, was of great use to him, but the Sultana Valide of still greater. The Sultans have a particular respect for their mothers, even beyond what nature prescribes. As Mohammed was full of this filial respect for his mother, she suborned witnesses who were glad to gain preferment by compliances that are often common enough in courts. The disaster at Vienna was imputed to persons far less criminal than the *vizier*. The Bashaw of Buda was strangled and lamented by the whole Ottoman Empire. It is true he had, on the present occasion, given up the *vizier* to the arms of the Christians but such a defection scarce ever happens but to a despised or detested general. The fault, however, was inexcusable and he paid for it with his head. Three other *bashaws* fell with him. The *cham* of the Tartars was deposed, a punishment which he could not have deserved under another *vizier*.

The same courier who was charged with these cruel orders brought the real criminal distinguished marks of his continuing still in favour; but it was upon condition of his repairing this misfortune. For, vanquished as he was, he still had an army far superior to that of the conquerors; and the lists were again opened.

★★★★★★

The King of Poland began his march on the 17th of September, to complete the destruction of his enemy, for he thought that nothing was done while anything still remained to do. He was followed by the German army, but not so numerous as it was at the battle before Vienna.

A body of some six or seven thousand Turks, all cavalry, had passed the Danube at Strigonia, in order to guard the head of the bridge belonging to that town. It was commanded by a young man who was the *bashaw*, named Kara-Mehemed, born for war, full of fire, ambition, and courage, and who was resolved to deserve his fortune.

The Polish troops always encamped before the rest of the army. The king flattered himself with the hopes of crushing this handful of Turks and taking the fort of Barcan at Strigonia; but, not choosing that the Germans should share in this victory, he concealed from them his march. The 7th of October was a day of blood. The Turks being covered with a rideau, the Polish vanguard did not think them so near and was attacked before it could draw up in order of battle. Disorder and confusion instantly seized the Poles; nothing was to be seen but flying parties and heads falling by the sabre. This seems to be but a reaction of what has often been known in the history of warfare. The bravest troops in the world, the best handled and the best led, will sometimes, when surprised, become panic stricken and become unmanageable and flee like cravens. An instance of this, later in the world's history, was the flight of Napoleon's old guard from the field of Waterloo.

In the midst of this disorder, the king came up with the main body of horse, but his presence did not stop the panic stricken troops. The young *bashaw* redoubled his activity, and the king had scarce time to form his line. He received the Turks with firmness and even charged them in turn. But the Turks opening their ranks to enclose the whole Polish line, and being stimulated with that rage which distinguished the Mohammedans under the first *cailiffs*, drove back the left wing, forced the right and penetrated the centre. The Towarisz were no longer that intrepid band which, about a century before, had said to their king: "What hast thou to fear with twenty thousand lances? If the sky should fall we would keep it up with their points."

In this universal disorder, when every moment added the dying to the dead and it became equally as dangerous to retreat as to resist, the Grand-General Jablonowski besought the king to escape with his son who fought by his side, and this was effected with the greatest difficulty.

When this battle was over, the calm that succeeded presented a deplorable scene. The Polish nobles, who had escaped the slaughter, with downcast eyes and dejected countenance, surrounded their master in mournful silence. The German generals also had an air of sadness; but the king knew what was in their hearts. He said, with that candour which is never found but in great minds

Gentlemen, I confess I wanted to conquer without you, for the honour of my own nation: I have suffered severely for it, being soundly beaten, but I will take my revenge with you, and for you. To effect this must be the chief employment of our thoughts.

This eloquence of the heart is perhaps superior to all the speeches in the world.

The young *bashaw*, proud of the advantage he had gained over so great a king, with an inferior force, was thinking, on his side, of gathering fresh laurels. He dispatched couriers the same night to Buda, with an account of his victory. The *grand-vizier*, without losing a moment, sent a body of twenty thousand cavalry, which arrived next day by the bridge of Strigonia, the distance being no more than eighteen miles.

The King of Poland, who had recovered his strength by a night's rest, employed the whole following day, which was the 8th, in collecting his scattered army, and counselling it for the misfortune of yesterday, in animating it to vengeance, in combining it with the Imperial troops, and in regulating the order of battle for the morrow.

The letter he wrote to the queen, dated this day, informing her frankly of his terrible disaster, was enough to freeze her blood. He told her that he was advancing towards the enemy and that she must expect the enemy to be defeated or bid him farewell forever.

Tekeli, who was ordered by the *vizier* to advance with thirty thousand men, had not arrived on the morning of the 9th when the engagement began. Anyone but the young *bashaw* would have avoided an action, or at least would not have fought it. It will scarce be believed that twenty-six thousand Turks, all cavalry, and without cannon, could venture a battle against fifty thousand Christians, provided with all the advantages of infantry, cavalry and artillery. The two *bashaws* of Silistria and Caramania, commanded the wings. The general, elated with his late victory and promising himself another, was in the centre.

The Christian Army outstretched that of the Turks, by a full half of its front, and was putting itself in motion to begin the charge, when the Turks, who were quicker, fell upon them with an impetuosity, attended with howlings, which it is impossible to describe. A torrent that tumbles from the top of a mountain's brow is neither more noisy nor more rapid. The Christians received them with such firmness that not a man lost his post and with such a terrible fire that brought men and horses to the ground. The Turks wheeled round to recover a little, and instantly returned with greater fury. It was owing to the *chevaux de frize*, placed at the head of the battalions of the Christian Army, that they were not broken. The Turks were often on the point of succeeding and as often repulsed. Never did squadrons perform their evolutions with greater dexterity and quickness nor was the excellence of the Turkish horses ever more fully displayed.

The *bashaws* that commanded the wings, both covered with blood, were made prisoners, but the general still did everything that could be expected from the most determined courage. He forced his way into the centre but being wounded at length in two places with a sabre, and perceiving that the strength of his troops was exhausted he thought of making his retreat.

The King of Poland, who observed his first disposition towards it, did not allow him time to execute his intention but advanced at the head of his cavalry to take him in flank and cut off his retreat. The first squadrons were already seen retiring over the bridge. The Christian Army now gave a great shout in its turn and, quickening its march, extended itself in the form of a crescent and came up with the enemy.

The whole was nothing now but a scene of slaughter to the Turks, whose sole object was to fly. Some got to the bridge, but the cannon swept it from end to end; and, being built of boats, it was soon overloaded and sunk under the weight. Others ran towards the fort but the fort could hold no more and drove them back. Many threw themselves into the Danube which was covered with men and horses, but the shot reached them even here, and the river swallowed them up. A body of eighteen thousand, who would not attempt this dangerous way, stayed upon the side of the river in much greater danger. The *Janazaries* in the fort were spectators of this slaughter and expected this to be their fate. They made all possible signals of surrender; hung out a white flag, and for fear it should not be taken notice of, tore off the sleeves of their shirts and fastened them to the ends of their weapons.

But this day was not a day of mercy. Their sentence of death was written upon their palisadoes, whereupon the Polish soldiers saw the bleeding heads of their brethren. The rage that seized them at this sight cost them fresh tears which they might easily have prevented. The *Janazaries*, upon the point of being forced when they offered to surrender, made a discharge which did great execution. It was an act of mere despair in the last moment they had to live. Of the twenty-six thousand Turks that were in this engagement, only two thousand escaped before the breaking down of the bridge. The young *bashaw* who would have deserved a second victory, if valour was a sufficient title to it, was one of the number.

Every circumstance of this engagement, the bloodiest of that age, was astonishing. A young warrior, who had never been in any command, venturing to combat with veteran generals and defying the hero of the age; twenty-six thousand Mohammedans fighting a pitched battle against fifty thousand Christians who were upon the point of being defeated; these same Mohammedans, more than men in the beginning of the action, and less than women in the end; Christians imbruing their hands after the victory in the blood of eighteen thousand men who begged for mercy; a truth which I would willingly suppress if my respect for the fidelity of history would permit it.

The extraordinary courage which Mohammed manifested in the beginning of this battle and in the battle of the day before, all proceeded from one man; the young Bashaw of Buda who was youthful, ambitious and filled with enthusiasm; he electrified his army. This was entirely the reverse of former contests and he almost snatched victory from the jaws of defeat. It is one of the marvels of history.

The taking of Strigonia put an end to the campaign and the armies separated. The Poles, before they could reach their native land, had a march of hundreds of miles. Christiana, then at Rome, wrote to the Conqueror that he had "made her feel, for the first time, the passion of envy, for she really grudged him the glorious title of deliverer of Christendom." This was the ex-Queen Christiana of Sweden, the daughter of the great Gustavus Adolphus, one of the greatest soldiers of his day and the champion of Protestant Europe; but his erratic daughter who succeeded him finally, after many misadventures, resigned her crown and entered the Catholic church and went to live and die at Rome.

The scene ended tragically on the side of the Turks. The deposition of the Cham of Tartary, and the sacrifice of four *bashaws* immediately after the affair at Vienna, was not sufficient to appease the murmurs of the Ottoman Empire. Tekeli was sent to Constantinople, bound hand and foot. Kara-Mustapha was strangled and his head carried to Constantinople, a fitting end to the general who had no sense of shame; a brute by nature, and possessed of very few qualities of manhood, who owed his elevation to favouritism alone.

LEONAUR

ALSO FROM LEONAUR

AVAILABLE IN SOFTCOVER OR HARDCOVER WITH DUST JACKET

THE FALL OF THE MOGHUL EMPIRE OF HINDUSTAN *by H. G. Keene*—
By the beginning of the nineteenth century, as British and Indian armies under Lake and Wellesley dominated the scene, a little over half a century of conflict brought the Moghul Empire to its knees.

LADY SALE'S AFGHANISTAN *by Florentia Sale*—An Indomitable Victorian Lady's Account of the Retreat from Kabul During the First Afghan War.

THE CAMPAIGN OF MAGENTA AND SOLFERINO 1859 *by Harold Carmichael Wylly*—The Decisive Conflict for the Unification of Italy.

FRENCH'S CAVALRY CAMPAIGN *by J. G. Maydon*—A Special Correspondent's View of British Army Mounted Troops During the Boer War.

CAVALRY AT WATERLOO *by Sir Evelyn Wood*—British Mounted Troops During the Campaign of 1815.

THE SUBALTERN *by George Robert Gleig*—The Experiences of an Officer of the 85th Light Infantry During the Peninsular War.

NAPOLEON AT BAY, 1814 *by F. Loraine Petre*—The Campaigns to the Fall of the First Empire.

NAPOLEON AND THE CAMPAIGN OF 1806 *by Colonel Vachée*—The Napoleonic Method of Organisation and Command to the Battles of Jena & Auerstädt.

THE COMPLETE ADVENTURES IN THE CONNAUGHT RANGERS *by William Grattan*—The 88th Regiment during the Napoleonic Wars by a Serving Officer.

BUGLER AND OFFICER OF THE RIFLES *by William Green & Harry Smith*—With the 95th (Rifles) during the Peninsular & Waterloo Campaigns of the Napoleonic Wars.

NAPOLEONIC WAR STORIES *by Sir Arthur Quiller-Couch*—Tales of soldiers, spies, battles & sieges from the Peninsular & Waterloo campaigns.

CAPTAIN OF THE 95TH (RIFLES) *by Jonathan Leach*—An officer of Wellington's sharpshooters during the Peninsular, South of France and Waterloo campaigns of the Napoleonic wars.

RIFLEMAN COSTELLO *by Edward Costello*—The adventures of a soldier of the 95th (Rifles) in the Peninsular & Waterloo Campaigns of the Napoleonic wars.

LEONAUR

ALSO FROM LEONAUR

AVAILABLE IN SOFTCOVER OR HARDCOVER WITH DUST JACKET

OFFICERS & GENTLEMEN *by Peter Hawker & William Graham*—Two Accounts of British Officers During the Peninsula War: Officer of Light Dragoons by Peter Hawker & Campaign in Portugal and Spain by William Graham .

THE WALCHEREN EXPEDITION *by Anonymous*—The Experiences of a British Officer of the 81st Regt. During the Campaign in the Low Countries of 1809.

LADIES OF WATERLOO *by Charlotte A. Eaton, Magdalene de Lancey & Juana Smith*—The Experiences of Three Women During the Campaign of 1815: Waterloo Days by Charlotte A. Eaton, A Week at Waterloo by Magdalene de Lancey & Juana's Story by Juana Smith.

JOURNAL OF AN OFFICER IN THE KING'S GERMAN LEGION *by John Frederick Hering*—Recollections of Campaigning During the Napoleonic Wars.

JOURNAL OF AN ARMY SURGEON IN THE PENINSULAR WAR *by Charles Boutflower*—The Recollections of a British Army Medical Man on Campaign During the Napoleonic Wars.

ON CAMPAIGN WITH MOORE AND WELLINGTON *by Anthony Hamilton*—The Experiences of a Soldier of the 43rd Regiment During the Peninsular War.

THE ROAD TO AUSTERLITZ *by R. G. Burton*—Napoleon's Campaign of 1805.

SOLDIERS OF NAPOLEON *by A. J. Doisy De Villargennes & Arthur Chuquet*—The Experiences of the Men of the French First Empire: Under the Eagles by A. J. Doisy De Villargennes & Voices of 1812 by Arthur Chuquet .

INVASION OF FRANCE, 1814 *by F. W. O. Maycock*—The Final Battles of the Napoleonic First Empire.

LEIPZIG—A CONFLICT OF TITANS *by Frederic Shoberl*—A Personal Experience of the 'Battle of the Nations' During the Napoleonic Wars, October 14th-19th, 1813.

SLASHERS *by Charles Cadell*—The Campaigns of the 28th Regiment of Foot During the Napoleonic Wars by a Serving Officer.

BATTLE IMPERIAL *by Charles William Vane*—The Campaigns in Germany & France for the Defeat of Napoleon 1813-1814.

SWIFT & BOLD *by Gibbes Rigaud*—The 60th Rifles During the Peninsula War.